Ageing in India

INSTITUTE OF ECONOMIC GROWTH, Delhi

Studies in Economic Development and Planning No. 66

General Editor
PROF. KANCHAN CHOPRA

For a list of titles published by the Institute of Economic Growth
in this series, see pages 285-288 (at the end of this book).

Ageing
in India

Socio-Economic and Health Dimensions

Moneer Alam

Academic Foundation
NEW DELHI

First published in 2006
by

ACADEMIC FOUNDATION

4772-73 / 23 Bharat Ram Road, (23 Ansari Road),
Darya Ganj, New Delhi - 110 002 (India).
Phones : 23245001 / 02 / 03 / 04.
Fax : +91-11-23245005.
E-mail : academic@vsnl.com
www.academicfoundation.com

Copyright © 2006 Institute of Economic Growth, Delhi
www.iegindia.org
www.ieg.nic.in

All rights reserved

No part of this book (including its cover) shall be reproduced,
stored in a retrieval system, or transmitted by any means, electronic,
mechanical, photocopying, recording, or otherwise, without the
prior written permission of the copyright holder and the publisher

Ageing in India: Socio-Economic and Health Dimensions
by Moneer Alam

ISBN 81-7188-535-7

Typeset and designed by Italics India, New Delhi

Printed and bound in India

To
little Fazil and my Mother

The former for making me realise the need for intergenerational bonds,
and the latter to help me realise my responsibilities towards the old

CONTENTS

1. An Overview of the Issues 29

1.1. Introduction

1.2. The Other Side of Indian Demographics:
Fertility-Mortality Transition, Added Life Span
and Growing Changes in Age Pyramids

1.3. India Gaining the Status of Both Young and Old

1.4. Ageing and its Emerging Issues

1.5. Public Policy Issues:
Reforms, Declining Returns to Saving and the Aged

1.6. Structure of the Study and Data Sources

2. Intra-aged Disparities and Outcomes: Some Empirical Findings 71

2.1. Introduction

2.2. Profiling Intra-aged Disparities by Major States:
Some Evidence from Secondary Data Sources

2.3. Ageing and Some Unanswered Dimensions:
Data Needs and Data Availability

2.4. The Elderly and their Care Providers:
A Survey of Urban Households in Delhi

2.5. Concluding Observations

3. Assessing Ageing Issues in Times of Change: A Survey of Households with Elderly Co-residents 115

3.1. Introduction

List of Figures, Tables, Boxes and Appendices

FIGURES

TABLES

BOXES

APPENDICES

Foreword

The Institute of Economic Growth has always been at the forefront of studying economic, social and demographic issues, as they emerge, sometime even before they seize the imagination of mainstream research. Ageing in India is one such issue. The UN Population Division predicts that the elderly population in India will rise from 85 million to over 300 million in another 40 to 45 years, an increase of almost three and half times over such a brief span of time. Further, the share of the older old—i.e., those in the 80+ age brackets—is likely to grow even faster, with a greater level of feminisation and increasing visibility of women at the later ends of the life span. Contrasting this, the overall growth of population is expected to register a declining trend with time. It seems India is not only graying at a pace faster than many of the industrialised societies but also with very limited resources–both physical and financial. Also, there is dearth of empirical literature on this issue.

Notwithstanding these resource gaps or lack of empirical research, changes in the age composition of this magnitude are bound to result in far reaching consequences. The problem may however be severe in terms of economic, social and health related consequences. Economically, for instance, aged may need a considerable amount of protective subsidies. These subsidies may particularly be more critical for the existing cohorts of the ageing population. As many of those who suffered large-scale deprivations in their formative years belong to these cohorts, they cannot be expected to manage without public support. Further, to believe that existing family support, especially for those from informal sector, may be able to find resources to meet all the necessities of elders may at best be an over-simplification.

In terms of health and a healthy life, the literature available does indicate serious morbidity issues with considerable loss of productive life. There are also indications that a big fraction of the morbid population includes older adults. What has however not been discussed in its required detail is the ramification of these diseases on the functional capabilities of the old. As diseases lead to frailty followed by functional incompetence and dependency on filial support, more and more ailing elders may need to rely on long-term care. With shrinking family size, and large-scale participation of all family members in economic or educational activities, this support is difficult to come by. Formal support and long term institutional care need to be developed.

Considering the fact that ageing is soon going to be an important socio-economic and medical challenge for India and most other South Asian economies, we have tried to analyse this issue with the explicit objective to make it useful in a wider context, though India remains the core concern. A significant contribution of this study lies in the attempt by the author to extend the study from its traditional concerns to the newer dimensions of ongoing economic liberalisation and the manner in which the old and non-old view liberalisation in the context of ageing. The study relied on household level data obtained from the National Sample Survey Organisation (NSS, 52nd Round for 1995-96). In addition, other important secondary data sources including the 2001 Population Census and the UN population projections have also been used. The author has also conducted a survey of over 1000 households in Delhi from different socio-economic backgrounds with respondents comprising both the young and the old from each sample household. Non-elderly respondents were asked to furnish their views on three broader issues: (i) care providing to the aged, especially in a situation of decelerating job market and increased casualisation of employment (ii) altruism in care giving, and (iii) self-ageing. Similarly, the aged were asked to respond to the range of questions especially their financial status, earning, sources, expenditure priorities, living preferences, grand parenting, declining interest earnings, old age health, functional disabilities, filial support to the disabled elderly and so on. Social security cover for the destitute elderly, proposed pension reforms and a host of other attendant issues were also discussed.

The study makes significant observations about the severe economic and health issues faced by the old people. This is observed both on the basis of the data obtained from the NSS 52nd Round, and the survey conducted by the author himself. There is also evidence to suggest that women are in a much disadvantageous position. They are largely dependent economically, suffer from poor health conditions, faced with major disabilities in their activities of daily living, and often have to contend with less congenial family environment—especially if they are functionally dependent. Government and civil societies are both lacking in terms of required support. Institutions of long term-care and other geriatric resources are yet to develop.

The study strongly recommends the development of a government supported social security system for the aged, with finances generated through a mix of public and private sources. It also makes out a case for evolving a system to tax a range of health hazardous and other selected ventures being used to create a fund for old age support provisioning. Interestingly, the study expects to see the political economy of ageing taking roots in the country in the near future.

A research grant from the Canadian International Development Agency (CIDA) supported the study. Given the policy relevance of the issues discussed and the conclusions arrived at, and in the interest of wider dissemination, the IEG decided to publish it.

I am hopeful that this book will help to fill some of the void in current economic literature on ageing in India, and also ignite a debate on this issue of immense public concern both with in and outside the country.

January 23, 2006

Kanchan Chopra
Director
Institute of Economic Growth

Preface

With persisting changes in many of its major demographic parameters, India is very much among the countries facing rapid growth in the higher age population—especially those beyond 60 years. While some of the emerging literature in recent years has been drawing attention to these age composition changes and increasing momentum towards societal ageing, very little has been done at the policy level to design appropriate responses except, for instance, such sporadic attempts like formulation of certain anti-destitution measures such as old age pensions or some travel subsidies to individuals aged 65 and above. A National Policy on Older Persons (NPOP) is also in place now, intuitively to comply with several national and international resolutions on ageing populations. In practice, however, many of the provisions described in this policy document await proper implementation. Of the many reasons for this neglect, a more significant perhaps is the lack of necessary understanding about the issues of ageing—especially against the backdrop of the ongoing pro-market reforms, persisting disparities, growing erosions in traditional values, low financial status, high prevalence of functional disabilities, lack of social support mechanisms, declining public welfare activities and so on. The underlying study was therefore designed to examine some of these issues with the help of household level data obtained in digital form from the National Sample Survey Organisation for 1995-96, and also by generating supplementary field-based information highlighting the views of the aged and non-aged on the vexed question of old age security in the emerging socio-economic paradigm.

Going by these considerations, the present study has been guided with the following three major concerns:

One is largely drawn from the fast growing economic-demographic changes in the country and a host of their ramifications over the coming years. One such ramification, for instance, may be the changes in the nature of the dependency burden with more of the poor and functionally impaired elderly dependents straining the caregivers both physically and financially.

Another focal concern of this analysis is to provide a situational assessment of the aged and their socio-economic and health disparities to bring out an important—though somewhat neglected—fact that the aged are mostly non-homogeneous and, therefore, differ if compared spatially (i.e., rural-urban), by sex or across different age groups (young old *versus* older old). The underpinning reason behind this whole argument is that the problems of ageing in India—and for that matter in most developing countries—cannot be handled effectively by evolving a single policy regime. The wide-ranging disparities and outcomes would need to be taken into account in designing multi-pronged strategies. The rural aged needs greater attention.

Finally, the third important concern of the study stems from the whole range of upcoming questions arising due to several recent changes in socio-economic dispensations including privatisation of major services, declining returns to savings, growing doubts about altruism in elderly care, inadequate income security to the aged, need for planned ageing, high prevalence of multiple diseases suffered by the aged, low quality of later life years, non-senescent functional disabilities, growing issues of care economy and so on.

Obviously, it was difficult to explore the third set of concerns with the help the data available from the existing sources. A sample survey of 1000 households was therefore conducted in Delhi to elicit views from elderly (60+) and non-elderly (15-49) respondents on many of these issues. The survey was also explicitly designed to ensure variability and representation of different socio-economic stratums drawn from all the nine districts of Delhi in close consultation with the Office of the Census Commissioner, and the Directorate of Census (Delhi Government).

This study is entirely the outcome of a research project—Health and Livelihood Issues of Ageing Indians: An Exploration towards Devising Old Age Security Measures—funded by the Canadian International Development Agency (CIDA) under its Socio-Economic Transformation Project (SETP).

A good part of the results presented in this study has been discussed in several conferences and seminars, both in India, especially at the Institute of Economic Growth (IEG), and abroad. I owe my utmost gratitude to fellow colleagues and seminar participants for their incisive comments and suggestions. Many of these suggestions have been used in subsequent revisions of the study.

I had the privilege of drawing encouragement from Professor B.B. Bhattacharya, (former Director of the IEG, and currently Vice-Chancellor of the Jawaharlal Nehru University), and Mr. Faisal Baig, Coordinator of the CIDA Programme (Canadian High Commission, New Delhi) at every stage of this work. Both of them have been extremely generous and have continued with their untiring support despite hiccups in the completion of the study. Professor Bhattacharya was exceptionally helpful and extended every possible support—both academic and logistic—during the course of this research. Professor Kanchan Chopra, who is currently heading the IEG, has remained equally concerned and taken keen personal interest in bringing out the study under the IEG publication series.

A great deal of the CIDA funded project was evolved in consultation with Professor Jean Dreze (CDS, Delhi School of Economics, Delhi University), Dr. Rohini Nayyar (Planning Commission) and Dr. Zachary Zimmer (Population Council, New York), the three members of a Research Advisory Committee constituted to advise and give direction to the study. This work owes considerable intellectual debt to each one of them.

A considerable amount of work on indexing the functional disabilities and support requirements of older persons was made possible because of the help received from Professors Steven M. Albert (Graduate School of Public Health, University of Pittsburgh) and M. Nizamuddin (Department of Socio-medical Sciences, Columbia University). My thanks go to Dr. Manisha Sengupta (Johns Hopkins University, and the US Census) who helped in designing the survey instruments including the questions used to generate data on functional incapacitations in the two major health domains—physical and sensory.

The entire survey work, used to collect information on several unconventional issues of ageing, is the outcome of invaluable assistance provided by the Directorate of Census (Delhi Government) on the advice of Mr. S. Banthia (Census Commissioner at the time of this study) and Mr. R.G. Mitra (Deputy Census Commissioner). Mr. Mitra was himself involved in finalising the sample design and its stratifications by using a set of identifiable socio-economic groups.

At the IEG, I had the privilege of discussing with colleagues including Professors M.N. Murty, P.N. Mari Bhat, R.P. Tyagi, Bhanu Murty, Sabyasachi Kar, S. Sakthivel and many others. Dr. Nihal Singh of the WHO (South-East Asia Region Office, New Delhi) has remained helpful in many ways and offered assistance in evolving the WHO's methodology on quality of survival and issues of functional impairments.

I held many discussions with Ms. Alia Saeed (Department of Social Welfare, Delhi Government) on old age support programmes administered by the state. I am thankful for all her assistance. Mr. Haseeb Ahmad (Director, Ministry of Social Justice and Empowerment) generously made himself available for clarifications on several policy related issues.

I must also mention the efforts made by my project associates— Ms. Mukta Mukherjee, Ms. Rini Lal and Mr. Tapan K. Nayak. They not only helped me through their untiring efforts, but also contributed by offering several useful ideas and computer generated solutions. Mrs. Suhasini Ramaswamy has helped me by going through the entire manuscript very meticulously and making several useful editorial changes to improve the clarity of ideas and uninterrupted reading.

Finally, I must express my gratitude to my family, especially my wife, who handled more than her share of distractions and responsibilities to free all my time and energy for my work.

Needless to say, all the errors that persist are my own. Also, CIDA, the funding institution, has nothing to do with the views expressed in the book.

Moneer Alam

Institute of Economic Growth
Delhi
January 2006

1

An Overview of the Issues

1.1. Introduction

Unlike the developed world, large scale ageing in many of the developing countries is a recent phenomenon. Until recently, most of these countries were in general tuned to problems of high fertility and its multifaceted socio-economic fallouts. Regarding ageing—it was simply individuals growing old without any indication about societal ageing or its complexities on account of persistent poverty, growing diminutions in older values and familial nuclearisation.

With its continuing decline in fertility along with a growing life span, India is also among the countries with many of the above traits. Simultaneously, the country is also in the process of economic transition with markets in a mediatory role. Jointly—and to an extent independently as well—these transitions may lead to many complex issues, a good number of them may arise owing to changes in the age composition of the population with accelerating growth of those aged 60 and more. Somewhat inexplicable, but these issues have been largely neglected in the current debate on socio-economic and demographic transitions in the country. This study basically draws its justification from this lack of concern, and attempts to explore the prospective issues of demographic ageing—especially against the backdrop of a changing social environment, poor old age health, erosion in familial norms and pro-market reforms. We however begin with a brief description of current and upcoming changes in the country's major demographic parameters with significant bearings on changes over-time in the age composition of the population. An interface between these and the emerging socio-economic situation will be taken up subsequently. A clarification about the database: we have used the UN population projections wherever we had to go beyond 2000 or 2001. For the rest of the analysis we mostly relied either on decennial population censuses or the National Sample Survey (NSS), 52nd Round relating to 1995-96.

1.2. The Other Side of Indian Demographics: Fertility-Mortality Transition, Added Life Span and Growing Changes in Age Pyramids

Barring a brief stretch of fifty years in the early twentieth century, India has hardly ever been a country with a high natural growth of population. Perpetual hunger, frequent famines, recurring epidemics, high infant and maternal mortality have for centuries ensured a 'very low' population growth in the country. Demographic historians, to illustrate, have estimated that the population in India grew at an average rate of only 0.03 per cent for about a millennium or so (Srinivasan, 2001). A reversal has however started since the early twentieth century—largely in response to the famine control and public health measures adopted by the Provincial governments under British rule. This later culminated in high fertility-mortality differentials (Figure 1.1) and the total population of the country grew from 238.4 million in 1901 to 361.1 million in 1951, and 1027.01 million in 2001—clearly a mind boggling 51.47 per cent increase during the first half, which later jumped to 184.41 per cent in the next half.[1] Such an unsustainable growth in population has left the country with no option but to reduce fertility through family planning and reproductive health measures. Having pursued these measures with great alacrity over the past fifty years, India is now on the recovery path with considerable improvements in its major population parameters—albeit with serious spatial disparities.[2]

As noted, over this entire process of demographic transition, India has passed through several distinct fertility-mortality stages: that is from a very high fertility-mortality situation to a gradual moderation in both these parameters—though fertility started declining with a significant time lag and has also remained sluggish if compared with mortality (see Figure 1.1). In the process, life expectancy has also increased—both at birth and later life years (SRS Statistical Report, 1998). Beside their implications for the size and future growth of population, these declining trends in fertility and mortality are significant from yet another angle—namely the embedding changes in

---

1. The annual average growth of population for 1901-1951 was 11.57 per cent. It rose to 12.5 per cent over the next 50 years.

2. A possible inference may therefore be that a single economic policy may not account for the demographic realities of the entire country.

age composition of population with bulging in adult ages. With the current process of fertility-mortality decline, which is likely to catch up with time, there is unanimity in population projections suggesting an accelerating pace of demographic ageing in India. In addition, this process does not completely end here and, over the coming years, the changes in population composition would cause India to differ from many of the world countries in some other respects as well.

Figure 1.1

Fertility-Mortality Differentials and Population Growth:
All India, 1901-2001

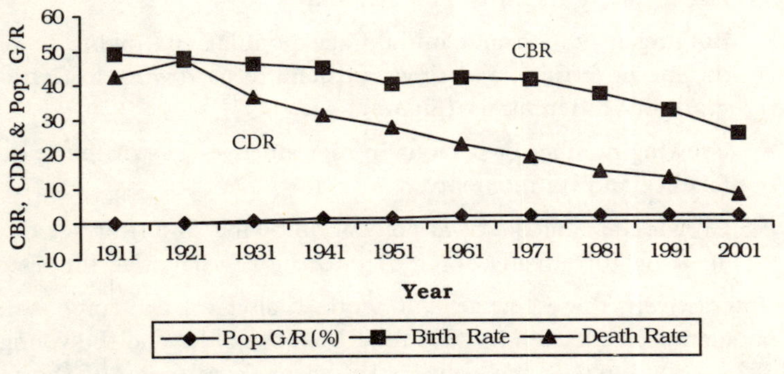

Source: Decennial Population Censuses and the *SRS Bulletins.* Cited in Alam (2001).

Table 1.1

Changes in Population Parameters: All India, 1950-2050

Time Period	TFR	G/R of Population**	e^0
1950-60*	5.95	2.13	40.65
2000-05	3.01	1.51	63.90
2010-15	2.46	1.20	66.30
2020-25	2.14	0.85	67.80
2030-35	1.92	0.54	70.00
2045-50	1.85	0.26	73.80

*Source: * UN World Population Prospects* (1998 Revision, Vol. 1). Information from 2000-05 onwards was obtained from the *UN World Population Prospects* (2002 Revision, Vol. 1).

** Average annual Growth Rate of Population.

Demographically, India has been able to reduce its fertility level from close to 6 in 1950s to about 3 as projected for 2000-05 (Table 1.1). A few of the recent projection exercises by Indian scholars reveal Total Fertility Rate (TFR) reaching the replacement level between 2015 and 2020. Also this trend of declining fertility is expected to continue even further with every passing decade as was shown in a comprehensive population projection by the Population Foundation of India (Natarajan and Jayachandran, 2001). Simultaneously, life expectancy in the country is also on the rise (Table 1.1)—more significantly for those in higher age brackets.[3] By implication, we have the following:

- Cohort to cohort increase in size of the elderly population with fast growing visibility in 'older old'.[4]

- Bulging in young and middle age populations owing to fast decline in fertility, and slow but definite narrowing in fertility-mortality differentials (Figure 1.1).

- Growing number of persons in reproductive ages owing to past fertility and its momentum.

- Growing size of the total population owing to fertility of those entering (or already entered) into the reproductive life span.

Interactively, these changes will work to alter the age composition of population in the country favouring both the older and the younger adults. It also makes the country different from many of the fast graying societies. Unlike many others, and for most of this century, India is expected to remain young and old simultaneously. But this may have several implications.

1.3. India Gaining the Status of Both Young and Old

Table 1.2 further illustrates the points made in the preceding discussion on temporal changes in age distribution of population. These distributions are also represented in the form of population pyramids to highlight the movements in age-specific bulges with time.

---

3. Based on the Sample Registration System (SRS) and its Abridged Life Tables, the expected life span at the age of 60 was 16.5 years during 1993-97. It becomes 10.8 years at the ages of 70 to 75 (see, SRS Analytical Studies Report No. 1 of 2000).

4. Throughout this study 'old, aged or elderly' are all used synonymously, and defined as those in age groups between 60 and 74. Similarly, those beyond 75 are defined as 'older old'.

Table 1.2

Changes in Share of Broad Age Groups: All India

Percentage

Age Groups	1960		2000		2020		2050	
	Male	*Female*	*Male*	*Female*	*Male*	*Female*	*Male*	*Female*
0-14	39.8	39.6	34.2	34.1	26.2	26.0	18.9	18.3
15-24	18.0	18.5	18.8	18.4	17.6	17.3	13.4	13.0
25-59	36.7	36.0	40.0	39.4	46.0	45.2	48.7	47.4
60-64	2.2	2.3	2.5	2.8	3.6	3.8	5.6	5.8
65-74	2.7	2.7	3.2	3.7	4.5	5.0	8.1	8.9
75+	0.6	0.9	1.3	1.6	2.0	2.7	5.2	6.7
Total	100.0	100.0	100.0	100.0	100.0	100.0	100.0	100.0

Source: UN *World Population Prospect* (1998 Revision & 2002 Revision), Vol. II.

Two interesting observations arise from Table 1.2. One, the first two age categories—namely 0-14 and 15-24—are likely to gradually decline in response to sustained reduction in overall fertility level. Their combined share, for example, is expected to shrink from 58 per cent in 1960 and a little over 52 per cent in 2000 to 33 per cent in 2050. Two, the population in the 25-59 age groups (almost all of them needing to participate in economic activities) is likely to grow substantially, and will be close to half of the country's total population by 2050 (Table 1.2). Even more striking growth may be noted for elderly persons—especially those exceeding 75 years of age. They are expected to be growing at an accelerating pace—resulting in substantial increase in age dependencies and demand for age related medical and non-medical services. The feminisation of ageing is also notable from the table under reference.

Similar observations arise from the four population pyramids given in Figures 1.2 (a) to 1.2 (d). These pyramids reflect several interesting changes in patterns of age composition over these years—from almost completely conical in 1960 to more or less fully cylindrical by the middle of this century. Given these, it may not be implausible to expect that: (i) demographically, India is going to remain both young and old for most of this century, and (ii) economically, both these age groups may undergo serious difficulties—one for lack of employment opportunities in high productivity sectors, and the other for lack of income and health security. We will however confine ourselves mostly to the latter aspect in the course of this analysis.

Figure 1.2

Changes in Population Pyramids: All India

(a) 1960

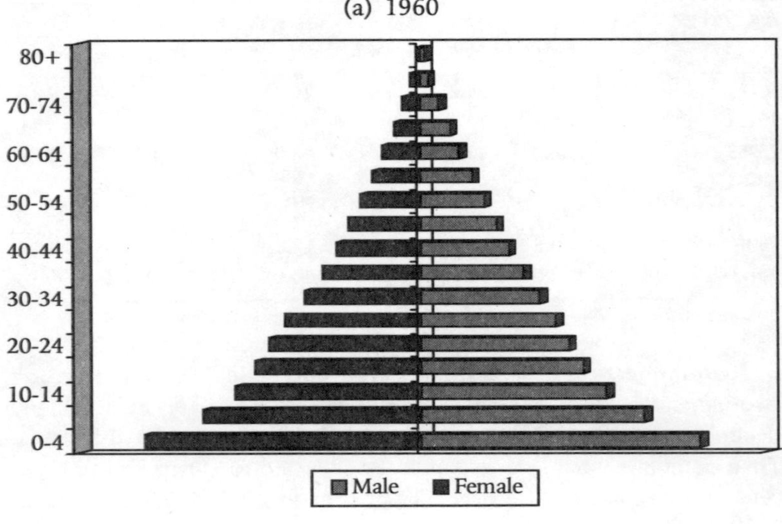

(b) 2000

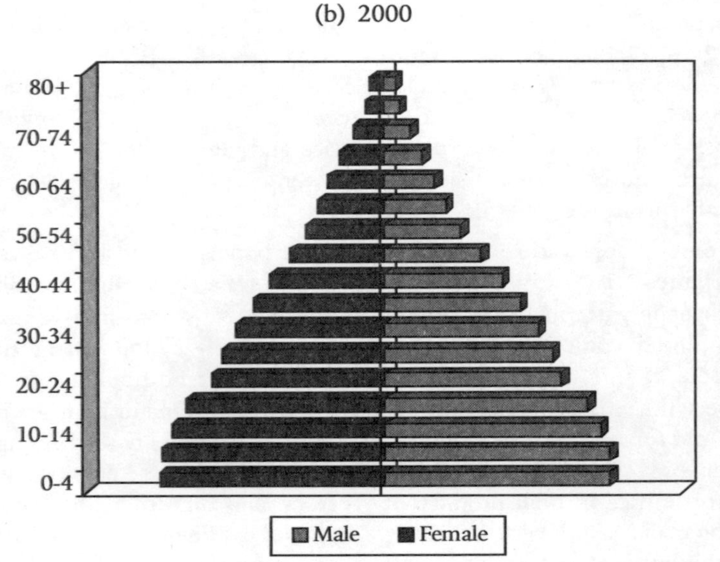

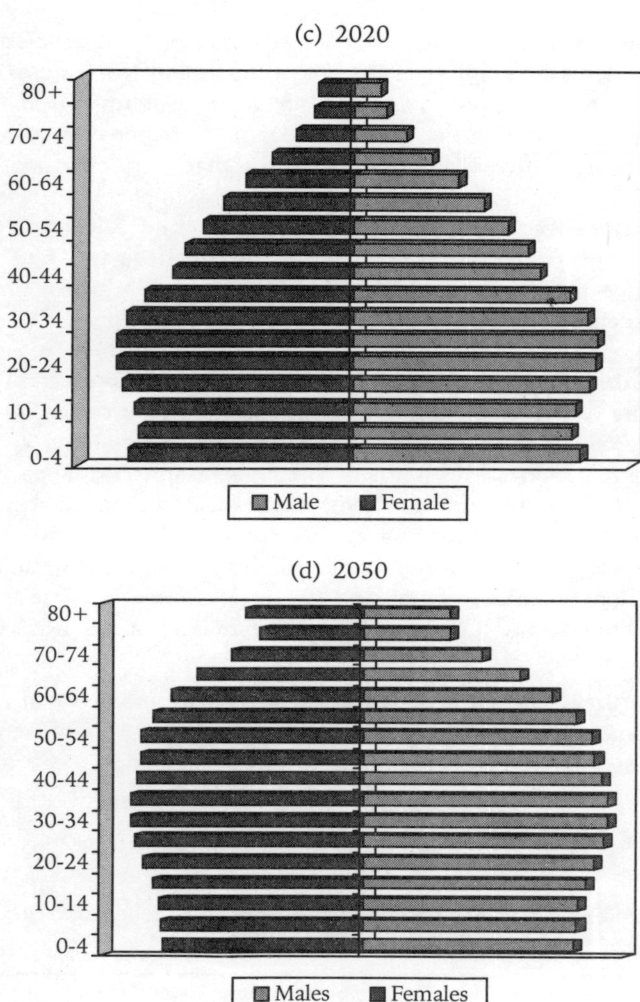

Source: UN World Population Prospects, 1998 & 2002 Revisions.
Note: Population in percentage.

1.4. Ageing and its Emerging Issues

In most traditional societies, ageing has never been a social phenomenon. As noted, individuals in these societies have passed through the typical human life cycle without any generalisation of their experience at the macro level. Two factors have basically contributed towards this phenomenon: (i) ageing, being involuntary was considered as a universal fact for all time, and (ii) families lent all support to their aged as a commonly accepted norm. Yet another reason for this was that these societies had never before changed their age composition drastically. India, and for that matter most of the South Asian countries, turn out to be typical examples with most of these traits. Even the industrialised countries of Europe, North America and part of the Asia-Pacific region have not had this experience before the early twentieth century. Following major advancements in the whole spectrum of human life, the last century has brought considerable pro-ageing changes in most of these developed regions with serious concern about social protection and well-being of the aged. This, *inter alia*, has led to a growing flow of literature on various aspects of ageing including the building up of a necessary support mechanism through major (and perhaps unsustainable) public transfers. Not many such mechanisms exist in most of the newly emerging ageing societies like India—partly because of a lack of proper understanding about ageing and its ramifications for the economy and for society. Some of these issues will therefore be taken up at a more elaborate level in the discussions that follow.

Departing from the past, the accelerating pace of ageing in many low-income societies like India (Table 1.3) presents a mix of complex issues—social, conceptual, economic, health related and those relating to public policies. An issue of considerable significance from the

Table 1.3

Annual Growth of Elderly and Non-Elderly: All India, 2000-2050

Percentage

Broad Age Groups	Annual Average Growth Rates	
	Males	*Females*
80+	4.04	4.27
75+	3.61	3.78
60+	2.80	2.84
0-14	-0.41	-0.38
15-59	0.89	0.96
Total Population	0.77	0.87

Source: Calculated on the basis of UN Population Prospects (2002 Revision), Vol. II.

conceptual viewpoint may, for example, be to define old age poverty. As ageing has generally been a concern of industrialised societies where perpetual poverty is exceptional and mostly covered under different plans, the conceptualisation of old age poverty has remained without causing much analytical concern.[5] This may however not be the case with countries spiked by high incidence of poverty and a big informal labour market with poor wages and absence of retirement benefits. Further, there are problems such as the prevalence of degenerating old age diseases without any insurance cover, growing cost of medical services owing to ongoing health sector reforms, declining returns to small savings affecting interest earners, and so on. Many of these issues have remained without serious investigation. And yet, the government and many non-government organisations are currently engaged in evolving old age policies. We therefore argue that many of these attempts may not fully conform to the existing realities and, as a result, remain superficial. This study is therefore designed keeping some of these issues in perspective.

Conceptual Issues: Problems in Defining Old Age Poverty

At the conceptual level, poverty is often defined as socially perceived deprivation with respect to basic minimum human needs. Economists have often perceived the issue of basic minimum human needs as a normative threshold level of goods and services that should be guaranteed to each individual. Hence, it can be inferred that those who fail to achieve this normative threshold level are deprived and, therefore, remain poor. But this whole concept may not remain entirely convincing if judged by taking into consideration some important basic differences among individuals. An example may be the age differentials that would change the basic minimum requirements of people—the basic needs of the young, for example, may largely differ from those of the aged. This poses a big question: can old age poverty really be judged on the basis of the generalised calorific norm?

Basic Needs Criterion and its Implications for the Aged

One of the critical issues in measuring poverty is to define the basic minimum needs basket and its composition. Commenting on this issue, (Sen, 1984) has argued that the material characteristics of

---

5. This is despite the fact that the concept of subjective well-being is now an area of growing interest.

the commodities need to be combined with the personal characteristics of the individuals while defining the minimum needs basket. In other words, the nutritional characteristics of a particular food item should be combined with individual specific factors such as age, sex, body weight, health conditions, etc. In a nutshell, it can be argued that the levels of commodity requirement to ensure capability are likely to differ, especially across major age groups.

The growing body of literature in recent years on 'subjective well-being' is an extension to account for some of these concerns. It also allows individuals to examine satisfaction with life as a whole or its identifiable domains including health, employment, living standards, and so on. (Clark and Oswald, 1994; Oswald, 1997; Pradhan and Ravallion, 2000 and Van Praag, 2002).[6]

Picking up the thread from these subjective considerations, we can argue that the elderly, being a group with certain age specific characteristics, may not fit into a generalised calorific-based poverty norm. A more focused study is therefore required to identify the specific needs of older persons and their respective weights before measuring old age poverty and its incidence. Some cursory attempts in this direction have been made in Chapter 5 of this study.

Current Measurement of Poverty and Ageing Studies

Poverty measurement starts with defining the minimum normative consumption of food on a per capita basis using nutritional criteria in the commodity space. This basket is evaluated at given prices to yield the minimum level of per capita food expenditure. One of the major drawbacks of this process in the underlying context is its failure to incorporate the age specific preference pattern while choosing the bundle of goods and services. To illustrate, health needs will be far more important for the aged than entertainment (see Chapter 4). Even if we assume entertainment as the preferred choice of elderly individuals, its nature would possibly be different from that of non-

---

6. Different domains of life, for instance, include satisfaction with health status, financial situation, nature of job (or job satisfaction), housing, etc. Satisfaction with life can be viewed more as an aggregate concept, and it can be partitioned into its domain components (Van Praag, 2002). The verbal evaluation of a particular domain like health (e.g., excellent, good or bad health) can be transformed into numbers on a specified scale. By doing this, one obtains points on a graph of individual's welfare function. There may however be difficulties with a big sample size. Moreover, the subjectivities involved may also be problematic.

elderly persons. An elderly person might prefer to participate in religious or philanthropic activities than the usual socialisation.

Another basic limitation of this poverty measurement is that it implicitly rules out the possibility of the 'above poverty persons' failing to meet many other essential needs—other than those included in their basic minimum food requirements. It is likely, for example, that a person fails to access medical care without lacking in terms of minimum food requirements. With the growing prices of medical care and gradual decline in real public health expenditure by states (Duggal, 1995a, 1995b), such a possibility cannot be completely ruled out. Since the measure of per capita monthly consumer expenditure, drawn on the basis of recent NSS data, does not incorporate expenses on medical and diagnostic care, it remains largely inadequate in explaining poverty incidence among the aged. Further, taking the elderly as part of a homogeneous cross-section of the population may not be quite realistic. With the risk of 'entitlement failure' looming large owing to growing changes in traditional systems and lack of publicly supported social security institutions, it is equally important to segregate the elderly as a special group and calculate poverty incidence among them by redefining their basic minimum needs basket. This is indeed an area that demands future research.

Economic Issues: Growing Old Age Dependency and its Implications

The preceding discussion on changes in age composition of population in India leads us to a few specific observations about: (i) societal ageing in the country with highest growth in the size of 'old old'—normally considered as the most vulnerable among the aged (see Table 1.3), and (ii) bulging in the working age populations—especially within 25-59 ages—with potentials to inundate the labour market. Yet another observation may be the negative growth of 0-14 population, though with a certain time lag. Besides several interesting ramifications of these changes on overall demand mix of various goods and services, it may also unfold into a reversal in young age dependency ratios in the country. A situation like this raises several questions. For example: how does it affect families or care providers? Does it fully or partially nullify the effects of corresponding increase in old age dependencies? These are important—though highly complex—questions and require working out the equivalence scales to suggest changes in consumption-mix because of changing dependencies and age compositions.[7]

Age-Dependency Relationship: Implications for Family, Government and the Economy

Often, dependencies (both young and old) are drawn on the implicit assumption of age–population relationship, dividing the over all population into economically dependent and independent. This distribution of dependents and independents is becoming increasingly significant from different considerations—intra-familial as well as for the government in the formulation of its socio-welfare policies. Three aspects are now gaining attention in the underlying context. These are:

- Changes in size and age composition of families: especially the changes in ratio of earning to non-earning family members may have bearings on intra-family relationship, altruistic exchange of resources and care giving.

- Changes in age composition of population and macro-economic management: while more of the younger population in 15-59 age groups may bring demand-supply imbalances in the labour market, a faster increase in 60+ would introduce changes in consumption needs, over all saving potentials of the economy, availability of domestic capital, etc.

- Changes in nature and magnitude of public transfers due to changes in population size and its age structure: these changes may also cause growing demand for health and income security provisioning, destitute pension and retirement linked benefits with considerable burden on government finances.

But these are not all; and it needs to be emphasised that an individual's age is linked with his or her dependency only partially. Between age and dependency there are many other factors as well. One is of course the biological ageing process and the physical condition of individuals. To illustrate, under the contrasting social environment, the same human biology can yield diverse health situations and longevity with varying dependencies. Physical incapacity can lead to greater and more severe dependencies with far more serious consequences—not to individuals or their families alone but

---

7. The UN Economic Commission for Europe and the United Nations Population Fund in their study "Social Aspects and Country Reviews of Population Ageing (Economic Study No. 6)" attempts to discuss such scales and relative consumption levels by different age groups. See, for example, Holzer and Fratczak (1994).

also for the public funded health care infrastructure. Another, and perhaps more significant, form of dependency may arise owing to lack of proper work opportunities.

Going by some available evidence, India is currently faced with many such issues. High burden of diseases—among the young and old alike (World Bank, 1993)—for instance, adds to aggregate dependencies in the country with very high direct and indirect cost to the affected families and society. Similarly, the growing informal labour market and decelerating work opportunities in high productivity sectors (Anant, Sundaram and Tendulkar, 1999; Alam and Mishra, 1998) erode the capacity to cope with dependency by low-income households (see Chapter 2 for more on this).

Age–Dependency Burden in India: Emerging Situation

Carrying some of these arguments further, the discussion to follow makes an attempt to examine three significant issues of ageing in the Indian context. These are: (i) over-time changes in the young and old age dependency burden on the 'labour force' and the 'working age' populations, (ii) saving-investment implications of ageing, and (iii) dependency and need for public support.

Tables 1.4a and 1.4b provide two forms of dependencies. The former is based on the conventional notion of demographic dependency—i.e., 60+ or < 15 populations in relation to those in 15-59 age groups. The latter is however different as it uses labour force in the denominator. An implicit assumption in the second formulation is that those outside the labour force are themselves dependent.

Table 1.4a

Dependency Burden on Working Age Population: Dependents Per Hundred 15-59 Persons

Year	Young Dependencies (M+F)		Old Dependencies (M+F)		Total** Dependencies
	Rural	Urban	Rural	Urban	
1971*	83.8	69.7	12.2	8.9	92.3
1981*	77.0	62.9	13.0	9.2	85.5
1991*	64.8	53.9	11.3	9.5	72.6
2001*	67.8	49.1	14.1	10.7	75.2

Note: * Based on Decennial Population Censuses.

** Combined all India young and old dependencies.

Source: 2001 Census figures were obtained from the data CD provided by the Office of the Registrar General, New Delhi.

Table 1.4b

Dependency Burden on Labour Force: Dependents Per Hundred Persons in Labour Force

Year	Young Dependencies		Old Dependencies		Total* Dependencies
	Rural	Urban	Rural	Urban	
1971	98.3	114.8	14.3	14.6	115.3
1975	93.0	102.9	14.4	14.1	109.1
1981	89.2	98.0	15.1	14.6	105.9
1985	87.1	95.9	14.8	15.3	103.8
1991	85.6	92.0	14.9	16.5	102.2
2000-01	67.8	49.1	14.1	10.7	75.2

Source: Alam and Agarwal (1999). 2001-01 dependency ratios were obtained by using population figures from 2001 Census, and NSS 56th Round providing data on labour force for 2000-01 (Report Number 476).

* Combined rural-urban and old and young dependencies.

Several interesting results follow from these two tables. One is the growing burden of old age dependency after 1971—especially in urban areas. The opposite is however true for the younger dependency, and this may be noted with some variation for both the rural and urban areas. Another notable result relates to the burden on the labour force. Judged by the observed levels of labour force participation rates (LFPR), there are indications that old age dependency on the labour force would significantly increase with time. If the average duration of unemployment in the country is high, and the quality of employment is low with high levels of casualisation in the labour market, this growing burden of dependency may be difficult to handle, especially by a large number of low-income families. A third interesting observation arises from the significant drop in combined dependency burden during the period under reference (last column in Tables 1.4a and 1.4b). This is true at both the levels: for the working age populations in 15-59 age groups, and the labour force.

The bottom line of the above scenario may act as a pointer towards the whole range of ageing issues in India; many of them are still in their infancy. With age-specific population projections suggesting acceleration in the process of ageing in India,[8] there is clearly a need to examine a number of related issues—especially the

---

8. Based on the UN population projections (1998 revision), the old age dependency in 2000 turns out to be 12.9 for every 100 persons in 15-59 age groups. It increases to 13.9 in 2010, 17.2 in 2020, 28.0 in 2040 and 35.8 in 2050. These ratios for 65+ are: 8.4, 9.2, 19.9 and 25.5 (see Alam, 2001b).

income and health security requirements of the aged. The argument that the aged may be looked after by families is gradually losing its relevance with increasing old age dependency, deceleration in quality employment and erosion in familial norms.

Further, some of the recent changes in monetary policies may also need to account for these developments and help to create (i) institutions, and (ii) assured saving instruments to ensure some degree of income security for the older people. While some feeble attempts in this direction have recently been made, the subsequent discussion will show that they are inadequate.

Dependency Burden and Aggregate Private Saving

The rapid population ageing in most developed countries has resulted in several macro-economic implications, more commonly in the form of changes in age composition of their labour force. While India is also in the process of moving in the same direction, its population dynamics and growing bulges in the working age groups (Figures 1.2 b, c and d) will help the country to delay many such implications for most of the 21st century. These bulges may also help the country to escape many of the fiscal and financial fallouts associated with societal ageing. To illustrate, the country may for quite some time be able to evade any possible decline in rates of domestic savings, a phenomenon sometimes linked with large scale ageing. Neo-classical empiricists have feared that this phenomenon may affect the supply of internally generated capital resources and reduce the over all investments in the economy (Hurd, 1997; Horioka, 1991, 1992; Auerbach, Kotlikoff, *et al.*, 1989 and Friedlander and Malul, 1980). Given the primacy of many such issues in the received literature on ageing, an attempt is made here to present a simple exercise to judge the effect of dependencies (old and young) on private domestic saving at the all India level.[9]

Several econometric models have been used in recent literature to examine the macro-economic effects of ageing.[10] As part of this

---

9. For further details, see Alam and Agarwal (1999).

10. Four types of models have been used in recent years to examine the macro-economic ramifications of age structure changes. These include: (i) Multi-country Macro-economic model (Masson and Tryon, 1990), (ii) the Neo-classical model (Noguchi, 1990), (iii) the general equilibrium type Overlapping Generation Model (Auerbach, Kotlikoff, *et al.*, 1989), and (iv) a Turnpike Model used by the Economic Planning Agency of Japan to provide long term projections of its economy under varying demographic scenario and age profile. Yet another - and simplest of all - is a single equation model used by Horioka in his studies (1991, 1992).

concern, attempts have also been made to investigate the changes in aggregate savings with shifts in age profile. Following a recent study by Horioka (1992)—which uses a single equation model to analyse the same for the Japanese economy—attempts have been made to report a similar—though cursory—exercise at the all India level.

A focal concern of this analysis is to present a relationship between aggregate private savings and the growing dependency burden at the all India level. Both young and old age dependencies are used as the two explanatory variables in the model, which are expected to bear inverse relationships with the level of aggregate private savings. In all, two specifications are used: (i) using simply the two dependencies as suggested by Horioka (1991), and (ii) a slightly modified model by including the real per capita income as an additional variable. This modification is made on the assumption that the growth in per capita income generally raises the level of savings in the economy. Thus, the second specification in our analysis uses the real per capita GDP along with the two dependencies to explain variations in the aggregate private savings. The time-series of private domestic savings and the GDP—all in real terms—have been obtained from the *National Accounts Statistics* (1994). The time series for the two dependencies have been drawn from Alam and Agarwal, (1999). In general, this relationship may be expressed as:

Saving S = f (young dependencies YD, old dependencies OD, per capita real GDP PC GDP),

Where dependency ratios (young 0-14 and old 60+) were calculated on the basis of the labour force data for the corresponding time-span—i.e., from 1971 to 1991 (see Alam and Agarwal, 1999), a trend variable was later introduced to capture the impact of time on saving. The estimates of the two equations are as below:

$$S = -2.26 - 53.800 \text{ OD} + 4.983 \text{ PC GDP} \qquad \qquad \ldots(i)$$
$$(-1.49) \quad (2.70)*$$

R^2 square = 0.48

$$S/Y = 100.9 - 7.455 \text{ YD} - 100.274 \text{ OD} + 0.228 \text{ trend} \quad \ldots(ii)$$
$$(-4.90)* \qquad \qquad (-1.31) \quad (0.70)$$

R^2 square = 0.60

(Values in brackets are the t – values. * denotes significance at 5 per cent level).

The estimates presented in equations (i) and (ii) indicate that old age dependency has so far no significant effect on private savings in the country. It may however be interesting to note that the coefficients of old age dependency bear a negative sign in both the equations.

Young age dependency is however found to be statistically significant with expected signs. It is true for the per capita GDP as well. Slightly stretching these results, one can possibly infer that the ageing dependents might also become a big dampener with time and reduce the saving potential of the households—especially those engaged in low paid informal economic activities.[11]

Health Issues: Disease Prevalence among the Old and Geriatric Care

As widely conceived in the literature, the relation between age and health bears a biological core and has nothing significant to do with the institutional arrangements like the retirement age. Need for old age health care or health expenditure of ageing societies therefore depends, *inter alia*, on a series of socio-economic and other factors including living standards, public health services, early life health stock, disease pattern and prevention mechanism, overall longevity, etc. With these, the implications of ageing for health care services in India are particularly complex for a mere extrapolation of current expenditure pattern to estimate the total monetary burden imposed by ageing. They depend crucially on genetic factors, living standards and the pattern of health status people experienced during their childhood and later life span.

Of late, evidences are mounting in India to suggest: (i) poor health status of its people along with significant increase in longevity and survival chances (e^0, for example, almost doubled from 32 years in 1951 to 63 years or more by now), (ii) high disease incidence among the elderly along with growing cases of multiple diseases (or co-morbidities), and (iii) growing treatment/diagnostic costs, lack of health services in rural areas. In addition, a significant amount of

---

11. Theoretically, this entire argument rests on the presumption that the income, spending and saving display a hump-shaped pattern, where all the three grow with time and then decline at the later end of the life cycle (Jackson, 1998). It often happens, though the life cycle models make no clear-cut theoretical predictions on the relationship between population ageing and aggregate saving. We premise that the rising burden of dependencies may affect the saving potentials of low-income households even during the peak of their earning cycle and, therefore, affect the aggregate saving rates in the economy.

literature now also exists to show the inadequacy of public health facilities.[12]

Health status and its quantification underlie many conceptual and data issues. While we do not intend to go into all those details, it ought to be noted that health status measurements require identification of sickness related losses both because of: (i) premature deaths (defined as the differences between actual age at the time of death and life expectancy at that age), and (ii) days of healthy life lost due to various communicable and non-communicable ailments. This concept was recently applied by the World Bank to derive the burden of diseases for different regions and major world countries such as India and China (World Development Report, 1993). The report clearly indicates a very high burden of communicable and non-communicable diseases suffered by large fractions of ageing and non-ageing population in India—especially children in the 0-4 age bracket.

Table 1.5 provides the burden of communicable and non-communicable diseases for different age groups. Besides indicating the continued high burden of communicable diseases and its attendant losses, this table also brings out another two issues, namely: (i) the predominance of early childhood diseases—especially in the 0-4 age group, and (ii) strong linkages between ageing and non-communicable diseases. Both these issues may have serious implications not only for the health sector or its management but also for many other aspects of the country's economy including labour productivity, workers' absenteeism, poverty trap, etc. However, leaving aside the economic issues for brevity sake, high incidence of early age diseases is in itself problematic and may leave many in poor health with greater risks of dependency and proneness to suffer from old age diseases in later life. These causalities obviously have implications for health sector planning involving, *inter alia*, financial resources for meeting the diagnostic and treatment costs of an ailing and ageing population—a large fraction of whom may comprise poor and 'elderly old' or both. A direct extrapolation of different population groups and their health requirements may not, therefore, be realistically true.

As against this pessimism, there has been evidence from many industrialised countries suggesting possibilities of a 'rectangularised

---

12. For a review of literature on the quality of health care provided by the Government, see Ellis, Alam and Gupta (2000).

Table 1.5

Burden of Communicable and Non-Communicable Diseases in India:
Broad Age Groups, 1990

Age Groups	Communicable, Maternal and Prenatal			Non-Communicable Diseases		
	DALYs* (in Million)	Percentage	Rate/1000 Population	DALYs*	Percentage	Rate/1000 Population
0-4	97.9	66.3	840.7	33.4	28.3	286.6
5-14	15.4	10.4	78.3	8.8	8.3	49.6
15-44	27.1	18.3	70.5	27.3	23.1	71.1
45-59	4.7	3.2	50.2	22.6	19.2	242.0
60+	2.6	1.8	44.8	25.0	21.1	425.2
All Ages	147.7	100.0	173.9	118.1	100.0	138.9

Source: World Bank (1993) (Table B-4, p.220)

* 'DALYs' refers to the loss of healthy life years due to disease related disabilities.

survival curve.[13] This curve premises that people are beginning to reach their full natural life span and do not therefore die at early ages on account of bad health or early childhood diseases. Given the figures in Table 1.5, such a situation for India is far beyond expectation. Hence, the optimistic approach found in the rectangularised (or near rectangularised) survival curve has limited applicability in the present context. But still some improvement or compression in the morbidity situation in the near future cannot be completely ruled out following a host of preventive measures such as improved diet, reduced smoking, growing awareness about a sedentary life style and environmental pollution (for further discussion on this, see Chapter 5)

High prevalence of old age diseases in India is not only observed by the World Development Report (1993), it has also been noted in many other studies—especially those based on the two recently held NSS for 1986-87 (42nd Round) and 1995-96 (52nd Round).[14]

---

13. Mortality statistics are depicted by a survival curve that plots the percentage cumulative survival of a birth cohort against its age. In such a curve, the survival rate is 100 per cent at the age 0, which then declines with increasing age until it reaches zero at an age when the entire cohort has died. This situation is described in the literature as 'rectangularised survival curve' – flattening out at lower ages due to very high survival rate and then falling away as the birth cohort enters old age (Fries and Crapo, 1981; Jackson, 1998).

14. Gumber and Berman (1995) provide a detailed description of the morbidity surveys conducted by the NSS since October 1953.

Despite growing data availability on the extent of old age diseases, nothing much has apparently been done in recent years to examine this issue by detailing the socio-economic and other characteristics of the morbid elderly. Attempts have also been lacking in making objective assessments about their health and non-health security requirements. For instance, the aged in most cases are considered as a homogenous group—without making them differentiable by certain cut-off ages (e.g. young old, mid old or older old). Similarly they were hardly studied empirically by taking into consideration their rural-urban distribution, social groups, work status, implications on activities of daily living (ADL), etc. While the next few sections of this study are exclusively devoted to some of these issues, the following details may further clarify a few of the points raised above.

Table 1.6

Aged with Chronic Ailments: Major States and All India, 1986-87 & 1995-96

Percentage

Major States	Rural: Persons		Urban: Persons	
	1986-87	*1995-96*	*1986-87*	*1995-96*
Andhra Pradesh	56.50	64.70	54.50	57.50
Assam	62.80	69.50	59.10	76.70
Bihar	43.20	43.00	43.70	40.90
Gujarat	30.80	41.80	34.60	48.00
Haryana	37.00	47.10	34.60	57.30
Karnataka	36.30	33.70	37.60	46.80
Kerala	69.30	68.90	71.90	61.40
Madhya Pradesh	40.40	44.50	39.80	42.00
Maharashtra	43.10	51.30	40.90	53.30
Orissa	48.80	58.70	51.60	51.10
Punjab	51.80	56.80	44.30	51.90
Rajasthan	39.20	45.00	40.30	39.10
Tamil Nadu	35.70	47.70	35.00	53.00
Uttar Pradesh	44.80	52.00	46.60	54.50
West Bengal	65.50	70.10	60.50	76.30
India	**45.00**	**52.00**	**44.80**	**54.40**

Source: For 1987-88: *Sarvekshna* (1991, Issue 49, p.116). For 1995-96: The Aged in India: A Socio-Economic Profile, NSS 52nd Round (July 1995-June 1996) Report No. 446 (52/25.0/3).

Table 1.6 serves to provide an idea about the extent of old age morbidity both at the all India level and for 15 major states. These details are also given over two points of time to judge the temporal changes. Disturbingly, most states suggest a rising trend in fractions of morbid elderly population. This share has particularly increased in states such as Andhra Pradesh, Haryana, Punjab, Madhya Pradesh, Tamil Nadu, Uttar Pradesh and West Bengal. They registered an increase in their ailing elderly in the rural as well as in the urban areas (see Figures. 1.3a and 1.3b). Increasing trends in old age morbidity may as well be noted for many of the prosperous states including Haryana, Gujarat and Maharashtra. With this increase, the all India figures in Table 1.6 reveal that more than half the rural and urban elderly (52 per cent in rural areas, and more than 54.4 per cent in urban areas) were reporting chronically ill in 1995-96.[15] As the aged in India are overwhelmingly rural (for further details, see Chapter 2), and also that the rural areas are severely lacking in terms of old age health care, this trend warrants consideration while planning for health care services and its pricing mechanism.

The striking level of morbidity among the rural elderly also deserves serious consideration. State level data, presented in Table 1.6, clearly reveal that in many states more than two-thirds of the total aged have reported as suffering from chronic ailments. This is especially the case with Andhra Pradesh, Assam, Kerala and West Bengal. Worse still, a large proportion of them suffer from multiple diseases.

Based on the 52nd Round of the NSS (1995-96), Tables 1.7a and 1.7b provide a distribution of the rural aged in 14 major states with or without any chronic ailments. As a further extension, we also generate information on single and multiple diseases suffered by those in 60-69 and 70+ age groups. This helps to make a judgment about the age-ailments relationship (Table 1.7b).

A number of distressing, though useful, observations can be derived from both the tables. Table 1.7a, for instance, suggests that the only state where chronically ailing elderly are less than half of their total rural population is Karnataka (see the ranks in brackets).

---

15. By definition, chronic illnesses or ailments are those requiring treatment for more than 30 days. Further, these were self reported ailments and may, therefore, suffer from subjectivities and exaggerations.

Figure 1.3

Chronically Sick Elderly: 1986-87 & 1995-96

(a) Rural

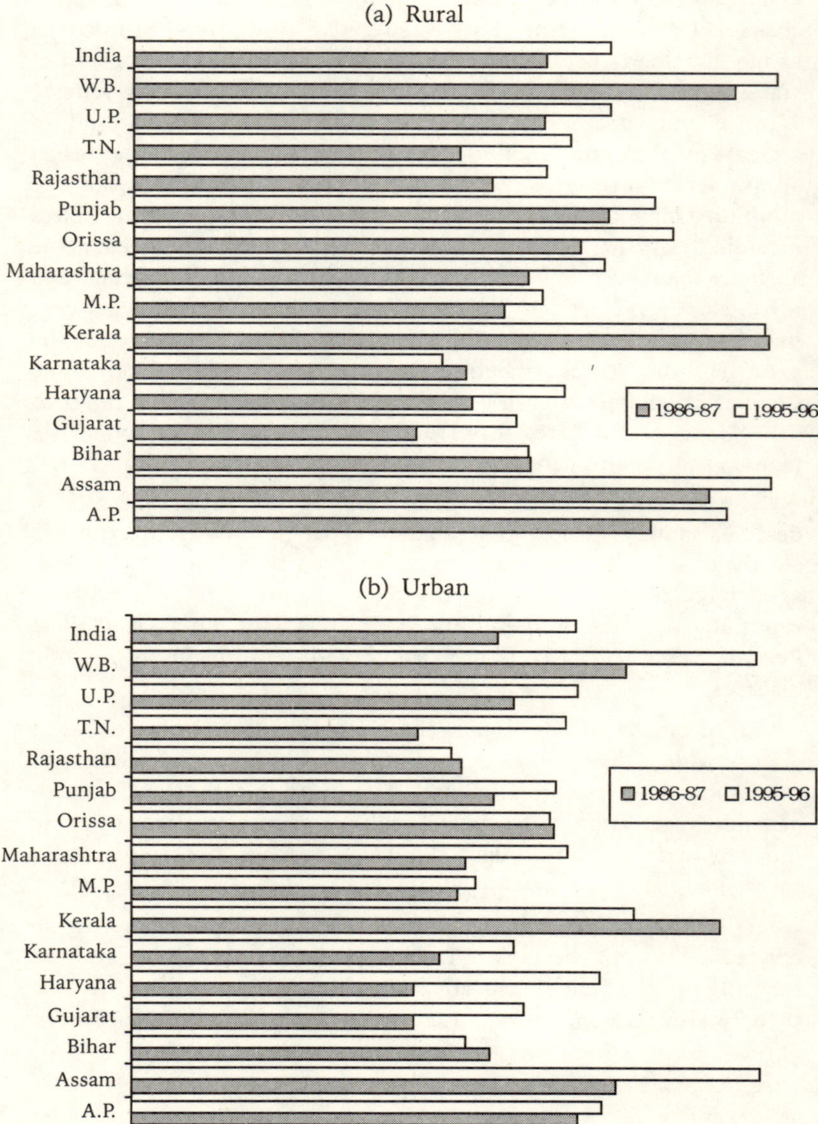

(b) Urban

Source: Table 1.6.

Table 1.7a

Distribution of 60+ with Single and Multiple Diseases: Rural

Major States	Number of Diseases (%)				Total	% Without
	1	*2*	*3*	*4 & More*	*(1 to 4+)*	*Disease*
Andhra Pradesh	30.4	22.8	11.5	10.4	75.1 (4)	24.9
Assam	27.1	24.0	13.6	11.7	76.4 (2)	23.7
Bihar	24.4	15.1	8.5	8.6	56.5 (13)	43.5
Gujarat	26.8	18.2	6.0	9.3	60.3 (10)	39.7
Karnataka	24.2	15.2	6.6	2.5	48.5 (14)	51.5
Kerala	27.5	20.6	13.3	14.6	76.1 (3)	23.9
Madhya Pradesh	23.0	16.1	7.0	11.2	57.2 (12)	42.8
Maharashtra	30.6	22.3	8.3	7.9	69.1 (6)	30.9
Orissa	29.2	12.1	13.0	15.1	69.3 (5)	30.7
Punjab	29.8	21.2	10.6	6.9	68.4 (7)	31.6
Rajasthan	25.2	20.6	6.8	7.4	60.0 (11)	40.0
Tamil Nadu	24.7	19.7	9.3	7.2	60.8 *(9)*	39.2
Uttar Pradesh	26.6	16.3	11.9	11.3	66.0 (8)	34.0
West Bengal	23.9	21.7	17.3	14.9	77.8 *(1)*	22.2

Source: NSS 52nd Round (1995-96) Household Data CD.

Note: 1. Computations based on household level data provided on CD by the NSSO.

2. Figures in bracket rank state-wise level of morbidity in descending order.

All other states far exceed this mark—notably Andhra Pradesh, Assam, Kerala, West Bengal, Orissa, Maharashtra, etc.[16]

With regard to multiple diseases, Table 1.7b clearly indicates that the fractions of those with two or more diseases are much higher in 10 out of 14 major states under consideration. No such pattern however emerges while comparing the two age categories of older persons (i.e., 60-69 and 70+), and a good fraction of higher age elderly suffers from multiple diseases in all the 14 states under observation. This brings quality of life as a significant issue to debate over. In addition, it also questions the usefulness of added longevity achieved by the country over the past decades. We will take-up this issue later in Chapter 5 of the study.

---

16. Notice that the level of old age morbidity in states such as West Bengal and Assam is higher than Kerala. This to some extent negates the argument that high morbidity in states like Kerala follows from its better literacy level and general awareness.

Table 1.7b

Distribution of 60-69 and 70+ by Single and Multiple Diseases: Rural

Percentage

Major States	Age Group: 60-69				Age Group: 70+				Single + Multiple Sickness (60-69)	Single + Multiple Sickness (70+)
	Single Disease	Multiple Diseases			Single Disease	Multiple Diseases				
		2	3	4 & More		2	3	4 & More		
A.Pr.	21.6	14.9	5.4	5.2	8.9	7.9	6.0	5.2	47.1	28.0
Ass.	21.0	17.9	7.7	6.2	6.0	6.1	5.9	5.5	52.8	23.5
Bih.	16.1	9.1	4.9	3.8	8.3	5.9	3.6	4.8	33.9	22.6
Guj.	18.0	10.6	2.4	3.6	8.7	7.6	3.6	5.7	34.6	25.7
Kar.	16.2	7.2	2.2	1.0	8.1	8.0	4.5	1.5	26.5	22.1
Ker.	16.1	12.0	6.8	6.0	11.4	8.7	6.5	8.5	40.9	35.1
M.Pr.	15.4	9.1	3.4	4.7	7.6	6.9	3.7	6.5	32.6	24.6
Mah.	19.9	13.6	4.3	4.2	10.7	8.6	4.0	3.7	42.0	27.0
Ori.	18.4	6.8	4.6	5.6	10.8	5.2	8.4	9.5	35.5	33.9
Pun.	15.0	9.4	3.8	2.4	14.8	11.8	6.8	4.5	30.6	37.8
Raj.	14.7	8.6	2.2	1.7	10.6	12.0	4.6	5.6	27.2	32.7
T.N.	16.2	9.9	4.2	3.8	8.5	9.7	5.0	3.4	34.2	26.6
U.Pr.	17.0	9.3	4.9	3.9	9.6	7.0	7.0	7.4	35.1	31.0
W. B.	15.0	15.3	10.5	6.1	8.9	6.4	6.8	8.7	46.9	30.9

Source: NSS 52nd Round Data CD (1995-96).

An important issue to identify in this context is the factor/s responsible for old age diseases of this magnitude in the country. Or, there is perhaps a need to investigate the socio-economic disparities and their health outcomes for the elderly. Though there has been growing interest among analysts on this issue in recent years, nothing much has emerged regarding the health of the elderly (DFID, 2003). We would come back to this and other related issues later.

A logical corollary of such high disease prevalence perhaps is to expect high amount of public spending on health and creation of gerontological infrastructure, especially in rural areas. While an attempt has been made to examine some of these issues at a subsequent stage, we present below two tables underlining the: (i) recent compressions in real per capita health expenditure by the Centre and states in response to their fiscal difficulties, and (ii) poor utilisation of public health care facilities—often because of poor quality of services, more waiting time, moonlighting by doctors (Sankar, 2001), and paucity of necessary medicines. These issues pose serious health security constraints for the aged in particular—especially in a situation of growing privatisation in the health sector and non-availability of any social health insurance cover for a sizeable majority of people in the country. A serious debate on providing some health insurance cover and its financial mechanism is therefore important.

Table 1.8 shows the real per capita health expenditure by the Centre and state governments and its annual growth over the years between 1990-91 and 1995-96. Going by this table, certain states have substantially increased their per capita health expenditure during this period, while the contrary has happened in many others. But the more interesting point relates to states such as Andhra Pradesh, Kerala,

Table 1.8

Real Per Capita Health Expenditure: Major States, 1990-91 & 1995-96

States	1990-91 (Rs.)	1995-96 (Rs.)	Annual Average Growth (%)
Andhra Pradesh	34.6	83.8	19.35
Bihar	25.4	21.9	(-) 2.92
Gujarat	50.9	52.7	0.70
Haryana	44.1	49.8	2.46
Karnataka	37.1	53.0	7.39
Kerala	51.2	63.7	4.47
Madhaya Pradesh	30.4	31.8	0.90
Maharashtra	58.4	61.7	1.11
Orissa	33.0	48.2	7.87
Punjab	54.9	57.7	1.00
Rajasthan	63.0	58.1	(-) 1.61
Tamil Nadu	70.2	72.8	0.73
Uttar Pradesh	33.1	29.4	(-) 2.34
West Bengal	41.6	34.4	(-) 3.73
Centre	9.2	4.7	(-) 12.57

Source: NSS, 52nd Round (1995-96)–Report No. 446.

Orissa, etc. While the growth of per capita expenditure in these states is substantially higher (19.3, 4.5 and 7.9 per cent per annum, respectively), they also suffer from high levels of old age morbidity. This raises several questions—particularly those relating to the utilisation of financial resources in these states and the effectiveness of their health delivery system. It would, however, require examining programme-wise allocation of financial resources made in rural and urban areas by the Centre and state governments. These data are however not readily available.[17]

Unlike in the past, the share of the public sector in hospitalised treatment seems to be declining in favour of private providers. This is clearly visible from Table 1.9, and holds for both rural and urban areas. A possible explanation of this might be the gradual decline in the quality of services in public facilities.

To sum up, this entire situation boils down to the following question: how efficiently can the health sector in India respond to the

Table 1.9

Share of Public & Private Sectors in Hospitalised Treatment

Percentage

Hospital Type	Rural		Urban	
	1986-87	*1995-96*	*1986-87*	*1995-96*
Government				
Hospital	55.4	39.9	59.5	41.8
PHC/CHC	4.3	4.8	0.8	0.9
Public Dispensary	-	0.5	-	0.4
Total Government	**59.7**	**45.2**	**60.3**	**43.1**
Non-Government				
Private Hospital	32.0	41.9	29.6	41.0
Nursing Home	4.9	8.0	7.0	11.1
Charity Institutions	1.7	4.0	1.9	4.2
Others	1.7	0.08	1.2	0.6
Total Non-Government	**40.3**	**54.7**	**39.7**	**56.9**

Source: NSS 52nd Round (1995-96), Morbidity and Treatment of Ailments, Report No. 441, November 1998, p. 28.

---

17. For a discussion on programme-wise health care financing in India and its various data limitations, (Alam, 1997).

fast emerging changes in age composition of the population and societal ageing—especially considering that the aged are predominantly rural, suffer from multiple diseases, are economically at a loss in the new pro-market dispensation, and socially are faced with erosion in traditional values. Social insurance is perhaps a possible solution, but it faces the uphill task of finding a sustainable financial mechanism. Unfortunately, much of the ongoing debate on these issues is urban centric—risking exclusions of the rural aged. Also, the Government's recent monetary policies remain completely non-committal on most of these problems.

1.5. Public Policy Issues: Reforms, Declining Returns to Saving and the Aged[18]

Social Security in India

Changes in the age composition of population in India are now widely accepted with recent attempts by the Centre and state governments to introduce specific welfare measures for the aged. These measures include the direct transfers in the form of monthly pension schemes (as part of Social Assistance Programme) by the Centre and state governments to protect the destitute elderly. This scheme also includes a recent initiative by the Union Government to provide a fixed quantity of grain (currently 10 kg) as a food security measure to the below poverty (BPL) aged.[19] The indirect form of support mechanism relies on subsidies provided on certain public services including travel by public transport, medical care, personal taxation, etc. Measures have also been taken to have separate windows in public offices for senior citizens.

Yet another mode of social security in India is the one that generally covers the retiring workers of major public and private sector establishments, and in many cases works on principles as followed internationally.[20] Many of these schemes are financed by joint employee-employer contributions and supplemented by the

---

18. A more comprehensive discussion on these aspects will follow in Chapter 7.

19. It refers to the 'Annapurna Scheme' announced by the Prime Minister in 1999. The functioning of this and all other anti-destitution schemes for the aged are however suspect and need follow-up studies (Alam and Antony, 2001).

20. For a comparison of various social security instruments in India and other countries, Singh (1997).

government. These, *inter alia*, include the Employees' State Insurance Scheme (ESIS), provident fund, pension and deposit linked insurance schemes, and so forth. Besides, there are a few non-contributory schemes covered under the Workmen's Compensation Act (1923) and Payment of Gratuity Act (1972). We describe some of these schemes in Chapter 7 of the study.

Many of these contributory and non-contributory schemes are currently faced with the problems of: (i) management inefficiencies, delays, cumbersome procedures, inadequate coverage, etc., and (ii) growing financial burden due to the added life span and increasing pool of retired pensioners. With the second phase of economic reforms in hand—which essentially requires more of fiscal pruning—this growing pressure on public finances is forcing the Centre and state governments to shed some of their future liabilities through pension reforms and privatisation of pension fund management. In a declining interest rate regime combined by factors such as long phases of depressed stock market, erosion in credibility of fund management agencies, and the country's weak regulatory mechanism, these new changes can become serious security issues even for the middle and higher income ageing population in the country.

National Policy on Older Persons (NPOP), 1999

Leaving aside the problems of growing economic pressure and competing demand for financial resources, it may be noted that Article 41 of the Indian Constitution has obligated the State to ensure the well being of the elderly. In addition, India is also a signatory of various UN backed International Agreements to protect the life and dignity of the aged.[21] Obligated by these provisions, the Government of India introduced a NPOP in 1999, seeking participation by the community at large to ensure financial security, health care, shelter, welfare and other important needs of the elderly. The policy also recognises the need for larger budgetary allocations to provide special attention to the aged suffering from life lack of resources and threatening impoverishment.

---

21. For example, the United Nations Principles for Older Persons adopted by the United Nations General Assembly in 1991, the Proclamation on Ageing, and the Global Targets on Ageing for 2001, etc.

Some of the important concerns of the NPOP are as under:

- Financial security: It *inter alia* requires extending the old age pension cover to the entire below poverty ageing population.[22] The realm of issues concerning the long-term savings and pension was also brought under this provision.

- Health care and nutrition: The NPOP is strongly committed to prioritise the health needs of the elderly. It specifically suggested strengthening the primary health units to meet the health care requirements of the rural aged.[23] In addition, involvement of health insurance agencies and private health providers was also discussed against the backdrop of existing subsidies including provisions of cheap land for private hospitals and concessions on import of medical equipment. Specialised geriatric training for medical and paramedical personnel was another area of major concern in the NPOP. The need to work for strengthening the services required for mental health was also highlighted.

- Assistance to geriatric care societies, NGOs, public charity and voluntary organisations was emphasised in the NPOP.

- Health education programme and involvement of mass media were regarded as significant in the context of healthy ageing.

- Shelter: It was recommended that 10 per cent of the allotments by major housing schemes be earmarked for the elderly—with provision to give them preference in allotment of the ground floor. Housing colonies were asked to consider the special needs of the aged in their construction layouts.

- Suggestions in regard to group housing societies and complexes for older persons.

- Priority in providing public utilities for the elderly.

- Education: Information and education material relevant to the lives of older persons was considered useful by the NPOP. It was suggested that such materials be widely disseminated.

- Welfare: It was especially considered necessary to identify the more vulnerable among the elderly cohorts—such as the

---

22. This is where the poverty norms for the aged need to be redefined.
23. The National Population Policy (2000) also suggests the same.

disabled, infirm, chronically ill or widows—and provide them with needed welfare services including institutional care.

- Creation of welfare fund for older men and women with assistance from different sources including government, corporate bodies, trusts, individual donors, and so on.

- Protection of life and property: The policy document pointed out the need to provide and strengthen the necessary provisions in the Indian Penal Code (IPC) against elderly abuse.

- Voluntary Sector: Special assistance to trusts, charities and other endowments to expand activities and services for the elderly.

- Family and familial support: The NPOP regards families as the main care providers with suggestions in the policy document to sensitise the younger generation towards their role in inter-generational bonding.

- Research on ageing and its ramifications: Emphasis was also placed on research in socio-medical gerontology and the required database.

Despite a good documentation on ageing issues and proposed safeguards ensuring the welfare of older persons, the NPOP is lacking in at least two major respects. First, it hardly attempts to specify measures required to ensure the security provisions listed in the document. Second, the document typically relies on supply side measures without inputs to look into: (i) the actual requirements of the aged, and (ii) how far these requirements can really be met by the care-givers, particularly in a situation of growing privatisation, deceleration in quality employment, informalisation of labour market with loss of labour rights and rising insecurity, sectoral reforms (e.g., health sector reforms with growing user charges), withdrawal of public subsidies, and so on. Also, large-scale disparities among the aged have not been fully recognised.

Ageing and Reforms: Risk of Economic-Demographic Mismatch

Economic Reforms

Beginning July 1991, the current phase of the reformist economic regime in India is essentially grounded into the twin concepts of: (i) structural adjustment, and (ii) fiscal stabilisation initiatives. Both of them have their roots in public economic policies, directed to reduce the level of internal and external deficits and allocative inefficiencies, especially in developing economies.[24] As both follow more or less a similar policy mechanism, the two concepts are generally distinguished by the time criterion—where stabilisation often refers to the short-term measures designed to reduce imbalances between domestic absorption and domestic supply. Structural adjustment policies, on the other hand, are relatively more time consuming and meant to improve allocative efficiencies, minimise distortions in factor and product markets, and make changes in ground rules of production and exchange with a view to accelerating GNP growth.

Like many other developing countries, India also began its structural adjustment programme with measures to reduce current account deficit—both fiscal and balance of payment—followed by attempts to minimise public liabilities on the premise of rationalisation measures. These measures entail cuts in two major components of the GDP, namely, consumption and investment. Algebraically, this is expressed as:

$$Y + NFI = C + I + X - M + NFI$$

Where Y denotes GDP, NFI represents net foreign income. C consumption, I investment, X export, M imports. An attempt to reduce the current account deficit by an increase in surplus—that is, X – M + NFI (the stabilisation effect)—may adversely affect the economy in terms of lower consumption and rising incidence of poverty. A way out might be to shift the pattern of expenditure from non-traded to traded goods and raise the stock of surplus with more exportable goods and lesser imports. This would obviously require a policy response in the form of structural adjustment, which *inter alia* seeks to ensure a decision-making role for the market. Some of these measures may however cause exclusions of vulnerable population groups including a big majority of illiterate or semi-literate labour market entrants, the physically weak and the aged. With decelerating employment in high productivity sectors, growing casualisation of the labour market, poor growth of social infrastructure, high level of morbidity, uncertainties of the money market, declining returns to

---

24. For a good discussion on evolution and various conceptual details of stabilisation and structural adjustment policies, see Stern (1991), Gaiha (1991), etc.

saving,[25] and so on, India has now already to face some of these problems (Prabhu, 2001; PROBE, 1999; Ghose, 1994 and Alam and Mishra, 1998). This whole situation is also fraught with the risks of a serious economic-demographic mismatch.

Economic-Demographic Mismatch

We pose a situation grounded into the following:

1. Changes in reproductive behaviour and added life years resulting in growing shares of young and old adults (Figures 1.1 and 1.2).

2. Shifts in economic paradigm with liberalised trade regime, competitive environment in the market and persisting deceleration in employment (i.e., the jobless growth).

3. Perennial poverty with the aged at the uppermost of the vulnerable segments. At an extended level, even the younger adults would be facing vulnerability with many serious labour market issues such as uncontrolled exit of sick industrial units, contractualisation of employment, non-compliance of labour laws or meagre wages due to demand-supply imbalances (Breman, 2003 and Breman and Das, 2000). We postulate that a situation like this may in many cases constrain the familial abilities to endure the burden of old age dependencies.[26] The largely held premise, especially advocated by the NPOP (1999), that the families and siblings would take the major responsibilities of their aged may not therefore be completely relied upon.

4. With none or at best grossly inadequate old age income security, the idea of downsising the family may lose some of its

---

25. While the implications of declining bank rates or uncertainties of the money market on the one hand, and the growing cost of various basic services such as power, water, transport, health care or the rising burden of several new taxes (e.g., taxes levied on whole range of services, proposed municipal taxes like parking tax or additional house tax, phasing out of tax breaks on home loans as suggested by the task force on tax reforms) has not been fully examined in relation to those largely dependent on interest earnings, some recent newspaper articles do suggest adverse fallouts for large segments of people including the retired elderly. This is particularly true given the lack of social security system in India. See, for instance, a write-up by J Mulraj in the *Times of India*, dated November 4, 2002 (New Delhi Edition).

26. Some of our subsequent findings suggest that the per capita consumption of households with financially dependent elderly are less than those where the aged have certain independent income.

logical moorings. It may also create a public-private conflict of interests.

We attempt to illustrate further the points raised above with the help of a flow diagram presented in Figure 1.4. Three situations are highlighted: one is the outcome of the ongoing economic liberalisation and pro-market regime (shown at the bottom of the flow diagram), while the second (shown at the top) relates to the shifts in various demographic parameters resulting in significant age structure changes. The third one—exemplifying certain broad areas of mismatch—are given in the middle and include issues such as the higher inflow of job seekers into the labour market, poor quality of employment, depressed wages, insecurity, and inadequate income transfers for the aged, old age poverty, distressed work related migrations, and so on.

Left unattended, we argue that these incompatibilities (or economic-demographic mismatch) would grow with time into major issues for different population groups. To the young and first timers into the labour market, for instance, it may turn into a demand-supply mismatch—especially in high productivity sectors. One of the fallouts of this situation may be the growing casualisation of employment and the labour market. A recent study by Breman and Das (2000) has already highlighted some of these issues. Besides, there may be lower wages, inadequate living standards, relative inequalities, higher migration to urban informal sectors with lopsided and unbalanced urbanisation, low equilibrium trap, poor intra household transfers and low bargaining capacity, etc. Such a situation may in many ways prove detrimental to the market and the economy.

The worst affected would perhaps be the ageing population—already faced with serious livelihood issues for lack of work opportunities, inadequate—if not completely missing—social securities, higher risks and poor returns to the accumulated savings, high rate of old age sickness,[27] lack of required health facilities, inadequate intergenerational transfer of resources especially among low income households (Alam, 2001), etc. Destitute and widowed women may suffer most from this mismatch, and perhaps with greater intensity.

---

27. More than 52 per cent of the rural and 54 per cent of the urban elderly suffer from chronic ailments-see 52nd Round of the NSS (1995-96, Report No. 446. p. 20). A detailed discussion on this is attempted in Chapter 2 of this study.

Figure 1.4

Economic-Demographic Changes and their Likely Mismatch: An Illustration

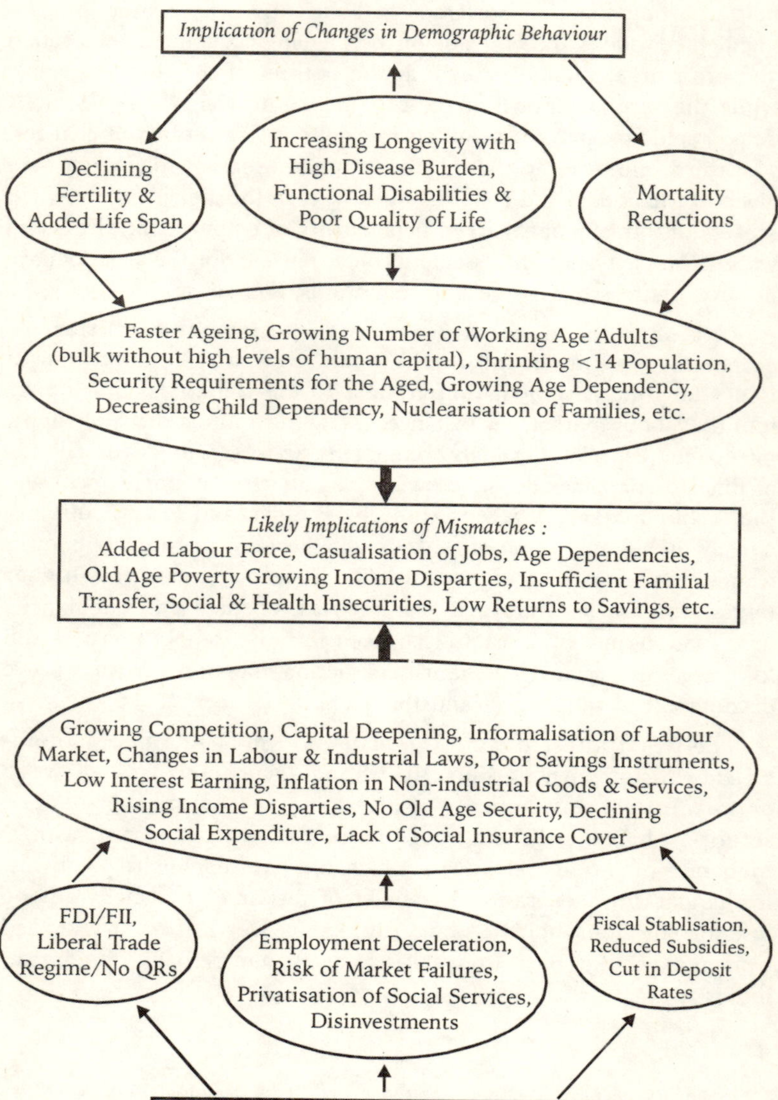

School or college participants may suffer from low quality of education provided through public institutions, poor linkages between the market and education, high drop out rates, absenteeism, unabated child labour, etc. All this may cause a large fraction of people to face perpetual risks of market exclusions and low paid casual employment.

While most of these issues need to be thoroughly examined to draw a definitive conclusion, a growing body of literature now already exists to support this premise. Demographically mediated age structure changes, for example, are now well documented (Kulkarni 2001). Ageing and its socio-economic ramifications have also been drawing attention (Alam, 2001b, 2000; Rajan, Mishra and Sharma, 1999; Kumar, 1998; etc.). An analysis by Mehrotra and Chaurasia (2001) comes out with considerable details about the limitations of education—both technical and general. Likewise, several disquieting facts about the decelerating growth of employment in high productivity sectors have already been addressed by a number of studies (ILO, 2005; Bhattacharya and Sakthivel, 2004; Planning Commission, 2002; Goldar, 2000; Anant, Sundaram and Tendulkar 1999; Alam and Mishra, 1998 and Ghosh, 1994). A recent study by Bhavani (2001) offers several details about the problems faced by smaller industrial units as a result of growing competition and dumping, increasing threats from patenting and Trade Related Intellectual Property Rights (TRIP) related controls. Similarly, a study by Visaria (1998) raises several questions about the growing cohort of first timers in the labour force. This study also underlines the mismatch between the growth of college graduates and the organised sector employment. Most of these studies agree that the employment scenario in the country over the coming years[28] is going to be difficult.

Communal Issues: Community Support for the Elderly

Two different, though interlinked, aspects of social security are 'protection' and 'promotion' from precarious conditions of living. The former, i.e., the protective form of social security, is considered particularly significant for preventing a large scale decline in living

---

28. A brief write-up by Dileep Padgaonkar 'Hard Times Ahead' in the Sunday *Times of India* (December 1, 2002) summarises a recent study by Sandeep Waslekar of the Strategic Foresight Group (Bombay). This study highlights the limitations of the current development model with potentials to generate a high amount of disparities across different population groups. The Waslekar study especially paints a grim picture about the employment scenario in the country due to the growing number of labour market entrants seeking more and more opportunities for work. The study suggests aiming for a 9 per cent pro-employment GDP growth rate.

standards in general, and in the basic conditions of living in particular (Dreze and Sen, 1991). In India, as in many other low-income countries, large sections of older persons are increasingly confronted with situations where even basic conditions of living are found wanting—often due to disruptions in old and mutigenerational family relationships. Modernisation theorists hold industrialisation and large-scale expansion of market-dominated formal services responsible for this disruption. They also agree that this process will grow further, leaving many of the existing informal services to be gradually taken over by the market. Despite growing recognition of these realities, countries like India have failed to respond effectively or to promote what is called 'a mixed economy of care' in which such care is shared between public and communal sources—particularly by non-profit voluntary organisations. This can be noted from the small coverage of the aged population by communally aided institutions or the lack of detailed evaluation of these institutions by analysts to judge the quality of services provided by them. This is also evident from the limited infrastructure available in the form of old age homes in the country.

As already pointed out, the available literature on the voluntary sector and its contribution to maintenance of the ageing population in India is extremely limited, inferences about its role in protecting the living conditions of older persons is not therefore possible. Nor is there any systematic information about its overall size across the country, growth pattern, nature and quality of services provided to the beneficiaries, and so forth. One of the few attempts to make an evaluation of this sector has been a recent study by Rajan, Misra and Sharma (1999). Using a limited survey of 186 old age homes from a few southern states in India, this study does not provide a very rosy picture about the contribution of this sector in caring for the elderly. One of its findings for instance, reveals that about half the sample homes (i.e., 46 per cent) did not provide any in-house medical care. Further, over 72 per cent of them had no vehicle to meet emergency situations. The study also suggests that many of the public funded institutions offer relatively better services than those run by religious or philanthropic institutions.

In order to supplement these findings, we tried to cull out certain information from the Helpage India Directory covering size and selected facilities provided by old age homes in most major states in India. This information, given in Table 1.10, reveals a few interesting

Table 1.10

Distribution of Old Age Homes by Size and Facilities: Major States

Percentage

Major States	Distribution of Homes (%)	Homes for Women	Intake Capacity (Nos.)			Type of Facilities			Availability of Medical Facility		
			< 25	25-50	>50	Free	Paid	Both	Orthopedic	Medical	First Aid
Andhra Pradesh	12.9	14.0	11.8	14.0	11.8	13.2	12.2	13.0	13.8	14.7	14.8
Assam	1.2	0.0	1.7	1.3	0.7	1.6	0.0	1.0	1.1	1.6	0.9
Bihar	0.2	0.0	0.8	0.0	0.0	0.3	0.0	0.0	0.4	0.4	0.3
Delhi	1.8	2.2	3.4	1.3	1.3	1.3	2.2	3.0	2.5	1.2	1.8
Gujarat	7.3	3.2	1.7	7.0	12.4	7.1	8.9	7.0	6.2	4.3	7.0
Haryana	0.6	0.0	0.8	0.9	0.0	1.0	0.0	0.0	0.7	1.2	0.9
Karanataka	8.4	5.4	13.4	6.1	8.5	6.1	10.0	13.0	9.8	7.4	8.5
Kerala	20.0	37.6	21.8	20.5	19.0	23.8	14.4	11.0	20.7	26.7	18.2
Madhya Pradesh	2.0	0.0	2.5	1.7	1.3	1.9	1.1	3.0	0.7	3.1	3.0
Maharashtra	9.8	10.8	6.7	7.0	13.7	6.8	13.3	17.0	10.5	3.9	6.1
Orissa	3.9	2.2	0.8	7.4	0.7	6.1	0.0	1.0	1.1	4.7	5.5
Punjab	3.3	1.1	4.2	2.6	3.9	3.9	1.1	4.0	5.1	2.7	4.5
Rajasthan	0.2	0.0	0.8	0.0	0.0	0.0	0.0	0.0	0.0	0.0	0.0
Tamil Nadu	19.0	17.2	23.5	17.5	18.3	18.6	25.6	15.0	19.3	17.8	17.3
Uttar Pradesh	2.5	1.1	2.5	2.2	3.9	1.9	4.4	3.0	2.2	3.1	3.0
West Bengal	6.9	5.4	3.4	10.5	4.6	6.4	6.7	9.0	5.8	7.4	8.2
Total	510	93	119	229	153	311	90	100	275	258	330

Source: HelpAge India (1998).

details. For instance, we notice that over 40 per cent of the total old age homes are located in just four Southern States—namely, Kerala, Andhra Pradesh, Tamil Nadu and Karnataka. States with high religiosity such as Uttar Pradesh and Bihar are far behind. In addition, female old age homes are particularly few—less than one-fifth of those reported, and more than half of them are located in only two states, Kerala and Tamil Nadu. Another interesting observation relates to their inmate capacity and basis of stay. We notice that a majority of the homes in the country are medium sized (capacity ranging between 25 and 50 persons) and free of charges. More than a quarter of the paid homes are in Tamil Nadu followed by Kerala, Maharashtra and Andhra Pradesh. Yet another observation from this table relates to medical facilities. While over 65 per cent of the reported old age homes are shown to have provided some kind of medical aid, their quality cannot be commented upon.

Clearly, the ongoing debate in national and international fora on questions of old age care lays heavy responsibilities on the community with large-scale participation from non-profit voluntary organisations. Recently, the UN sponsored Second World Assembly on Ageing (April 2002) has further reiterated this argument. India too as one of the member countries has agreed to pursue this line of approach. The NPOP (1999) held similar views on this.

Notwithstanding these international recommendations and government endorsements, the big question relates to the financing of all such activities. There are also other issues such as free *versus* fully or partially paid facilities, their mix, management, mobilisation of enough community support, areas of public-private participation, nature or extent of subsidies by government to make private facilities more affordable, a regulatory mechanism, and so on. Given the high prevalence of old age poverty in the country, these are indeed questions that need serious examination. Table 1.11, which gives an idea about the level of per-capita monthly consumption expenditure of the urban elderly, might serve as a pointer in this direction.[29] It may be disquieting to notice from this table that in most states a very large fraction of the aged survive at an expenditure level far below the international poverty norm (i.e., below 1 US $ a day). In addition, states like Bihar and Orissa present a very grim situation. Paid old age

---

29. Similar information for the rural elderly is far more appalling.

Table 1.11

*Distribution of Elderly by Per Capita Monthly Consumption
Expenditure: Urban Persons, 1995-96*

Percentage

Major States	Expenditure Levels (Rs.)			
	< Rs. 250	*Rs. 250 – 399*	*Rs. 400 – 600*	*> Rs. 600*
Andhra Pradesh	9.04	27.44	31.3	32.50
Assam	NA	NA	NA	NA
Bihar	23.69	41.36	20.99	13.96
Gujarat	2.53	19.85	36.34	41.28
Karnataka	12.8	32.01	30.19	25.00
Kerala	6.93	34.55	32.05	26.47
Madhya Pradesh	12.39	38.98	30.94	17.68
Maharashtra	6.68	22.91	28.61	41.80
Orissa	15.53	40.73	30.64	13.10
Punjab	1.71	15.65	35.51	47.13
Rajasthan	5.89	28.01	37.56	28.54
Tamil Nadu	9.83	29.54	33.77	26.87
Uttar Pradesh	12.53	32.85	30.35	24.27
West Bengal	8.71	25.38	32.96	32.96
All India	9.04	27.44	31.03	32.50

Source: NSS 52nd Round Data CD.

homes in these or similar other states may therefore be able to serve
only a tiny fraction of the older population. The community has
therefore a prime role.

1.6. Structure of the Study and Data Sources

Of the many, at least three important points emerging from the
preceding discussion need to be re-emphasised. These include:
(i) India is already on the verge of societal ageing with many serious
implications, (ii) inadequate attention has been paid to many of these
issues by empiricists and development planners, and (iii) the ongoing
macro-economic and sectoral reforms are apparently adding to the
problems of insecurity among the aged and non-aged with the former
obviously at a greater risk. This study, as was already noted, is
designed to address some of these issues empirically.

At almost every level—constitutionally, politically, socially and culturally—India remains fully committed to resolve the problems of social deprivation and poverty. In pursuance of this, India has to its credit a long history of publicly funded welfare enhancing anti-poverty programmes. A great deal of concern in most of these programmes has however been directed to the generation of employment and asset building among the poor (World Bank, 1998). The special needs of the elderly—that may be central to decide about their poverty problems, and also the nature of social protection required by them[30]—have however remained largely neglected.

To be precise, the following questions have remained almost completely unattended:

- Is it plausible to overlook the age-specific differences while deciding about the basic requirements of an individual?

- Is it plausible in the emerging economic environment to expect low-income families to provide health and income security for their elderly without a well-designed and financially sustainable public support mechanism?

- Is it plausible for a country like India to ignore the risks of market failure for a sizeable ageing population who suffer from serious disparities including health impairments owing to multiple diseases, low per capital consumption level, declining participation in economic activities, dwindling health infrastructure in public sector, and no idea (even at the discussion level) about a social health insurance system?

- With fast emerging changes in the value system, is it plausible to expect altruism in parental (or elderly) care?

- Do the existing pillars of income security for the aged make the elderly feel secured?

---

30. Social protection is now used in most societies to combat poverty or negative consequences of social contingencies including age related loss of earnings. With growing financial burden that led to several modifications in social protection schemes, focus has now been shifted in most societies to social insurance (i.e., publicly backed contributory benefit schemes) rather than social assistance. The latter—i.e., social assistance—is generally directed to persons of small means to ensure a minimum standards of needs for them. In India, the question of ageing and its support mechanism may not be properly considered unless the basic requirements of the elderly are examined in greater detail followed by an assessment of elderly population with smaller (or larger) means.

If what has been raised above makes sense, the question that needs to be examined is whether the required security measures based on realistically drawn health and financial needs of the ageing population are likely to grow with time at an accelerating pace. Allied to this would be to evolve a sustainable delivery and financing mechanism. Moreover, because demographic ageing is likely to abound in South Asia sooner than later, these questions have a much wider significance. This study is therefore largely devoted to the former issue, and attempts to provide an empirical assessment about the health and livelihood issues of ageing Indians. Their financial status and reliance on filial support are also examined.

Indeed, any such analysis would require to generate age and sex specific data on older persons including the details of various intra-elderly heterogeneities, their living status, ailments, nature of disabilities, own income sources,[31] expenditure preferences, family support, health requirements, utilisation of public health services, and so on. Unfortunately, the recent health and expenditure surveys by different organisations including the NSS do not probe many of these issues for details. An independent survey of households with elderly co-residents is therefore required. In addition, the available data sources do not provide the viewpoints of the non-elderly persons on care giving. This study, therefore, proposes to hold a comprehensive survey of the old and non-old in the city-state of Delhi.

Going by these considerations, the rest of this study has been divided into seven broad chapters, each converting many of the issues highlighted so far into further discussion—hoping that some of these discussions will help in raising the sights for India's elderly. Chapter 2 of the study, therefore, attempts to provide state level details about the aged and their socio-economic disparities. Some of the health and non-health outcomes of these disparities were also examined using household level data obtained from the NSS, 52nd Round for 1995-96.

As noted earlier, the NSS or any other secondary data sources do not provide many necessary details about elderly persons—especially their views on recent economic changes, expenditure preferences, functional health, dependence on filial support in their self-

---

31. Problems associated with income and expenditure measures are fully documented in the literature hence we refrain from going into these details. For a recent discussion on this, see Montgomery, *et al.*, (1999).

maintenance, and the like. We, therefore, conducted a structured survey of over 1000 urban households with elderly co-residents from all the nine districts of the National Capital Territory of Delhi (NCT of Delhi). One of the interesting features of this survey is that apart from the old, it attempts to elicit the views of the non-aged as well; especially the way they foresee their own ageing and its planning needs. The survey also attempts to go into the questions of altruism *versus* exchange relations in elderly care. This entire survey including its sampling frame, key questions, choice of study area, socio-economic characteristics of the sample households and data analyses constitutes the bulk of the discussion that follows. An exclusive chapter (chapter 7) has also been devoted to describe the public responses to income security issues of the aged. Three issues constitute this discussion: (i) support provision by the Centre and states for the destitute elderly, (ii) proposed pension reform, and (iii) the soft interest rate regime including its underlying arguments and their suitability in the context of interest reliant older persons. Finally, a few broad policy interventions are suggested, for consideration and further debate.

2

Intra-aged Disparities and Outcomes: Some Empirical Findings

2.1. Introduction

Much of the preceding discussion was directed at highlighting the prospects of rapid ageing in the country accompanied by a range of unattended issues—conceptual, behavioural, socioeconomic and health related. Part of it was also devoted to describe the possibilities of an economic-demographic mismatch in the country caused by the bulging of working age adults, and retiring old. It was argued that this risk was likely to get aggravated by the presence of large-scale socio-economic and health related disparities in the country—especially among the aged. As India and many other developing economies are moving to follow a liberalised market-driven economic regime without creating adequate safety provisions—especially for the old—this mismatch can drive them beyond most of the opportunities created by the market. To make this argument more explicit, an attempt is made here to profile the intra-aged disparities in a set of major states, and their health and non-health outcomes. Some of these outcomes, as posited earlier, may tend to produce vulnerabilities and cause the existing cohorts of the aged to suffer the risk of exclusion. This whole analysis relies on two major data sources—the decennial population censuses, and the household level data from the NSS 52nd Round for 1995-96. The latter will particularly be used to examine the health outcomes of the disparities.

Besides the issue of disparities and their health outcomes, this part of the analysis may also help to provide a genesis for the rest of this study—especially the one presented in chapters 3 to 6 that deals with several unconventional issues of ageing including the views held by the non-elderly on self-ageing, altruism *versus* exchange relation in elderly care, ageing and declining interest rate regime, health of the elderly, frailty, incapacitation in activities of daily living (ADL) and dependence on filial support, and so on. A survey of over 1000 multi-generational households with elderly co-residents was conducted to carry out this analysis.

2.2. Profiling Intra-aged Disparities by Major States: Some Evidence from Secondary Data Sources

Until recently, population ageing was considered as an issue related to developed nations alone. Developing countries, despite seeking to achieve fertility transition and higher longevity, have failed to respond effectively to changes in their age composition or their ramifications for the economy—especially in terms of health or income security requirements of the old. A great deal of this non-response still persists—especially in India. This is despite a few recent attempts by analysts to caution about the threat of market exclusion if the security requirements of the aged have failed to receive public recognition (Alam, 2001b). To clarify, consider the following. Take the case of India where age structure changes are taking place in favour of the working age adults too. It will inevitably result in excess supply of labour—creating pressure on the labour market and its clearance mechanism (Visaria, 1998). Although neo-liberal policies focus on increasing labour demand by fostering economic growth, it remains open to question whether such growth can fully absorb the excess supply of labour including the cumulated backlog. If not, it will eventually lead to growing market pressure, casualisation of employment, work insecurity and poor wages (Alam and Mishra, 1998). With a simultaneous increase in ageing, the dependency burden will also increase at the household level. An economic agent, under these circumstances, is likely to face the problems of increasing age dependency along with a shrinking income. With less income and more mouths to feed, a possible outcome would be the uneven distribution of familial support, with the aged—especially the women—at the receiving end.

Like India, most other developing nations in South Asia—have remained slow in recognising large-scale ageing and its protective security requirements. While some attempts were made in this direction after the First World Assembly on Ageing in Vienna in 1982,[1] most of them are yet to be taken up for serious implementation. Recently, the Valencia Forum (Valencia, Spain, April

---

1. For details of the Vienna Conference (1982) and its recommendations, see Bose and Shankardass (2004), Chapter 7. This work also provides details of the Second World Assembly on Ageing in Madrid (2002).

2002) has drawn attention to many of these issues, and concretised them academically as well as at the policy levels. The Madrid Declaration, adopted after the Second World Assembly on Ageing in April 2002, was largely a formalisation of the technical inputs received at Valencia. The broader policy paradigm, adopted consensually in the Madrid Declaration (April, 2002), made it necessary for all the participating countries including India to ensure:

- the full participation of the aged in the development process and its benefits;

- the protection of health and well-being of the aged; and

- the creation of an enabling and supportive environment for the aged.

Obviously, these standpoints were adopted in the Declaration to provide the national governments a broad policy direction on various ageing issues.[2] As will be evident from this analysis, India is lacking significantly in each of them. Also, this situation persists despite increase in societal ageing over the past decades. A few simple facts will confirm this.

A brief re-look into the age composition of population in India will reveal that the process of ageing in the country has been gaining strength since the early 1980s. In certain states it started even earlier.

Beginning from 1971, the share of elderly persons has risen more perceptibly in the total population (Figure 2.1). The inter-censul comparison of age composition further reveals that in the 1970s this share grew faster. This is in conformity with the trend of the declining overall fertility and increasing chances of survival—both at birth and in later life years. Disaggregating at the state level, we find a similar situation—although with considerable variations (Table 2.1).

Table 2.1 clearly reveals that the share of the elderly population registered an increase in almost every major state under reference. Only Bihar, U.P. and Kerala showed a somewhat different pattern. In the 1980s and 1990s for instance, the share of the elderly in Bihar has actually declined. Over the same period, U.P. has somehow managed to keep its elderly share constant. Whereas in Kerala it may be the out-migration of its working population—leaving most of the higher age people back home. In addition, the state is known for its distinct socio-demographic parameters and longevity.

---

2. For further details and more specific recommendations of the Madrid Declaration (2002), see Appendix 2.1.

Figure 2.1

Share of Elderly Persons in Total Population: 1971-2001

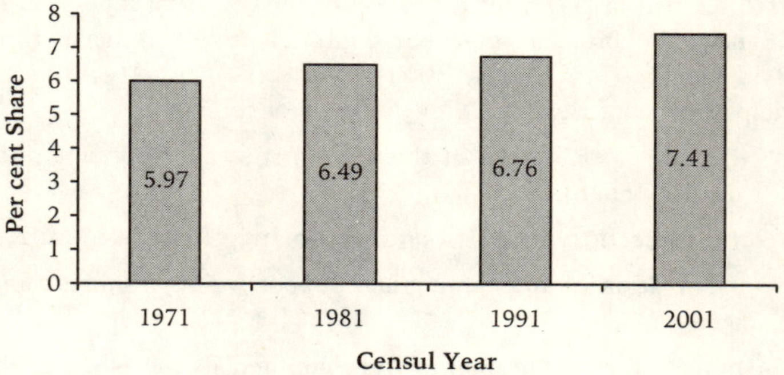

Source: Census of India, Series I, Social and Cultural Tables (corresponding years). For 2001 Census, age data available on CD from the Registrar General's Office (Government of India).

Table 2.1

Share of Elderly Population by Major States: 1971-2001

Percentage

States	1971	1981	1991	2001*
Andhra Pradesh	6.4	6.7	6.8	7.6
Bihar	6.3	6.8	6.3	6.6
Gujarat	5.3	6.0	6.4	6.9
Karnataka	6.1	6.6	7.0	7.7
Kerala	6.2	7.4	8.8	10.5
Madhya Pradesh	5.8	6.5	6.6	7.1
Maharashtra	5.7	6.4	7.0	8.7
Orissa	6.0	6.4	7.2	8.3
Punjab	7.5	7.8	7.8	9.0
Rajasthan	5.5	6.0	6.3	6.7
Tamil Nadu	5.7	6.4	7.5	8.8
Uttar Pradesh	6.8	6.8	6.8	7.0
West Bengal	5.3	5.6	6.1	7.1
All India	6.0	6.5	6.8	7.4

Source: Census of India (Series 1, Social and Cultural Tables) for respective years. * For 2001 Census, age data available on CD from the Registrar General's Office (Government of India).

Like variations in the size of the elderly population, the existing and up-coming cohorts of the aged are also believed to differ in many ways with major health and non-health consequences. Unfortunately, however, this aspect has so far remained without much analytical concern. In view of this, and also because of its policy relevance, this part of the study attempts to present a distribution of the aged in India and major states over different census years by taking into consideration their:

- age structure e.g., young old *versus* older old,

- rural-urban distributions,

- health conditions (i.e., sick *versus* non-sick or those with multiple sicknesses),

- socio-economic profile, and

- gender dimensions in the form of their sex-wise break-up.

Drawing upon data from the NSS 52nd Round (1995-96) for households with elderly members, attempts have also been made to examine certain outcomes of various socio-economic disparities suffered by the old. An important conclusion emanating from this entire analysis is that the aged can in no way be treated as a homogeneous entity and, therefore, need a different policy regime.

Age Structure of the Elderly: Inter-state Variations

Often, policies targeted towards specific population groups rely on assumptions of homogeneities within the group. In many cases, however, such assumptions remain implausible. The evidence presented below clearly supports this argument and reveals considerable heterogeneity faced by the aged. To illustrate, their age and sex compositions, health status, and consumption expenditure are all shown to vary in many different ways. We go into these details by using: (i) decennial population censuses to make over-time comparisons, and (ii) NSS 52nd Round in a cross sectional context and to study various health and non-health outcomes of disparities.

We begin by examining the state-wise distribution of older persons into three broad age categories, namely: 60-69 (young old), 70-74 (old), and 75+ (older old). Figure 2.2 presents this distribution.

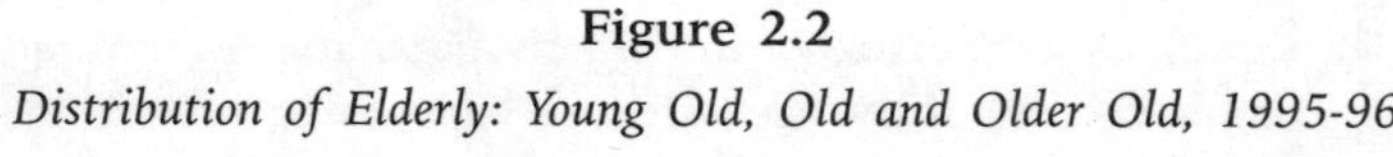

Figure 2.2

Distribution of Elderly: Young Old, Old and Older Old, 1995-96

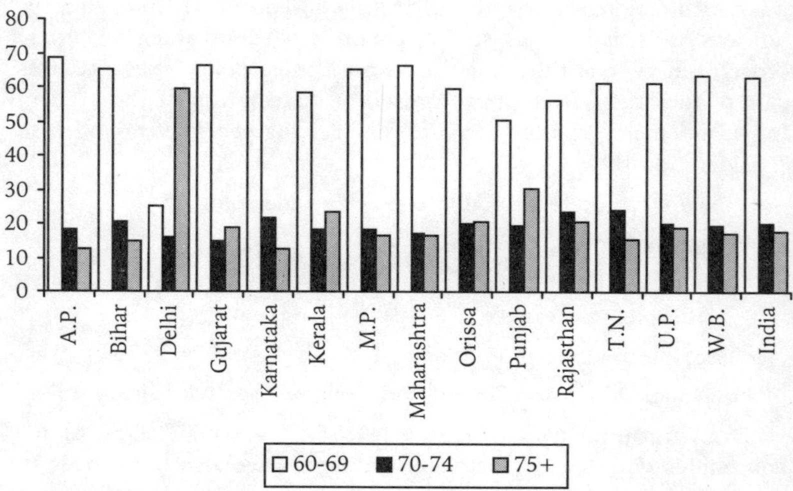

Source: NSS 52nd Round, 1995-96.

We notice from this distribution that the share of the young-old (60-69 age group) at the all India level is as high as 63 per cent of the total elderly population. The share of the older old (75+) is however far less, and does not exceed 18 per cent of their total population. Barring Delhi and to some extent Punjab or Kerala, most other states follow a similar pattern. Andhra Pradesh and Karnataka are the lowest. Two significant points follow from these comparisons: (i) unlike most developed countries, the elderly population in India is still predominantly young (i.e. in the 60-69 age group), and (ii) given the variations in the composition of elderly populations, an identical old age policy regime for the entire country may not be feasible. To illustrate, states like Gujarat, Punjab, Madhya Pradesh, etc., with more of 75+ may need to think more in terms of long-term care (LTC) requirements. Also, a large share of the young old may serve to provide a big and cost-effective pool of human skills—especially for the private sector.

Attention may however be drawn in regard to the poor health condition of the younger old. If the aged reporting chronic ailments at the time of the NSS 52nd Round were grouped into the three age categories under reference, we notice that over half of them (i.e., 55 per cent) lie in the lowest age bracket (Figure 2.3). This contradicts our earlier contention of using the younger old as a cost-effective pool of human skills. This also brings the quality of survival in later ages at the centre of the ageing debate. Any old age policy framework therefore requires attention on worsening health conditions of the old. But this is not all, and the variations in income or consumption levels of the older persons are yet another critical issue, especially to draw certain inferences about old age poverty. These issues are also significant as they are linked with the discussion on old age income security in Chapter 7 of this study.

Figure 2.3

Distribution of Sick and Disabled Elderly: Young Old, Old Old and Older Old, 1995-96

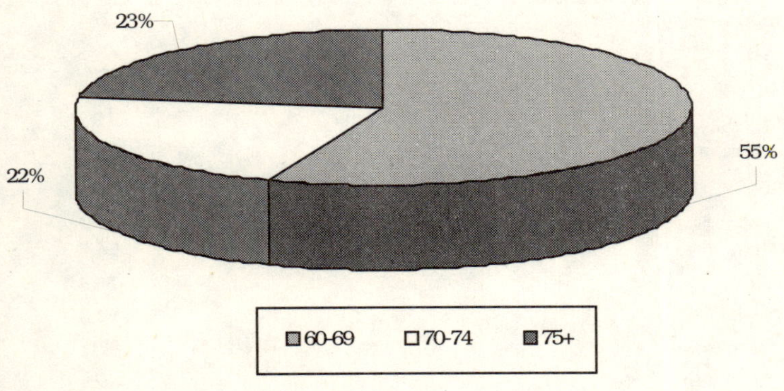

Source: NSS 52nd Round, 1995-96.

Diversity in Economic Conditions of the Old

Based on the NSS 52nd Round, we report below the all India and inter-state variations in per capita monthly consumption expenditure (PCMCE) of households with at least one family member over 60. Two exercises were conducted—one for the households with only young old in 60-69 age group[3] and the other without any such discrimination (Table 2.2). Both the exercises reveal large variations

---

3. Younger old might work and contribute to the family income.

in average consumption expenditure of households. Furthermore, this holds true for most of the states. We also notice that this variation is higher for households with younger old in 60-69 age (all India coefficient of variation increases from 68 to 72 per cent). Going by individual states, we observe the South and West Indian states including Tamil Nadu, Maharashtra, Kerala, Andhra Pradesh, and others, have yielded higher variations in per capita consumption level. These results clearly indicate that the aged in India face very diverse economic conditions.

Table 2.2

Variations in Per Capita Monthly Consumption Expenditure (PCMCE): Households with Elderly Family Member/s, 1995-96 (All India)

Major States	All Aged (60+)	Young Old (60-69)
	CV*	CV*
Andhra Pradesh	73.7	80.3
Bihar	51.9	68.6
Delhi	56.9	61.7
Gujarat	58.5	61.3
Karnataka	63.4	66.4
Kerala	68.8	58.3
Madhya Pradesh	54.7	66.5
Maharashtra	83.7	74.8
Orissa	53.1	70.4
Punjab	48.1	62.3
Rajasthan	47.4	60.1
Tamil Nadu	66.3	89.1
Uttar Pradesh	65.4	72.9
West Bengal	67.4	70.2
All India	**68.0**	**72.0**

Source: NSS 52nd Round Household Data.
Note: * CV = s/$\overline{x}$ *100

In a nutshell, the evidence drawn from the preceding discussion suggests that:

- the aged in India are largely comprised by the younger old,
- a majority of the younger old suffer from poor health conditions, and

- judged by the per capita monthly household consumption expenditure (an important surrogate for income distribution and poverty) there are very high variations in economic conditions of the old. In addition, this is true for all the observed states. South Indian states are relatively more uneven.

Rural-Urban Distribution of Elderly Population

Often income or consumption disparities are also affected by the locational pattern of individuals. Conventional wisdom suggests that the likelihood of being economically better off increases if an individual is located in an urban centre with access to income generating opportunities. With older persons it particularly helps in terms of:

- better socio-economic conditions,

- easier access to medical facilities, and

- availability of LTC including old age homes.

Going by these considerations, a brief investigation into the spatial distribution of the elderly population in India would reveal the share of those in a relatively better situation. Figure 2.4 provides this distribution as obtained from the 2001 Census. It can be noticed from this figure that the aged in India are overwhelmingly rural with about three-fourths of them residing in villages. A majority of them would presumably be failing to access many of the LTC and health care services.

Figure 2.4

Rural-Urban Distribution of Elderly Population (60+): All India, 2001

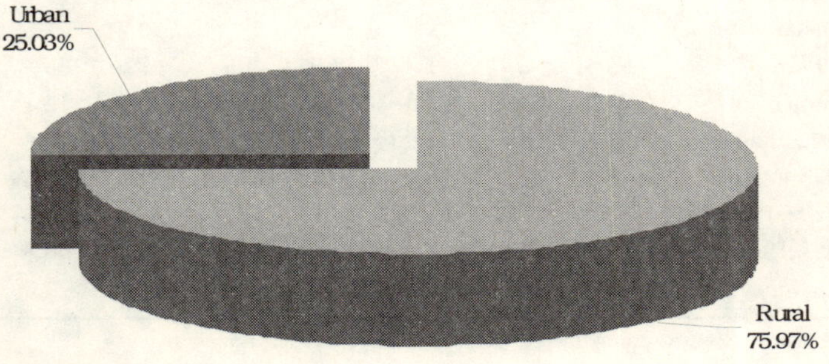

Source: 2001 Census.

Extending this analysis further, a similar pattern holds for most other states as well, especially those located in the North and Northeastern parts of the country (Table 2.3). Interestingly, however, this table also reveals an over-time shift in the residential pattern of the aged. The share of the urban aged, for example, is showing a rising trend in most of the states during the period between 1971 and 2001. This change in locational pattern however raises a question: namely, does shifting to urban areas really help? Or, do the urban elderly enjoy a better life than their rural counterparts? To find a tentative answer, we try to examine the nature of diseases suffered by the aged in rural and urban areas. Supposedly, these details may help to infer about the severity of diseases suffered by people from the two areas. As these details are not provided in the census, we relied on household data from the NSS 52nd Round relating to 1995-96.

Table 2.3

Changes in Rural-Urban Distribution of Elderly Population: All India &
Major States, 1971-2001

Percentage

Major States	1971		1981		1991		2001	
	Rural	*Urban*	*Rural*	*Urban*	*Rural*	*Urban*	*Rural*	*Urban*
Andhra Pradesh	85.0	15.0	82.0	18.0	79.0	21.0	77.8	22.2
Bihar	92.1	7.9	90.9	9.1	89.7	10.3	90.3	9.7
Delhi	-	-	-	-	8.0	92.0	5.9	94.1
Gujarat	74.5	25.5	72.8	27.2	70.2	29.8	66.3	33.7
Karnataka	79.8	20.2	75.1	24.9	74.2	25.8	71.1	28.9
Kerala	84.4	15.6	83.4	16.6	74.3	25.7	74.3	25.7
Madhya Pradesh	85.9	14.1	84.1	15.9	81.3	18.7	76.3	23.7
Maharashtra	75.3	24.7	72.1	27.9	69.3	30.7	67.5	32.5
Orissa	93.6	6.4	91.4	8.6	90.4	9.6	88.3	11.7
Punjab	81.9	18.9	78.3	21.7	76.4	23.6	72.1	27.9
Rajasthan	83.4	16.6	81.9	18.1	80.8	19.2	79.4	20.6
Tamil Nadu	72.9	27.1	70.2	29.8	68.7	31.3	58.5	41.5
Uttar Pradesh	88.7	11.3	85.8	14.2	84.5	15.5	82.6	17.4
West Bengal	76.7	23.3	72.9	27.1	70.3	29.7	66.8	33.2
All India	83.4	16.6	85.04	15.0	78.0	22.0	75.0	25.0

Source: Socio-Cultural Tables, Census of India (respective years).

This distribution shows that the rural aged mostly suffer from conditions involving joint pains, visual impairment and chest congestion (Figure 2.5). More than a fourth of the ailing elderly in rural areas, for instance, suffered from some form of joint problems. While these problems are equally pronounced in the urban elderly, they also register a higher incidence of lifestyle diseases including low or high blood pressure and coronary diseases (Figure 2.6). Around 13 per cent of the urban elderly suffer from these. As a whole, the urban old do not seem to be in much better health.

A more significant point to be noticed from these figures is in the two common ailments of ageing: (i) poor functioning of joints, and (ii) visual impairment. Yet another common problem relates to phlegm formation suggesting high chest-lungs problem faced by the aged from the two areas. What does this imply in terms of health care infrastructure—especially in the rural areas? What will be the future demand-supply implications for various geriatric services in the country? Who will provide LTC to the ailing old? These are certain issues that need more in-depth studies.

Figure 2.5

Distribution of Diseases-Rural Aged

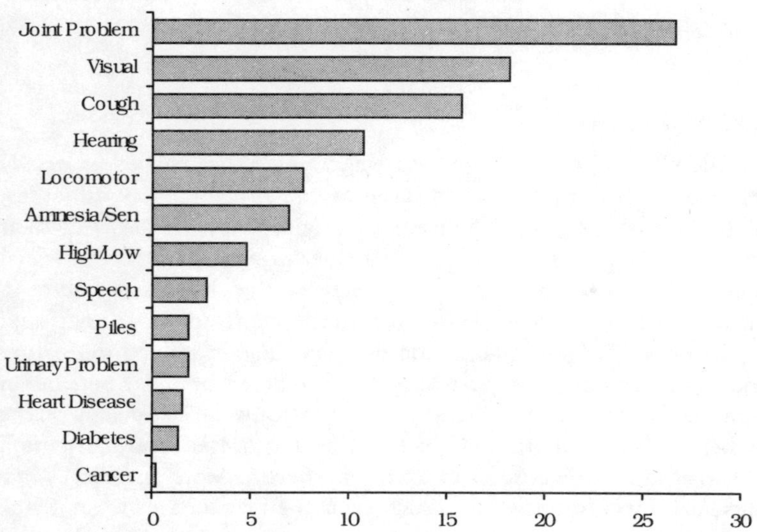

Source: NSS Data CD, 52nd Round: 1995-96.

Coming once again to the earlier question about the relative advantages of living in urban areas, it may be noticed that large fractions of the aged from both the areas suffer from many crippling diseases. This makes the on-going debate on healthy and active ageing in India inconsequential.

Figure 2.6

Distribution of Diseases-Urban Aged

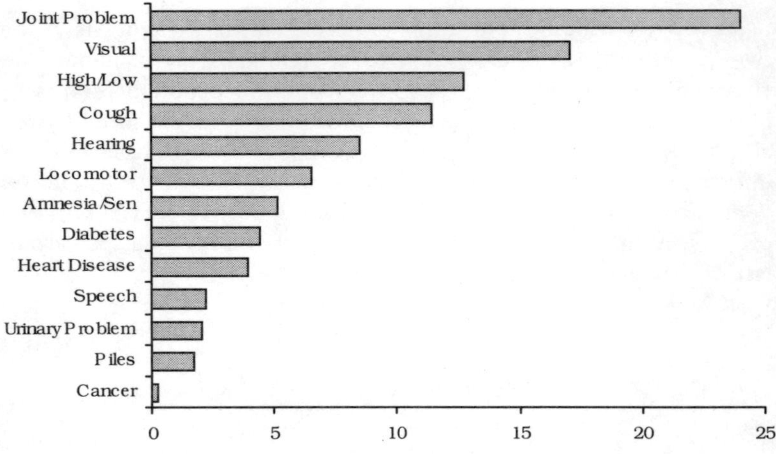

Source: NSS Data CD, 52nd Round (1995-96).

Health Disparities

The physical and psychological well being of the people, especially the aged, has always been an issue of concern for many. Illnesses, frailty and poor health conditions constrain people in terms of their ability to support themselves and to perform their expected social roles. Impairments and disabilities increase the chances of failure in performing vital social roles, and drive many to face functional dependence. The previous section has, *inter alia,* examined the nature and magnitude of self-reported ailments suffered by older persons in rural and urban areas. This section is basically an extension of the earlier analysis and attempts to focus on the overall health situation of the aged and the effects of ageing on health. More specifically, we present below the results of certain econometric exercises to show the health outcomes of the socio-economic diversities suffered by the aged in rural and urban areas.

The following issues relating to the elderly health are under examination:

- Health status and its causal risk factors,
- health care utilisation, and
- health expenditure.

As was stated, the household level data for these analyses were drawn from the NSS 52nd Round, separately for rural and urban areas.

Health Status of the Elderly and Causal Risk Factors

Irrespective of advancement in understanding about nutritional needs, disease prevention, diagnostics and health care, the aged seem to make greater demands on health establishments. Further, this demand may grow steadily—especially in countries with greater socio-economic disparities and poor health conditions like India. Because of this, it is perhaps essential—especially on policy considerations - to analyse the health conditions of older persons including the share of those with single and multiple diseases, and their causalities. We shall try to carry out this analysis in two ways. One is through descriptive statistics providing proportionate distribution of the aged suffering from: (i) none, (ii) single, and (iii) multiple diseases/disabilities in major states. This will be followed by a set of econometric exercises to explore their causalities. Based on NSS 52nd Round, these exercises employ the Count Data Model (CDM) using (i) Poisson distribution and (ii) Negative Binomial.[4] We begin by the descriptive statistic.

Tables 2.4(a) and 2.4(b) present the share of elderly population with and without ailments. Those sick have been further distributed by number of diseases—namely, single or multiple. For brevity, these details are presented only for two broad age groups—namely 60-69 and 70+.

Several interesting observations emerge from these two tables. One is, for example, a positive association between the onset of multiple diseases and ageing—irrespective of the place of residence. We observe from both the tables that the prevalence of multiple diseases is higher at the later ages. Another interesting observation may arise while comparing diseases in rural and urban areas. Though, in most cases, the two seem to differ only marginally, states such as

---

4. For certain methodological details and limitations of the CDM, see Appendix 2.2

Table 2.4.a

*Age-wise Distribution of Rural Aged by Single
and Multiple Diseases: 1995-96*

Percentage

Major States	60+ Number of Diseases			60-69 Number of Diseases			70+ Number of Diseases		
	None	Single	Multiple	None	Single	Multiple	None	Single	Multiple
Andhra Pradesh	24.9	30.4	44.7	31.5	31.4	37.1	10.3	28.3	61.3
Assam	23.7	27.0	49.3	26.2	29.3	44.4	17.2	21.3	61.6
Bihar	43.5	24.4	32.1	47.8	24.7	27.5	35.5	23.8	40.7
Gujarat	39.7	26.8	33.5	47.6	27.3	25.0	24.3	25.8	50.0
Karnataka	51.5	24.2	24.3	59.6	24.6	15.8	36.0	23.5	40.6
Kerala	23.9	27.5	48.5	29.6	27.7	42.7	16.1	27.3	56.6
Madhya Pradesh	42.8	23.0	34.2	50.2	23.6	26.3	28.9	21.8	49.3
Maharashtra	30.9	30.6	38.4	36.6	30.0	33.4	19.7	31.8	48.5
Orissa	30.7	29.2	40.1	40.1	31.2	28.8	17.1	26.3	56.5
Punjab	31.6	29.7	38.7	39.4	29.7	30.9	23.6	29.8	46.5
Rajasthan	40.0	25.2	34.7	51.5	26.1	22.4	25.4	24.1	50.6
Tamil Nadu	39.2	24.7	36.1	44.0	26.5	29.4	31.6	21.7	46.7
Uttar Pradesh	34.0	26.5	39.5	42.5	27.8	29.6	20.6	24.5	54.9
West Bengal	22.2	23.9	53.9	25.9	23.7	50.5	16.0	24.3	59.8

Source: NSS 52nd Round (1995-96) Household Data CD.

Table 2.4.b

*Age-wise Distribution of Urban Aged by Single
and Multiple Diseases: 1995-96*

Percentage

Major States	60+			60-69			70+		
	Number of Diseases			*Number of Diseases*			*Number of Diseases*		
	None	*Single*	*Multiple*	*None*	*Single*	*Multiple*	*None*	*Single*	*Multiple*
Andhra Pradesh	33.9	29.4	36.7	39.5	30.9	29.6	23.4	26.5	50.1
Assam	19.6	30.5	49.9	22.8	32.4	44.7	11.3	25.3	63.4
Bihar	46.3	25.8	27.9	52.7	23.8	23.5	35.5	29.1	35.4
Gujarat	31.9	34.3	33.8	38.2	31.4	30.4	22.0	38.8	39.2
Karnataka	42.0	25.3	32.7	45.0	25.5	29.5	36.3	24.9	38.8
Kerala	32.2	29.1	38.7	36.5	33.2	30.3	25.7	23.0	51.3
Madhya Pradesh	44.0	23.3	32.7	51.0	24.4	24.6	30.7	21.2	48.1
Maharashtra	33.5	29.8	36.6	40.0	31.1	28.9	21.2	27.5	51.2
Orissa	40.4	24.5	35.1	49.4	25.4	25.3	23.0	22.9	54.1
Punjab	36.8	23.8	39.4	37.7	27.5	34.8	35.7	19.6	44.7
Rajasthan	43.2	26.7	30.1	48.8	29.4	21.8	36.6	23.5	39.9
Tamil Nadu	36.8	27.0	36.2	40.2	28.6	31.1	31.2	24.3	44.5
Uttar Pradesh	34.1	27.5	38.3	40.9	27.7	31.4	23.5	27.3	49.3
West Bengal	16.2	29.1	54.7	19.8	35.1	45.2	11.2	20.8	68.1

Source: NSS 52nd Round (1995-96) Household Data CD.

Assam, West Bengal and Maharashtra have reported greater prevalence of multiple diseases among the urban aged—especially those over 70. Furthermore, in most states, the share of non-ailing elderly does not exceed much beyond two-fifths of their total population (Tables 2.4a and 2.4b).

Important policy implications of these observations relate to poor health infrastructure in rural areas where most of the sick elderly live.

Multiple Diseases: Socio-economic Risk Factors

In addition to physiological factors, what other factors—especially of a socio-economic nature—may lead to poor health conditions, especially multiple diseases?[5] We tried to explore this question with the help of certain exercises based on two different specifications of the count data model (CDM): (i) Poisson distribution, and (ii) Negative binomial. Both the specifications have been recently used in the literature by bio-statisticians and medical analysts. We begin by a brief description of the Poisson distribution and its limitations. The negative binomial was therefore employed as improvement. We however present both results so that readers can make their own judgment.

In applied work, models based on Poisson distribution are restrictive in many ways. First, they are laid out on the assumption that events (in our cases diseases) occur independently over-time. This assumption however breaks down in several cases, as successive health events are mostly dependent. One disease, for instance, causes many other collateral conditions. Contagion models in biometric literature consider this possibility more explicitly. Secondly, the assumption that the conditional mean and variance of Y_i given X_i are equal may also be strong and, therefore, fail to comply with real life situations. Applied econometric literature therefore suggests considering generalisation of the basic Poisson models to ensure greater flexibility in situations of over dispersions, arising due to heterogeneous populations (Cameron and Trivedi, 1986). We therefore attempted to extend our analysis and used the negative binomial in addition to Poisson distribution. It allows us greater heterogeneity across different population groups.[6] Both these models are specified in Box 2.1.

---

5. In all, NSS identifies 8 major diseases and 5 disabilities. These are listed in Table 2.14.

6. A further discussion of these models is provided in Appendix 2.2.

Box 2.1

Specification of Count Model: Number of Diseases Suffered by Aged

Count Model Specifications	Dependent Variable	Explanatory Variables
I) Poisson Model	Number of disease/s suffered	Age, Age^2, Sex dummy (Male = 1),
II) Negative Binomial Model	by an elderly person	Literacy dummy (Literate = 1), Drinking water dummy (Tap, Tube well & Hand Pump = 1), Toilet Type dummy (Flush system = 1, All others = 0), Household monthly consumption expenditure (HHMCE)

As already noted, we have estimated these models on the basis of the 52nd NSS Round household level data for 1995-96. Further, these estimates have been obtained for the 60+ populations from the rural and the urban areas separately.

Model Findings

It is clearly evident from these results that there is a positive correlation between risks of suffering from a larger number of diseases and age, though this relationship is completely reversed with age^2 as its coefficient turns out to be negative. Moreover it is true for both the Poisson and Negative binomial (Table 2.5). In simple words, it implies that people are susceptible to multiple diseases up to a certain critical age limit, and thereafter these susceptibilities taper off. How far this explanation is justifiable requires sifting through genetic or biometric literature. These results also reveal that the rural elderly from higher consumption expenditure households enjoy fewer risks. This is shown by a negative but statistically significant relationship between household consumption expenditure, a commonly used indicator of poverty, and the number of diseases. Similar relationships exist between diseases and the public health variables represented by the drinking water and toilet dummies in the model. In other words, better public health and proper hygiene may help to bring down the disease risks. Literacy level may also significantly help to reduce the risks of multiple diseases. Compared to the males, probabilities of suffering from a greater number of diseases or disabilities are apparently low for females. Is this really true? Perhaps not, and suggests under reporting or reporting biases in the data. It may as well be pointed out that both the specifications yield more or less similar results (Table 2.5).

Table 2.5

Results of the Count Data Model-Rural Persons
Dependent Variable: Number of Diseases/Disabilities

Explanatory Variables	Poisson Regression		Negative Binomial	
	Coefficients	St. Error	Coefficients	St. Error
Constant	-5.920795	0.00928	-5.900393	0.012076
Age	0.144337*	0.00025	0.143742*	0.00033
$(Age)^2$	-0.000742*	1.71E-06	-0.000738*	2.26E-06
Sex Dummy	-0.056483*	0.00029	-0.056446*	0.00037
Literacy Dummy	0.025358*	0.00036	0.027533*	0.00045
Drinking Water Dummy	-0.111998*	0.0003	-0.111574*	0.00038
Type of Toilet Dummy	-0.005719*	0.0018	-0.008248*	0.00226
HHMCE	-1.28E-06*	1.11E-07	-6.21E-07*	1.40E-07
Log likelihood	- 59047012		- 57354987	

*Coefficients significant at 1 per cent level of significance.

Table 2.6

Results of the Count Data Model-Urban Persons
Dependent Variable: Number of Diseases/Disabilities

Explanatory Variables	Poisson Regression		Negative Binomial	
	Coefficients	St. Error	Coefficients	St. Error
Constant	-5.199179	0.018988	-5.146724	0.024086
Age	0.1299909*	0.000522	0.128663*	0.000666
$(Age)^2$	-0.000685*	3.55e-06	-0.000675*	4.56e-06
Sex Dummy	-0.061899*	0.000580	-0.0608274*	0.000716
Literacy Dummy	-0.106916*	0.000598	-0.107109*	0.000740
Drinking Water Dummy	-0.068589*	0.000942	-0.0738475*	0.001180
Type of Toilet Dummy	-0.020776*	0.000599	-0.0220192*	0.000742
HHMCE	8.14e-06*	1.40e-07	8.15e-06*	1.74e-07
Log likelihood	-16465040		-16007593	

*Coefficients significant at 1 per cent level of significance.

Table 2.6 presents the results for the urban old. Barring the variable representing consumption expenditure (HHMCE), all other variables in both the specifications conform closely to the preceding results and yield similar explanations. The HHMCE, which differs in terms of the sign observed in Table 2.5, shows that persons of higher expenditure brackets are also susceptible to multiple diseases—perhaps owing to poor life style.

Utilisation of Hospital Services by the Elderly

Of late, some attempts have been made by economists to address explicitly the health care issues of the elderly in India. One of the studies by Gupta and Sankar (2002), for example, tried to examine the nature of diseases suffered by the older persons and their influencing factors. They also tried to examine the health seeking behaviour of the aged. Moving further with some of these attempts, we tried to carry out a similar exercise using a set of socio-economic factors being responsible in accessing hospital services—basically hospitalisation services—by the aged in rural and urban areas.

Logically, like any other age group, the aged can also seek health care with or without hospitalisation. Often, however, their chances of using any of these services vary for a variety of reasons, and hence need investigation. Using the multivariate regression analysis, inferences can be drawn about the factors influencing the utilisation of in-patient hospital facilities by older persons.

Following this, we attempted to carry out a probit exercise examining the factors associated with the utilisation of in-house hospital facilities by the elderly in rural and urban areas. The socio-economic variables are listed in Box 2.2.

As the probability of getting ill and taking resort to hospitalised care increases with age, this model also tries to incorporate age as one of the explanatory variables. The nonlinearity aspect is accounted for in this exercise by using the age-square. Use of hospitalisation care may vary with respect to sex, age, literacy level and individual's income. The dummies representing economic independence and higher consumption expenditure can explain the effect of income level on the probability of accessing hospitalisation services. It may so happen that the aged from higher income/consumption categories are more likely to opt for hospital care, and *vice versa*. The results are presented in Table 2.7.

Box 2.2

Probit Regression Specification: Likelihood of
Accessing Hospitalisation Care by Aged

Type of Model	Dependent Variable Binary	Explanatory Variables
Probit Regression	Whether or not any hospitalisation services used over the last 365 days.	Age (60+), Age^2, Sex Dummy (male = 1), Literacy Dummy (literate = 1),
	Dependent Variable = 1 if at least once hospitalised, 0 otherwise	Per Capita Monthly Per Capita Monthly Dummy (PCMCE),Economic Independence dummy (economically independent = 1, dependent and partially dependent = 0)

The Results

As expected, the results in Table 2.7 suggest a positive relationship between the chances of utilising hospital care and the age. In other words, the likelihood of accessing hospital care increases with age. This can be noticed for both rural and urban areas. Particularly from the demand-supply viewpoint, this may be an interesting finding with an underlying message to keep creating hospital infrastructure with increase in ageing. On the gender side, our results reveal that the older males are more likely to visit hospitals as compared to the older females. Monthly per capita consumption expenditure (PCMCE), used as a proxy for income level, shows a positive relationship with the probability of accessing in-door hospital care. This signifies the fact that in the present set-up the richer have better chances of using hospital facilities than the poorer. Similar results are obtained for literates. Surprisingly, however, the reverse is true for those in urban areas—urban literates are shown to have lower probabilities of utilising in-patient care in a hospital. A possible, though somewhat tentative explanation for this may be that owing to better lifestyle and awareness the urban literate might carry fewer risks of hospitalisation. Another inexplicable result in Table 2.7 relates to a negative relationship between economic independence and the likelihood of availing oneself of in-door hospital care. Does this mean that the dependent elderly have better chances to get hospitalised? Or, does this phenomenon again reflect the awareness effect? The financially independent are assumed to be more literate and hence more informed with lower hospitalisation risks. At least the NSS data available to us do not answer either of these questions. We may therefore try to pick up this question later while working with our own survey data.

Table 2.7

*Probit Regression Results: Use of Hospitalisation Services
Dependent Variable, Use of Hospitalisation Services by 60+
(User of Services = 1, 0 Otherwise)*

Explanatory Variables	Rural		Urban	
	Coefficients	*St. Error*	*Coefficients*	*St. Error*
Constant	-5.471211	0.032669	-576619	0.051903
Age	0.082316*	0.000907	0.102274*	0.001444
$(Age)^2$	-0.000531*	6.24e-06	-0.000646*	9.96e-06
Sex Dummy	0.248915*	0.000972	0.180099*	0.001540
Literacy Dummy	0.236077*	0.000972	-0.025877*	0.001530
PCMCE	0.001044*	1.68e-06	0.000347*	1.52e-06
Economic Independence Dummy	-0.272597*	0.001039	-0.219059*	0.001661
Log likelihood	-4837139.2		-2070845.3	

* Coefficients significant at 1 per cent level of significance. Number of observations is as in Table 2.6.

Yet another question in this context may be the choice of facilities by the users of inpatient hospital services. Will they have greater chances of using the public sector facilities? If yes, what socio economic

---

Box 2.3

*Specification of Probit Regression: Choice between Public
and Private Hospital Services*

Model	Dependent Variable Binary	Explanatory Variables
Probit	*Choice of facility:* Dependent Variable=1 for Government run facilities/ hospitals including PHCs, charitable institutions run by public trusts, ESI/CGHS facilities, etc. = 2 for Private hospitals, nursing homes, etc.	Age, $(Age)^2$, Sex dummy (male = 1), Literacy dummy (literate = 1), PCMCE, Income, Public/private hospital dummy, Economic independence dummy (ecinpd: independent = 1), Employment dummy (emp. = 1) Social group dummy (soclgrd: SC/ST=1)

Table 2.8

Probit Regression Results: Utilisation of Public Sector Hospital Services Dependent Variable, Utilisation of Public Sector Hospitalisation Services by 60+ (1 for Government run facilities, 0 Otherwise)

Variables	Rural		Urban	
	Coefficients	St. Error	Coefficients	St. Error
Specification 1: with only socio-economic dummies				
Constant	4.115039	0.0978626	- 0.239461**	0.138042
Age	- 0.087683**	0.002721	0.026291**	0.003853
Age^2	0.000552**	0.000019	- 0.000323**	0.000027
Aexd	- 0.169323**	0.002537	0.339128**	0.003779
Litd	- 0.108750**	0.002415	-.347972**	0.003846
PCMCE	- 0.001395**	5.12e-06	- 0.000220**	3.12e-06
Ecinpd	0.121784**	0.002717	- 0.047026**	0.004160
Log likelihood	-877951.82		-416224.15	
Specification 2: also with social group & employment dummies				
Constant	1.721377	0.097806	0.020119	0.138407
Age	- 0.017973**	0.002725	0.030149**	0.003863
Age^2	8.16e-06	0.000019	- 0.000342**	0.000027
Sexd	- 0.098519**	0.002604	0.328387**	0.003851
Litd	- 0.127946**	0.002416	- 0.332581**	0.003838
Ecinpd	0.351276**	0.003151	- 0.079591**	0.004452
Social groupd	- 0.504055**	0.002848	- 0.644549**	0.005091
Empd	- 0.535560**	0.003187	- 0.116313**	0.005158
Log likelihood	- 889170.33		- 410252.83	

** Significant at 1 per cent level.

and caste attributes do they possess? An answer to this question was obtained by carrying out two probit exercises, differentiated by two sets of specifications, namely, with and without caste and employment dummies (Box 2.3). Estimates of both these specifications suggest poor, socially deprived and unemployed older persons relying more on the public run facilities (Table 2.8). Further, it holds for the rural as well as the urban areas. Given the serious issues of deprivation and old age poverty, these results are significant for health care management of the growing old.

Socio-economic Disparities

Earlier we have made references about the growing threat of exclusion faced by a large segment of the deprived and socially under-privileged including the aged. Further, an earlier chapter has also highlighted the growing momentum in societal ageing followed by erosion in traditional institutions, high old age poverty, socio-economic backwardness, illiteracy and none—or negligible—public support for the aged. Here a brief attempt has been made to find further justification for these arguments offering instances of large-scale socio-economic backwardness suffered by the elderly population in the country, making them susceptible to changes in current economic policies and increasing the role of private institutions without an adequate safety net. The following two aspects are examined briefly:

- literacy level among the aged, and
- their livelihood issues including family status.

Literacy level will help to conjecture about the fraction of the aged who may actually be able to seek information and participate in the market mechanism. Livelihood issues, on the other hand, will help to highlight their actual position and hierarchy within the family or household.

Literacy Level among the Aged

According to the household data collected during the NSS 52nd Round, the literacy level of the elderly population in India was merely 36.5 per cent in 1995-96 (Table 2.9, also see Figure 2.7). Further, three fourths of the rural aged were totally illiterate. Contrasting this, the aged in urban areas were found to be better educated as over half of them (or about 58 per cent) had some formal schooling. The share of college graduates was less than 3 per cent of their total population. At the same level, the share of semi-literate persons (i.e., those below or up to 5 years of schooling) was highest. The situation in rural areas where three quarters of the country's aged live appears much worse. As it is, it throws open many serious questions—both at the macro and micro levels. At the macro level, for instance, it may be difficult for the semi-literate to share the developmental processes as desired nationally and internationally, and especially in the Plan of Action adopted by the Second World Assembly on ageing in Madrid with Indian endorsement.

Yet another issue that needs consideration in the underlying situation is the income security of the elderly. With growing nuclearisation of families, and high rates of unemployment or under-employment, will the government be willing to provide a public pillared old age income security? This is indeed a big question with serious financial implications. We will go into this question more specifically later in this study.

Table 2.9

Literacy Level among the Aged: 1995-96

Percentage

Education Levels	Rural	Urban	Total
Illiterate	77.0	41.7	63.5
Literate (Read and Write)	2.6	3.3	2.9
Below Primary	8.0	11.2	9.3
Primary	7.0	14.3	9.8
Middle	3.2	10.6	6.0
Secondary	1.5	9.7	4.6
Higher Secondary	0.3	2.8	1.3
Graduate	0.3	6.4	2.7

Source: NSS 52nd Round data CD.

Figure 2.7

Literacy Level among the Aged: 1995-96

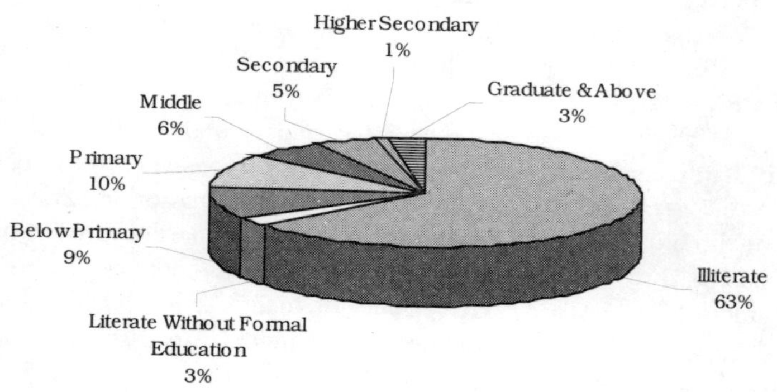

Source: NSS 52nd Round data CD.

Livelihood Issues of the Aged

Despite increasing standards of living and per capita real income, millions of people all across the globe die every year prematurely from deprivation and undernourishment. Major developmental programmes, launched to support the weaker segments of the population, often remain unsuccessful for different reasons (Dreze and Sen, 1991). The elderly, being one of them may have to considerably bear the brunt of poverty and deprivation in the changing scenario. Lack of ability to be a part of the workforce—often because of illiteracy or poor health conditions or both—leaves many of them dependent on household support for survival. It would therefore be interesting to examine the size of the elderly dependents living under the same roof. This may well give us an idea about the prevalence of dependence and co-residence. Within this perspective, we decided to go in to: (i) the patterns of elderly living, and (ii) some of its key influencing factors. An all India situation drawn on the basis of data from the NSS 52nd Round is presented in Figure 2.8.

Figure 2.8

Living Arrangements of the Elderly: All India, 1995-96

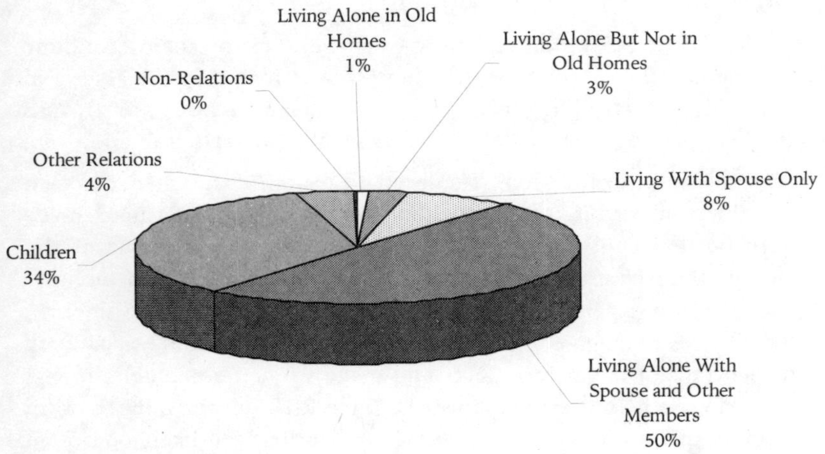

Source: NSS 52nd Round data CD.

Clearly, around half of the total elderly population in India lives together with spouse and other family members including children. In contrast, only 34 per cent of them stay with children. Staying in old age homes still remains an unusual phenomenon with barely three per cent of the total elderly population in such homes. Another interesting fact drawn from this figure is that in 1995-96 around 8 per cent of the elderly were living alone with their spouses. While this fraction may not appear high in comparison with many other societies, for a country like India it seems to be a significant fraction and needs to be reckoned with. In addition, this fraction is expected to increase with growing migration and erosion in the traditional family system. Nevertheless, it cannot be denied that a majority of the aged in India still lives jointly in a multi-generational family set-up.

Despite the high prevalence of inter-generational living in the country, there are questions about the hierarchical position enjoyed by the elderly co-residents within the family. To make an assessment about this issue, we present below a few exercises with an implicit question—namely: are the elderly marginalised in their families? Because of their lower bargaining strength, this question cannot be completely ruled out. The analysis reported below is therefore an attempt to shed some light on this important issue.

Living Arrangements of the Elderly

The exercises reported below examine a set of socio-economic factors, and the extent to which these factors may help the elderly in terms of: (i) familial hierarchy (say as head of household), and (ii) living arrangements. Box 2.4 specifies the postulated relationship.

The first specification attempted to examine the chances of an older person heading the household. It was expected that households with better acquired attributes including economic status of the elderly, their educational background and higher per capita monthly consumption expenditure (PCMCE) would not only help to improve the chances of an elderly person to lead the family, but may also work to neutralise the gender effects and make women acceptable in that role. However, the results shown in Table 2.10 do not fully conform to our expectations. For example, we notice that the likelihood of an elderly person being the head of a household applies more with males as the coefficient of sex dummy turns out to be the most dominant along with a positive sign. It is also significant at the 1 per cent level. In addition, it holds both for rural and urban areas. But this is perhaps a reality in most traditional societies where males hold decisive positions. Literacy and economic independence are the other acquired attributes associated positively with chances of an elderly person becoming head of the family. The per capita household monthly expenditure also works to the same effect—though only in rural areas. In urban areas, the opposite may be true implying rural-urban differentials in the value system. Most of these coefficients are however too small in magnitude.

Box 2.4

Specification of the Probit Regressions: Likely factors enabling the old to act as head of household, and factors promoting the chances of living with adult children or family

Regression Type	Dependent Variable (Binary)	Explanatory Variables
Probit: Probability of the elderly being head of the household	Head of household = 1, = 0 otherwise	Sex dummy, Income level (per capita con. exp.), Literacy dummy, Economic independence dummy
Probit: Living arrangement—living alone or as inmate of an old age home	Elderly Living alone = 1, = 0 otherwise	Sex dummy, Income level (per capita con. exp.), Literacy dummy, Employment dummy, Widow/widower dummy, Caste dummy Economic Independence dummy
Probit: Living arrangement–living with spouse	Elderly Living with Spouse = 1, = 0 otherwise	Sex dummy, Income level (per capita con. exp.), Literacy dummy, Economic independence dummy
Probit: Living arrangement–living with children, spouse and others	Elderly Living with adult child = 1, = 0 otherwise	Sex dummy, Income level (per capita con. exp.), Literacy dummy, Economic independence dummy

---

In addition to the question of heading the household, the probit exercises reported below further aim to explore the factors responsible for differences in the living arrangements of the older people (Box 2.4). In all, three different forms of living arrangements were considered for this analysis: (i) living alone in own house or old age home, (ii) living with spouse, and (iii) living with spouse and adult children. Several specifications were tried out to see the interactive effects of various explanatory variables presented in Box 2.4.

Table 2.10

*Probit Regression Results: Elderly as Head of Household,
All India Persons*

Variables	Rural		Urban	
	Coefficients	*St. Error*	*Coefficients*	*St. Error*
Dependent Variable = Elderly as the head of household				
Constant	-1.441790	0.000692	-1.089775	0.001014
Sex dummy (Male = 1)	1.743138*	0.000556	1.550392*	0.001040
Literacy dummy (literate = 1)	0.336944*	0.000694	0.153413*	0.001086
Per capita monthly expenditure	0.000510*	1.65e-06	-08.00091	1.40e-06
Economic independence dummy	0.880324*	0.000613	0.854826*	0.001127
Economically independent = 1				
Log likelihood	-14117255		-4372453.6	

Source: NSS 52nd Round data CD.

Note: * Significant at 1 per cent level.

An analysis relating to the living arrangements of the elderly is often premised on the notion of growing nuclearisation of families and declining trends in multi-generational living. As a fallout of growing urbanisation and industrialisation, younger couples are living in nuclear households, affecting the overall living arrangements of the elderly. At times, it can also work to reduce the size and flow of transfer income to the older persons, and make them more susceptible to entitlement failures. While in most traditional societies the pace of these changes is often expected to remain slower, the probit results shown in Table 2.11 are somewhat striking and conform to our earlier premise that the aged in India are on fast losing ground.

The relationship between gender and living alone is indeed striking. We observe from Table 2.11 (specification 1) that males are less expected to live alone. Or, in other words, it is the females who

Table 2.11

Probit Regression Results on Living Arrangements: All India (Persons)

Variables	Rural		Urban	
	Coefficients	*St. Error.*	*Coefficients*	*St. Error.*
Dependent Variable = Living Alone (in own house or as old age inmates)				
Specification 1				
Constant	-1.980558	0.000807	-1.845244	0.001393
Sex dummy (Male = 1)	-0.625338*	0.000967	-0.697190	0.001916
Literacy dummy (literate = 1)	-0.281233*	0.001179	-0.244103	0.001732
Per capita monthly consumption exp.	0.000918*	1.68e-06	0.000324	1.67e-06
Eco. indep. dummy (eco. indep. =1)	0.623164*	0.000916	0.902462	0.001776
Log likelihood	-5716637.7		-1638336.8	
Specification 2				
Constant	-1.915843	0.000983	-1.716693	0.002057
Sex dummy (Male = 1)	-0.539748	0.000934	-0.450504	0.001752
Literacy dummy (literate = 1)	-0.255537	0.001160	-0.150083	0.001658
Employment dummy (employed = 1)	0.398562	0.000878	0.457152	0.001778
Social group dummy (Non-SC/ST = 1)	-0.071058	0.000874	-0.115162	0.002068
Per capita monthly consumption exp.	0.000972	1.65e-06	0.000452	1.60e-06
Log likelihood	-5989368.1		-1761613.5	
Specification 3				
Constant	-2.630364	0.001198	-2.303563	0.001984
Sex dummy (Male = 1)	-0.044354	0.000933	0.017546	0.001783
Literacy dummy (literate = 1)	-0.165861	0.001227	-0.107974	0.001694
Per capita monthly consumption exp.	0.001033	1.70e-06	0.000390	1.64e-06
Widow dummy (Widow/widower = 1)	0.971631	0.000994	0.756033	0.001734
Log likelihood	-5519268.6		-1690331.3	
Specification 4.1				
Constant	-1.976260	0.000792	-1.754222	0.001314
Sex dummy (Male = 1)	-0.433564	0.000858	-0.296764	0.001578
Literacy dummy (literate = 1)	-0.205167	0.001159	-0.167414	0.001623
Per capita monthly consumption exp.	0.001034	1.64e-06	0.000421	1.58E-06

Contd...

...Contd...

Variables	Rural		Urban	
	Coefficients	St. Error.	Coefficients	St. Error.
Emp. dummy (Casual worker = 1)	0.675270	0.001053	0.492290	0.003301
Log likelihood	-5911321.5		-1799366.9	

Specification 4.2

Variables	Rural		Urban	
Constant	-1.872375	0.000760	-1.744073	0.001301
Sex dummy (Male = 1)	-0.358373	0.000895	-0.338771	0.001673
Literacy dummy (literate = 1)	-0.263634	0.001140	-0.194214	0.001622
Per capita monthly consumption exp.	0.000961	1.63e-06	0.000423	1.58e-06
Emp. dummy (Self-employed = 1)	-0.000497	0.000988	0.232011	0.002065
Log likelihood	-6099815.9		-1789218.9	

Specification 4.3

Variables	Rural		Urban	
Constant	-1.872234	0.000758	-1.736000	0.001293
Sex dummy (Male = 1)	-0.358484	0.000830	-0.326395	0.001612
Literacy dummy (literate = 1)	-0.263428	0.001139	-0.196492	0.001628
Per capita monthly consumption exp.	0.000961	1.63e-06	0.000411	1.59e-6
Emp. dummy (Wage earners = 1)	-0.028192	0.005386	0.640243	0.003127
Log likelihood	-6099802.2		-1776731.5	

Dependent Variable = Living with spouse

Specification 5

Variables	Rural		Urban	
Constant	-0.342878	0.000521	-0.443633	0.000860
Sex dummy (Male = 1)	0.770463	0.000493	0.831019	0.000960
Literacy dummy (literate = 1)	0.281752	0.000600	0.366080	0.000953
Per capita monthly expenditure	1.18e06	1.31e-06	-0.000182	1.19e-06
Economic independence dummy (Economic independence = 1)	0.382138	0.000537	0.290865	0.001031
Log likelihood	-21613570		-5971993.3	

Dependent Variable = Living with children

Specification 6

Variables	Rural		Urban	
Constant	1.312437	0.000591	1.196944	0.000972
Sex dummy (Male = 1)	0.142857	0.000567	0.296879	0.001157
Literacy dummy (literate = 1)	0.244028	0.000656	0.137251	0.001117
Per capita monthly expenditure	-0.001130	1.36e-06	-0.000450	1.25e-06
Economic independence dummy (Economic independence = 1)	-0.537303	0.000568	-0.597540	0.001140
Log likelihood	-16691170		-4390980.3	

All coefficients are statistically significant at 1 per cent level. Variables are defined in Box 2.4.

Source: NSS 52nd Round household data CD.

might live by themselves.[7] The relationship with the literacy dummy is also interesting—illiterates are shown to have greater chances of living alone. Further, this is turning out to be true irrespective of the place of residence. If these results are accepted at their face values, it might imply a growing problem of non-altruism in the living arrangements of the aged in India. Are the males, literates and economically independent going to be more acceptable by families or care providers? If so, is it because of their superior worth? We will try to revert back to this question later. Here, however, we have tried to go deeper into this issue by introducing three additional dummies in our probit exercises—namely a caste dummy that divides the aged into three social groups: (i) scheduled caste/scheduled tribe and the rest, (ii) a widow or widower dummy, and (iii) a dummy representing the nature of employment held by a working old (i.e., casual, salaried or self-employed workers). The idea was to take into account the caste, employment and widowhood factors in explaining the chances of older persons living alone. The results presented in Table 2.11 and specifications 2 to 4 reveal that apart from females, the chances of living alone are also higher for (i) widows or widowers, (ii) the socially backward old from rural areas, and (iii) low paid casually employed elderly persons (specifications 2 and 4.1, Table 2.11). The opposite may however be the case with rural self-employed or wage earners (specification 4.3). As a whole, living alone appears to be a phenomenon associated closely with the aged belonging to the socially deprived and economically weak. This makes the general belief that families would look after their aged a proposition fraught with major uncertainties.

Males and the literate elderly are shown to bear higher chances of family living—especially in urban areas. The economically independent aged are less likely to be staying with family or children. They would either be loners or live with spouse. Apparently, therefore, multi-generational living in India is going to be a tradition of the past.

Gender Dimensions of Ageing

Besides many other disparities, the aged population in India also suffers from gradual feminisation and serious gender disparities. The

---

7. A simple data analysis with frequency distribution of loners by male and female also confirms this result.

feminisation of ageing is especially evident from the growth pattern of elderly females, which remained varying over the past decades. In the 1970s and 1980s, for instance, the number of elderly women increased rapidly (Figure 2.9). The situation however changed in 1991, and both the genders grew almost uniformly. In 2001, however, women have overtaken men once again. This is further confirmed by the state-wise figures. These figures reveal that in many cases, ageing tendencies are much higher among females. Barring states such as Punjab, Tamil Nadu, Bihar and Uttar Pradesh, it can be noticed for most of the states considered. Why do women surpass men in terms of ageing? Obviously, they have certain advantages in terms of longevity, which is apparently on the rise (Table 2.12). Unfortunately, however, they are facing serious morbidity issues as can be noticed from Table 2.13. To illustrate, barring the rural areas of Gujarat, Karnataka, Madhya Pradesh, Rajasthan and Tamil Nadu, and the urban areas of Kerala, Tamil Nadu, Maharashtra and Uttar Pradesh, all other states suggest larger proportions of women with co-morbid conditions. Hence their post-menopausal longevity advantages may be

Figure 2.9

Share of Aged Men & Women in Total Population:
All India, 1971–2001

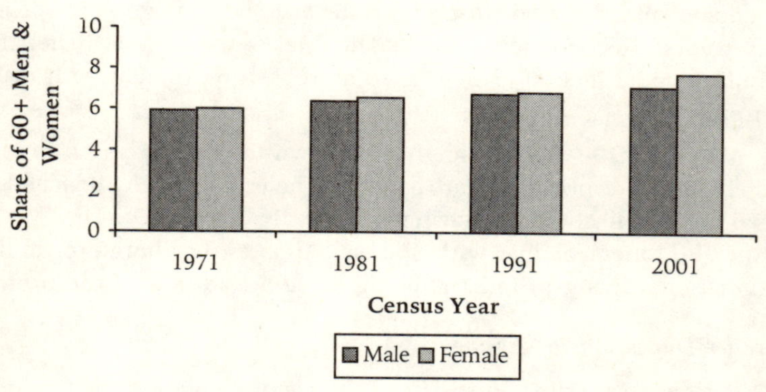

Source: Census of India (Series 1, Social and Cultural Tables) for corresponding years. For 2001 Census, age data available on CD from the Registrar General's Office (Government of India).

Table 2.12

Gender-wise Share of Aged in Total Population: States and All India, 1971-2001

Percentage

	1971		1981		1991		2001	
	Male	*Females*	*Male*	*Females*	*Male*	*Females*	*Male*	*Females*
Andhra Pradesh	6.3	6.4	6.5	6.8	6.6	6.9	7.2	8.0
Bihar	5.7	6.1	6.8	6.8	6.5	6.0	6.8	6.5
Delhi	4.3	4.3	4.4	4.6	4.6	4.8	4.8	5.7
Gujarat	5.0	5.6	5.5	6.4	6.0	6.8	6.2	7.7
Karnataka	6.1	6.1	6.5	6.8	6.8	7.2	7.2	8.2
Kerala	6.0	6.5	6.9	7.8	8.3	9.3	9.6	11.3
Madhya Pradesh	5.5	6.1	6.1	6.8	6.5	6.8	6.7	7.6
Maharashtra	5.5	5.9	6.1	6.7	6.7	7.3	7.8	9.7
Orissa	5.8	6.3	6.1	6.7	7.2	7.2	8.1	8.5
Punjab	8.2	6.6	8.3	7.3	8.1	7.6	8.6	9.5
Rajasthan	5.5	5.5	5.8	6.3	6.1	6.5	6.2	7.3
Tamil Nadu	5.8	5.7	6.5	6.3	7.7	7.3	8.7	8.9
Uttar Pradesh	7.0	6.5	7.1	6.6	7.2	6.5	7.1	7.0
West Bengal	5.0	5.6	5.3	5.8	5.9	6.2	6.7	7.5
India	**5.9**	**6.0**	**6.4**	**6.6**	**6.8**	**6.8**	**7.1**	**7.8**

Source: Census of India 1971, 1981 and 1991 (Social and Cultural Tables). Figures for 2001 were obtained from the data CD provided by the Registrar General Office (Government of India).

Table 2.13

Gender Differentials in Single and Multiple Diseases: 60+

Major States	Rural (Percentage)				Urban (Percentage)			
	Males		Females		Males		Females	
	Single	Multiple	Single	Multiple	Single	Multiple	Single	Multiple
Andhra Pradesh	30.2	42.5	30.6	46.7	27.3	34.4	31.1	38.7
Assam	28.2	46.6	25.5	52.8	33.7	46.9	26.5	53.5
Bihar	24.0	31.8	24.8	32.5	22.2	25.6	29.4	30.2
Gujarat	14.1	49.1	29.3	34.0	29.3	33.5	28.4	40.4
Karnatake	23.6	32.9	27.6	19.8	27.2	30.7	38.4	34.1
Kerala	19.6	30.5	29.2	49.0	26.4	39.3	23.3	34.9
Madhya Pradesh	25.5	48.0	22.9	37.0	24.4	31.9	31.4	38.3
Maharashtra	23.0	31.2	32.0	38.9	28.6	37.1	22.1	33.6
Orissa	29.3	38.0	32.2	39.8	25.5	31.8	31.0	36.2
Punjab	26.4	40.4	28.7	41.7	25.8	35.1	23.6	38.3
Rajasthan	30.7	35.7	24.7	33.0	26.4	29.9	21.5	44.2
Tamil Nadu	25.9	37.1	25.9	31.2	29.2	37.7	27.0	30.2
Uttar Pradesh	23.7	40.2	26.2	40.5	24.5	35.3	24.8	34.6
West Bengal	26.9	38.5	24.3	60.7	31.3	49.4	30.2	41.0

Source: NSS 52nd Round data CD.

more a phenomenon caused by certain bio-medical factors. The discrepancy between this and some of our earlier econometric exercises may be the result of certain reporting biases—especially in backward states. The gender-wise activities of daily living (ADL) disabilities, derived on the basis of our survey results, may help us to take a more specific view on this issue.

We further tried to look into the nature of male and female diseases in an attempt to highlight the gender dimensions of the health of the elderly. Table 2.14 gives this distribution separately for men and women.

Several interesting observations follow from Table 2.14. Most of the sick elderly males and females suffer from joint problems followed by lung related diseases, poor vision and hearing impairment. They also suffer from locomotor disorders and amnesia. Males seem prone to many lifestyle diseases such as blood pressure, heart problems and diabetes.

Table 2.14

Size of Older Men and Women Suffered by Major Diseases: All India

Percentage

Nature of Diseases/Disabilities	Male	Female
Visual	17.0	18.6
Hearing	9.4	10.3
Speech Related	2.5	2.5
Locomotor Disorder	6.8	7.6
Amnesia	5.8	6.7
Cough	16.0	12.2
Piles	2.3	1.3
Joint Problem	23.8	27.3
Blood Pressure	7.7	7.9
Heart Problem	3.0	1.9
Urinary Problem	2.5	1.4
Diabetes	2.9	2.0
Cancer	0.2	0.2

Source: NSS 52nd Round Data CD.

At the end, two significant points emanating from this entire discussion bear consideration. The aged in India can in no way be treated a homogeneous category—especially at the policy level. Secondly, given the fast emerging socio-economic and demographic changes in the country, health and livelihood issues of the aged in India may not remain as before. Many new issues are expected to crop up with time. The data available from existing sources like the census or the NSS may not help to examine many of these issues. Therefore, new data sets will have to be created. We shall try to look into this aspect.

2.3. Ageing and Some Unanswered Dimensions: Data Needs and Data Availability

A number of new questions arise from what has been observed so far. While the worsening conditions of the aged in the country are clearly evident, this whole issue is also mired in the questions emanating from section 1.5. To be precise: what are the ongoing perceptions about these issues among a cross-section of the aged and non-aged? Are they concerned about the on going changes? How do they react about major shifts in the economic environment? What are the views of the non-aged on (i) their own ageing, and (ii) care giving to the aged? Is there altruism in care giving? What fractions of the aged are functionally impaired and dependent in their activities of daily living? Who should manage old age pensions? Should it be privately managed as favoured by many? Who benefits from public supported old age programmes? There are an endless number of similar questions, and each of them is significant for devising old age support mechanisms. Unfortunately, none of these questions can even partially be examined on the basis of the information available from secondary sources. We therefore conducted a household survey in Delhi with a structured questionnaire—designed to elicit views on many of these issues. We also tried to collect information on ADL impairments from the elderly respondents and the assistance received by them from their families.

2.4. The Elderly and their Care Providers: A Survey of Urban Households in Delhi

Our comprehensive survey of over 1000 Delhi based households had at least one elderly co-resident. A two-part questionnaire was designed to obtain information from the older participants and their care providers with the following major issues:

Part A of the Questionnaire

- Sections 1-3: Household details including housing and other socio-economic characteristics including living conditions and asset holdings,

- Section 4: Views of the non-elderly about caring for the aged (especially against the background of increasing cost of old age care on the one hand, and large scale informalisation of the labour market with growing labour insecurities on the other), and their perceptions about the need for planned ageing with early participation in old age income and health security instruments,

- Section 5: Familial Transfer: Altruism *versus* exchange relationship,

- Section 6: Migration Status

Part B of the Questionnaire

- Sections 7-16: Elderly related issues including their familial and non-familial earning sources, activity status, coverage in old age pension plan, asset holdings, health issues, diseases and functional impairments, itemised expenditure, utilisation of health care, decline in interest earnings and emerging problems, grand parenting, problems faced by widows, etc.

The details of the sample design, choice of Delhi as the survey area, and some of the major findings of this survey are discussed in a later part of this study.

2.5. Concluding Observations

This chapter was designed with an expressed objective to highlight a few of the major disparities suffered by the elderly population both at the all-India level and across a set of major states. This part of the analysis draws its justification from the fact that it helps to negate the popular perception characterising the aged as a homogeneous group. Our analysis—both over the censual years and across major states from all over the country—reveals all kinds of disparities among the Indian old. The aged, for example, suffered considerable variations in their age composition by states. Some of the states, particularly Kerala, have a much higher share of the older old. Obviously these states may need more medical and long-term care institutions. The aged also vary in terms of their health status identified by multiple disease conditions. Obviously, states with a higher share of the aged inflicted with multiple diseases need their health policies to be formulated keeping this fact in view. Health sector reforms in these states may be tailored accordingly. Interestingly, many of the better-off states suffer with a larger share of elderly population reporting multiple diseases. This may partly be due to their superior knowledge and health consciousness. Similar variations are noted in case of the economic environment faced by the aged across the states. Of all, perhaps the most disturbing is the gender dimension of ageing. Older women were found to be on losing ground—they suffer more from co-morbid conditions, lack chances to become heads of households and bear the risks of living alone.

APPENDIX A-2.1

Resolution Adopted in the Madrid Declaration:
Madrid, April 2002

Political Declaration

Article 1: We, the representatives of Governments meeting at the Second World Assembly on Ageing in Madrid, have decided to adopt an International Plan of Action on Ageing, 2002 to respond to the opportunities and challenges of population ageing in the twenty-first century and to promote the development of a society of all ages.

Article 2: We celebrate rising life expectancy in many regions as one of humanity's major achievements. We recognise that the world is experiencing an unprecedented demographic transformation and that by 2050 the number of persons aged 60 years and above will increase from 600 million to almost 2 billion and that their proportion is expected to double from 10 to 21 per cent.

Article 3: We reiterate the comments made by our heads of State at major UN conferences and summits.

Article 4: We emphasise that in order to complement national efforts to fully implement the International Plan of Action on Ageing 2002, enhanced international cooperation is essential.

Article 5: We reaffirm the commitment to spare no efforts to promote democracy, strengthen the rule of law and promote gender equality.

Article 6: We recognise that concerted action is required to transform the opportunities and the quality of life of men and women as they age and to ensure the sustainability of their support systems. All attempts should be made to include older persons in all walks of life and productive activities.

Article 7: We recognise the importance of placing ageing in development agendas, as well as in strategies for the eradication of poverty and in seeking to achieve full participation in the global economy of all developing countries.

Article 8: We commit ourselves to the task of effectively incorporating ageing with social and economic strategies, policies and actions while recognising that specific policies will vary according to conditions within each country.

Article 9: We commit ourselves to protect and assist older persons in situations of armed conflict and foreign occupation.

Article 10: The potential of the older person is a powerful basis for future development and, therefore needs to be harnessed.

Article 11: We emphasise the importance of international research on ageing and related issues.

Article 12: The expectation of older persons and the economic needs of society demand that older persons be able to participate in the economic, political, social and cultural life of their societies. Older persons should have opportunities to do these all as long as they wish or are able to.

Article 13: We stress the primary responsibility of the Governments in promoting, providing and ensuring access to basic social services, bearing in mind the special needs of older persons.

Article 14: We recognise the need to achieve progressively the full realization of the right of everyone to the enjoyment of the highest attainable standards of physical and mental health.

Article 15: We recognise the important roles played by families, volunteers, communities, etc., in providing support and informal care to elderly persons in addition to services provided by the Governments.

Article 16: We recognize the need for inter-generational solidarity.

Article 17: Governments have the primary responsibility for providing leadership on ageing matters and on the implementation of the International Plan of Action on Ageing 2002.

Article 18: We underline the important role of the UN system, including the regional commissions, in assisting the Governments at their request in the implementation, follow up and national monitoring of the International Plan of Action 2002.

Article 19: We invite all people in all countries from every section of society, individually and collectively, to join in our dedication to a shared version of equality for persons of all ages.

Madrid International Plan of Action on Ageing, 2002:
Major Recommendations

Three broad policy directions were adopted as part of the Madrid International Plan of Action on Ageing, 2002. These included the following:

A. Priority Direction 1: Older Persons and Development

Older persons must be full participants in the development process and also share in its benefits. No individual should be denied the benefit from development.

B. Priority Direction 2: Advancing Health and Well-Being into Old Age

Good Health is a vital individual asset. Similarly, a high over all level of health of the population is vital for economic growth and the development of societies. The full benefits of healthy longevity have yet to be shared by all humanity, evidenced by the fact that entire countries, especially developing countries and certain population groups, still experience high rates of morbidity and mortality. Older persons are fully entitled to have access to preventive and curative care, including rehabilitative and sexual health care. Health care and services need to include the necessary training of personnel and facilities to meet the special needs of older persons.

The growing need for care and treatment of an ageing policy requires adequate policies. This must ensure health promotion and well being throughout life.

C. Priority Direction 3: Ensuring Enabling and Supportive Environments

The promotion of an enabling environment for social development was one of the central goals agreed upon at the World Summit for Social Development. It was renewed and strengthened at the twenty-fourth special session of the General Assembly on social development. Realisation of all these and other aspects of an enabling environment and the economic growth and social development to which they contribute will make possible the achievement of the goals and policies agreed upon in the Madrid International Plan of Action on Ageing, 2002.

APPENDIX A-2.2

Assumptions of the CMD, Poisson and Negative Binomial Regression Models

Count Data Model (CDM)

In a count model the dependent variable takes non-negative discrete values corresponding to the number of events occurring in a given interval. Gilbert (1979) and Hausman *et al.*, (1984) used this technique by taking the number of purchases per period and the number of visits to doctors as dependent variables, respectively. Cameron and Trivedi (1986) used this technique on Australian Health survey data (1977-78). They used the number of consultations with a doctor or specialist in a two-week reference period as the dependent variable. Some of the important explanatory variables considered by them included sex distribution of the respondents, their age, age-square, income and illness dummies. We also tried to incorporate these variables in our analyses directed to examine the health outcomes of various socio-economic disparities.

The count type of models has two variations: (a) *Poisson type* and (b) *Negative Binomial type*. We briefly describe them in the following section.

Poisson and Negative Binomial Regression Models

Assumptions of Poisson: The Poisson model is a non-linear regression model and relies on the assumption that: (i) the observations of the dependent variable (here the discrete number of diseases suffered by the older persons) drawn from a Poisson distribution with mean and variance equal to 1, and (ii) the conditional mean and variance of the dependent variable are equal.

The model is estimated by maximum likelihood estimation. In modelling the count data, it is desirable to supplement estimation with additional tests to determine whether the fitted model is adequate or not. Hence, specification tests to test the hypothesis of choosing between Poisson and more general models may be carried out using the Wald test, the Likelihood Ratio and the Score (Lagrange Multiplier) tests.[8]

---

8. For a detailed discussion on this, see Cameron and Trivedi (1986).

Limitations of the Model: The assumed equality of the conditional mean and variance functions is typically taken to be the major shortcoming of the Poisson model, especially in a situation of over-dispersion in the data. Another limitation of the model relates to its assumption about independence between preceding and successive events. This again does not hold in reality. It may particularly not hold in our case where co-morbid conditions are usually inter-linked.

The most common alternative in this situation is the *Negative Binomial* resulting from the Bernoulli process. It is a generalisation of the Poisson model by introducing an individual, unobserved effect into the conditional mean (i.e., Ln $\lambda_I = X_i \beta + \varepsilon$). Here the exp (ε) follows a gamma distribution with mean 1 and variance χ .

Logistic Regressions: Probit Model

Probit (or logit) models are used when the response variable is dichotomous (binary or 0–1 type). The predictor variables may be quantitative, categorical or a mixture of the two. The basic form of the logistic function is:

$$P = 1/1+e^{-Z}$$

Where Z denotes a set of predictor variable ($Z \equiv b_0 + b_1X_1 + b_2X_2 + \ldots + b_kX_k$), and e is the base of the natural logarithm (Retherford and Choe, 1993). These models rely on the assumption that: (i) the error term follows normal distribution with zero mean and standard deviation (ii) the number of counts of the dependent variable follows a normal distribution, and (iii) the distribution is symmetric for the Probit model. There are also some problems with the measures of the Pseudo R^2, the traditional indicator of the goodness of fit in logistic regression. Many authors do not therefore present values of Pseudo-R^2 (for further discussion on this, see Retherford and Choe, 1993, pp. 140-42).

3

Assessing Ageing Issues in Times of Change: A Survey of Households with Elderly Co-residents

3.1. Introduction

Delhi—the national capital and the city-state chosen for this analysis—has a population of 13.8 million according to the 2001 Census. More than 5 per cent of this population (or about 764,000 people) was reportedly over 60 years of age. As it is virtually impossible for a study of this size and concern to bring into consideration every single detail about as many people, the option to work on the basis of a well identified sample was taken—seeking to characterise a few of their more important traits including living conditions in a situation of changing environment, major income sources—self and transferred, preferred pattern of expenditure, health practices, altruism as the basis of inter-generational relationship, implications of growing economic hardships on familial transfers, available public support mechanism, and the like. Some of these details were collected from a sample of 1000 households with elderly co-residents from all the nine districts of the National Capital Territory of Delhi (NCT of Delhi).

We begin with a few basic details about the survey, especially the sample design and selection of households recruited from each of the nine districts in Delhi. This will help to provide a genesis about the data and its efficacy for drawing inferences on issues under consideration. A discussion on the socio-economic characteristics of the sample households follows next.

3.2. Survey Design, Population Stratums and Choice of Study Area

The sampling frame of this exercise was designed with two central objectives: one, to ensure the representative character of the sample, and second, to bring about variability across the sample households.

As well documented in the sampling literature, a survey with one of its objectives to yield estimates of certain parameters needs to rely on a probability sampling in which the units are selected with known and non-zero probabilities.[1] It however requires far more resources and the background details, which are often hard to access. We have adopted a mix of procedure and safeguards, and used a multi-stage sample design to make this study more reliable.

Study Area

In India, poverty or insecurity—general or age-specific—is seldom area specific. It is almost a universal phenomenon, and differs only in terms of intensity (Table 3.1). Ideally, therefore, a study of our concern must include—if not all—most of the critical states and regions. For obvious reasons this was not possible, and we had to be more selective.

Table 3.1

Population Characteristics: Urban Population, 60+ Population and Below Poverty Population, All India & Major States

Major States	Population Characteristics: 2001#		Below Poverty Pop. 1999-00 (%)
	Share of 60+ (%)	Urban Population(%)	
Andhra Pradesh	7.6	27.3	15.8
Assam	5.9	12.9	36.1
Bihar	6.6	10.5	42.6
NCT of Delhi	5.2	92.2	8.2
Gujarat	6.9	37.4	14.1
Haryana	7.5	28.9	8.7
Karnataka	7.7	34.0	20.0
Kerala	10.5	26.0	12.7
Madhya Pradesh	7.1	26.5	37.4
Maharashtra	8.7	42.4	25.0
Orissa	8.3	15.0	47.1
Punjab	9.0	33.9	6.2
Rajasthan	6.7	23.4	15.3
Tamil Nadu	8.8	44.0	21.1
Uttar Pradesh	7.0	20.8	31.2
West Bengal	7.1	28.0	27.0
All India	**7.4**	**27.8**	**26.1**

Source: State-wise urban and 60+ populations are obtained from the Census of India (2001): Final Population Tables (Series I, India), May 2004, pp. 6-7. For the below poverty populations, see Economic Survey (2001-02), p. 239.

---

1. In many instances, the non-probability sampling including purposive or quota samplings may yield reasonable estimates, but they cannot provide the confidence that is necessary in the event of unexpected results (*Sampling Manual*, DHS, Phase III, No. 6, 1996).

While there may be several ways to decide about the study area[2], the following three appeared more plausible in the context of this study:

- Share of the elderly population in a state.

- Share of impoverished and below poverty line (BPL) population—assuming that a good fraction of the poor is constituted by the older people.

- Level of urbanisation in a state—assuming that urbanisation leads to dilution in family values and creates major hiccups for the elderly.

Table 3.1 provides these details for 16 major states and the National Capital Territory (NCT) of Delhi.

Table 3.1 suggests Kerala and Punjab among the states with highest share of elderly population. By way of contrast, Delhi is at the bottom with only 5.2 per cent of older persons. Two other states with very low proportions of 60+ are Assam (5.9 per cent) and Bihar (6.6 per cent).

Using the level of urbanisation as a criterion, the choice may shift to the western or the southern states such as Tamil Nadu, Maharashtra, Gujarat or Karnataka. Delhi turns out to be another highly urbanised state with more than 92 per cent of its population residing in urban areas. The eastern states, in contrast, remain at the bottom (Table 3.1).

Replacing poverty over the preceding two criteria leads to a markedly different position with the two eastern states—namely, Orissa and Bihar—topping the list. Considering that the below poverty population also comprise a good fraction of non-adult children, a choice of Orissa or Bihar seems less plausible.

Delhi is a highly urbanised state with a good mix of different population groups, which made it a good choice for a study area.

Distribution of Sample Households; A Methodological Note

This survey was essentially designed to elicit views from the aged and the non-aged in a household on the following broad issues:

---

2. Yet another criterion may be to concentrate on a few mega cities like Delhi or Bombay to know the effects of cosmopolitanism on elderly status.

- Views of the non-aged on caring for the aged, and their perceptions about own ageing in a changing family structure and environment.

- Major income sources of the aged and a few of their critical expenditure items.

- Their health issues including incapacitation due to frailty and poor health.

- Dependence in their activities of daily living (ADL).

- Their livelihood issues—especially on account of declining returns to small savings.

- Grand parenting.

- Familial transfers and their basis: altruism *versus* exchange relationship.

- Financial status of the elderly.

- Public transfers.

- Declining interest rate regime and interest reliant old.

Clearly, most of these issues required views from a cross-section of people with diverse socio-economic and cultural backgrounds. It required a wider coverage of areas to ensure variations in responding households. Two formulations were considered useful to meet these objectives.

Formulation 1:

Two major steps were involved here, each requiring several details about the population and its socio-economic characteristics. To illustrate:

It first divides the NCT of Delhi and its population into N urban districts/sub-districts (D^u_1, D^u_2, —— D^u_N), and uses the proportionate share of population in each district to distribute the (pre-determined) sample of 1000 households, i.e.,

$$S\left(D^u_i\right) = Pop^{2001}(D^u_i) / \sum_{i=1}^{N} Pop^{2001}_{i=1}(D^u_i) * 1000 \ (\text{where } N = 9) \quad \dots (1.1)$$

where N=9

Another step would be to distribute the district-wise populations (i) by age groups, and (ii) by certain socio-economic characteristics to stratify the sample of households (S^{hhd}) in i^{th} district (D^u_i). No such information was however available for recent years – in particular at the district level.

Formulation 2:

This formulation differs from the earlier one in one important respect—instead of population, it rests more on the household characteristics for stratification of the sample. To be more specific:

1) Like formulation 1, it also distributes the overall population into N urban districts (D^u_N).

2) This is followed by a distribution of all the districts (D^u_i) into an identifiable set of enumeration blocks (EBs^u)[3]—carved out in every district by the census officials as the primary data collection units.

3) Finally, these EBs are distributed into 4 distinct socio-economic classes ($J= j^1, j^2, .., j^4$):

   (i) EBs with predominantly high-income households (h^g),

   (ii) identified slums (l^d),

   (iii) government colonies and residential apartments (g^e), and

   (iv) localities with mixed income households (o^h).

Table 3. 2

Distribution of Households by Districts and
Socio-Economic Categories

N Districts	Distribution of District into EBs^u with Dominantly			
	HIG Households (h^g)	*Slums Households* (l^d)	*Government Households* (g^e)	*Mixed Households* (o^h)
D_1	h^g_{D1}	l^d_{D1}	G^e_{D1}	o^h_{D1}
D_2	h^g_{D2}	l^d_{D2}	g^e_{D2}	o^h_{D2}
.	.	.	.	.
.	.	.	.	.
D_N	h^g_{DN}	l^d_{DN}	g^e_{DN}	o^h_{DN}

---

3. Enumeration blocks (EBs) were distributed identically with each EB comprising 125 to 140 households.

The Directorate of Census (Delhi) has collected these details from all the nine administrative districts at the time of its house listing operations for the 2001 Census.

By this logic, the ith district may be expressed as summation of all the 4 categories of EBs:

$$D^u_i = h^g_i + l^d_i + g^e_i + o^h_i \qquad \qquad \text{...(2.1)}$$

Also, the sample of 1000 households may be distributed as:

$$S(D^u_i) = \{EB(D^u_i) / \sum_{J=1}^{4} EB \ (D^u_i)\} * 1000 \qquad \qquad \text{...(2.2)}$$

Where $\sum_{J=1}^{4} EB \ (D^u_i)$ is the same as in (2.1) above.

A stratum-wise break up of D_i may be written as:

$$S(h^{gj}_i) = \{EBs(h^{gj}_i) / \sum_{J=1}^{4} EB \ (D^u_i)\} * 1000 \qquad \qquad \text{...(2.3)}$$

$$S(h^{gj}_i) = \{EBs(h^{gj}_i) / \sum_{J=1}^{4} EB \ (D^u_i)\} * 1000 \qquad \qquad \text{...(2.4)}$$

$$S(h^{gj}_i) = \{EBs(h^{gj}_i) / \sum_{J=1}^{4} EB \ (D^u_i)\} * 1000 \qquad \qquad \text{...(2.5)}$$

$$S(h^{gj}_i) = \{EBs(h^{gj}_i) / \sum_{J=1}^{4} EB \ (D^u_i)\} * 1000 \qquad \qquad \text{...(2.6)}$$

We decided to follow this formulation for two basic considerations: (i) availability of reliable data from the Registrar General's (RG) Office and the Directorate of Census (Delhi), and (ii) it helps to stratify the sample of households more convincingly.

Distribution of Sample Households by Districts and Socio-Economic Categories

As already noted, the Census 2001 has distributed Delhi into nine districts, all overwhelmingly urban. This exercise is therefore solely confined to the urban areas after netting out the rural EBs. Table 3.3 provides these details.

Table 3.3

District-wise Distribution of Sample Households

Districts	District-wise Population (R+U) (million)	District-wise Urban Population (million)	District-wise Share of Urban Pop. (%)	District-wise Share of Urban EBs (%)	Distribution of Sample Households (Number)
1. North-West	2.8	2.6	20.16	19.68	197
2. North	0.8	0.7	5.72	5.10	51
3. North-East	1.8	1.6	12.65	9.10	92
4. East	1.4	1.4	11.16	13.64	136
5. New Delhi	0.2	0.2	1.34	3.14	31
6. Central Delhi	0.6	0.6	5.02	4.63	46
7. West Delhi	2.1	2.0	15.87	14.33	143
8. South-West	1.7	1.5	11.90	11.81	118
9. South	2.3	2.1	16.18	18.56	186
Total	**13.8**	**12.8**	**100.00**	**100.00**	**1000**

Source: Census of India 2001, Series 8, Delhi (paper 2 of 2001), and records of the Delhi Directorate of Census.

Table 3.4 serves to provide the socio-economic stratification of the sample households across all the nine districts. We used these details

Table 3.4

Socio-Economic Distribution of EBs: 2001 Census

Percentage

Districts	HIG (h_i)	Slums (l_i)	Government (g_i)	Mixed (o_i)	Row Total
1. North-West	0.53	13.69	1.52	84.25	100
2. North	1.37	41.53	5.46	51.64	100
3. North-East	0.00	8.19	0.54	91.28	100
4. East	3.37	13.94	0.51	82.18	100
5. New Delhi	3.76	16.37	3.54	76.33	100
6. Central	3.46	77.14	4.21	15.19	100
7. West Delhi	1.02	8.65	0.87	89.46	100
8. South-West	4.01	5.96	7.20	82.83	100
9. South	11.71	15.98	8.33	63.98	100

Source: Computation based on information from the Directorate of Census (Delhi).

to obtain the final distribution of our sample in Table 3.5. This table also represents the spread of our sampling units both spatially and by four different socio-economic categories or strata.

Table 3.5

Distribution of Sample Households by Stratums

Districts	HIG (h_i)	Slums (l_i)	Government (g_i)	Others (o_i)	Total Households
1. North-West	1	27	3	166	197
2. North	1	21	3	26	51
3. North-East	1	7	0	83	92
4. East	5	19	1	112	136
5. New Delhi	1	5	1	24	31
6. Central	2	35	2	7	46
7. West Delhi	1	12	1	128	143
8. South-West	5	7	8	98	118
9. South	22	30	15	119	186
Total	39	164	35	762	1000

Source: Based on Table 3.4.

Figure 3.1

District-wise Distribution of Sample Households

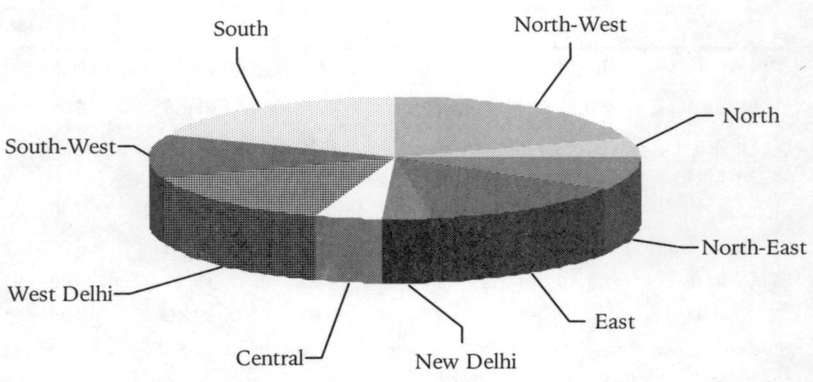

Source: Table 3.5

Areas and EBs Covered under the Survey

As we have pointed out earlier, identification of slums or government colonies does not pose any serious difficulty because of their well-identified locational status. But the HIG (h_i) and the mixed households (o_i) were problematic. Fortunately, however, the Census Commissioner's office has provided district-wise lists of localities/EBs with asset holding status of their households.[4] We used these details to pick up the HIG households from the posh localities of the districts in question. Most of these households included the owner residents along with personal cars and an operational bank account. The middle or the lower middle class categories may or may not own a car or a house, and were essentially drawn from the lower level residential areas, identified by the Census officials.

Despite these safeguards and a multistage sampling design, the size of high-income households (HIG) in our sample is relatively low and comprises only about 4 per cent of the total sample size. The largest share of the respondents comes from the lower and the middle-income households (o_i).

3.3. Ageing Issues: Questions from the Elderly and Non-elderly

This survey was directed to elicit views from elderly as well as non-elderly respondents. From the elderly, obviously the focus was on issues relating to their self-worth and experiences including asset holdings, financial status, physical and functional health, access to health care, expenditure preferences, declining returns to saving, sense of security with or without a bigger family with several siblings, etc. The below 60 (or non-aged) respondents, on the other hand, were asked questions relating to their own ageing—particularly their views on planned ageing owing to growing nuclearisation of families, fewer number of children, out migrations, and lack of public support for the aged. They were also prompted to react about the motivational factors responsible in transfer of income to the older dependents, families and their role in elderly care, altruism in caring for the aged, etc. Their views were elicited on the growing labour market issues because of

---

4. These lists were generated from the House Listing Schedules for the 2001 Census.

the ongoing economic shifts, and some of their difficulties in finding resources to meet the elderly care. Variations in responses across the four socio-economic categories were expected.

3.4. Sample Households and their Characteristics

The Setting

Socio-economic and health disparities among the aged in India raise a range of unanswered questions. Many of these relate to the non-aged as well.[5] Broadly, two sets of such questions are subjected to scrutiny in the forthcoming analysis.

One, will the future cohorts of the elderly (i.e., non-aged now) be more prepared to face old age contingencies—especially those relating to their income or health security aspects? This question basically stems from the belief that future cohorts of the aged may not be facing the kind of difficulties confronted by their peers today. Or, in other words, with the phasing out of the existing aged, many of the ongoing issues would taper off.

The second set of questions is mostly drawn in the context of the inter-generational transfers—i.e., caring for the aged and its burden on non-elderly caregivers. These questions draw much of their justifications from the recent economic changes and growing informalisation of the labour market that is likely to result in more and more low paid and insecure employment. The burden of old age dependencies on low paid persons may eventually be a constraining experience—especially if there are also young age dependencies. A question that arises is: will such difficulties make old age care less altruistic? If yes, the aged with better economic means and self-worth may draw better familial care and respect. The inheritance factor may also have a role in offering care to the aged.

Likewise, there are several unexplored issues linked with the older population as well. One of the foremost perhaps is the declining interest rate regime which erodes the cash earnings of those relying on their past savings. By contrast, the cost of daily living—especially the tariff structure of major services including water, power, transport, health care, etc.,—is on the rise.

---

5. Non-aged includes those below 60.

There are also many specific issues relating to the health, poverty, financial status, functional impairments, and livelihood aspects of the aged including their preferred pattern of expenditure, grand parenting choices, destitute pension, and so on.

Clearly, most of these issues can hardly be examined with the available data sources. We therefore relied on the underlying household survey to derive some the tentative inferences on many of these issues, though we refrain from making generalisations in view of the limited sample size.

The discussion is at two levels. Firstly, the characteristics of the surveyed households are described. An analysis of the ageing issues as perceived by the aged and the non-aged is attempted thereafter. Questions such as altruism in old age care or linkages between the health of the elderly (proxied by functional incapacitations) and poverty will also be discussed.

Sample Households and their Characteristics

Comparisons from the household survey will help explore the intra-aged disparities as was noted in a few recent studies conducted on off-shore aged of Indian origin (Burholt, Wenger, *et al.*, 2003 and Evandrou, 2000).

Distribution of Households by Districts and Socio-economic Groups

A total of 4,525 persons, aged 14 and above, were covered from a sample of 1,019 households.[6] A fifth of them were from the Northwest district with a mixed income background. The next largest district in terms of its overall share in the sample population was South Delhi (with 18.14 per cent share) followed by the South-West (13.43 per cent) and the East Delhi districts (13.38 per cent). The lowest coverage of just 4.07 per cent (or 183 persons) was from the New Delhi area.

---

6. It ought to be noted that the total sample population covered in the survey was 6060. Of this, a total of 4525 were 14 or above, and the remaining 1535 below the age of 14. As this analysis is not very much concerned with below 14 populations, we omitted them from most of our discussions except, for example, while analysing the average household size or its variations by different stratums.

Table 3.6

Distribution of 14+ Population by Districts and Stratums: NCT of Delhi

Districts	Number of Persons by District & Stratum				Total Persons
	HIG	Slums	Government	Others	Covered
1. North-West	0	107	7	796	910 (20.16)
2. North	11	95	16	112	234 (5.20)
3. North-East	3	29	9	337	378 (8.40)
4. East	17	75	5	510	607 (13.38)
5. New Delhi	0	25	5	153	183 (4.07)
6. Central	9	157	10	21	197 (4.16)
7. West	0	44	3	540	587 (13.05)
8. South-West	64	29	63	448	604 (13.43)
9. South	94	125	60	546	825 (18.14)
Sample	198	686	178	3463	4525 (100.0)
Population	(4.40)	(14.85)	(3.96)	(76.79)	(100.0)

Source: IEG/CIDA Ageing Survey (2002).

Note: Figures in bracket are percentages.

Most of the high-income respondents in the survey are either from South Delhi or those located in the South-West District. Similarly, most of the slum respondents were mainly residents of the Central Districts with a sizeable proportion coming from the residential areas of old Delhi. Respondents employed in government services and living in public colonies were mostly located in South and Southwest Delhi (Table 3.6). Some of these colonies also housed senior and middle level officials of the Central and state governments.

Another important point in the context of this survey is the share of households from the mixed income localities and residential areas. Together they add up to more than three quarters of the sample population. This ought not to be overlooked while interpreting the survey results.

Sex and Age Composition of Respondents

Unlike a very unfavourable sex ratio for urban Delhi,[7] the proportion of women in our sample turns out to be marginally higher

---

7. According to the 2001 Census, the aggregate sex ratio in urban Delhi was 822 (Census of India 2001, Series-8 (Delhi), Paper 2 of 2001).

—i.e., 2,266 women (50.08 per cent) and 2,259 men (49.92 per cent). However, this distribution does not hold for all the nine districts (Figure 3.2). At least five of them—the Northwest, Northeast, East, New Delhi and Southwest—drew larger shares of men. The remaining four—particularly the West and the Central districts—suggest a sex

Figure 3.2

*Districts-wise Distribution of Sample Males
and Females: NCT of Delhi*

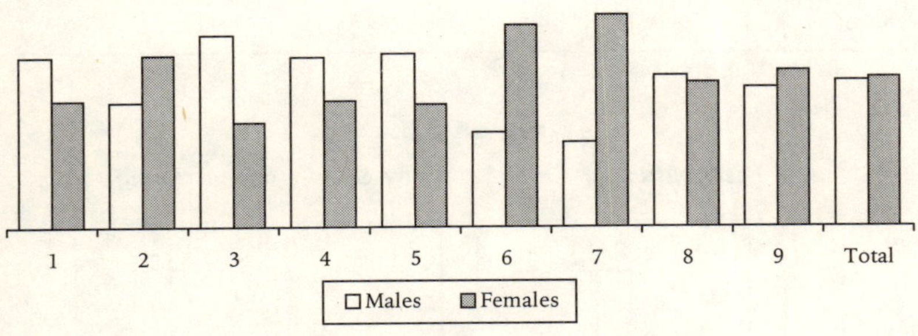

Source: IEG/CIDA Ageing Survey (2002).

ratio favouring women. Incidentally, both these districts have also registered better sex ratios in the 2001 Census.

In terms of the age distribution, Table 3.7 shows that the number of persons aged sixty or more is substantially higher in our sample than is factually true. But this is precisely because of the nature of this survey and its pre-condition of at least one elderly co-resident per household. The 60+ therefore constitutes between 22 and 28 per cent of the stratum-wise populations—maximum 28 per cent among the HIG households. The share of 75+ is also highest among the high-income group. As can be expected, the slum population lags behind in terms of 60+ and tops with the highest share of younger population in the 0-14 age bracket. Working age persons of 14-59 are about half of the sample population in each stratum (Figure 3.3a).[8]

---

8. National Family Health Survey (NFHS, 1998-99) provides the following age distribution of population for urban Delhi: 0-14 (32%), 15–59 (61%) and 60+ (7%).

Table 3.7

Age Distribution of Sample Population by Socio-economic Groups

Percentage

Age Groups	HIG	Slums	Govt.	Mixed	Total
0 - <14	18.2	31.1	21.6	24.6	25.3
14 – 59	53.7	47.2	55.9	52.5	51.8
60 – 69	15.3	15.7	13.2	13.6	14.0
70 – 74	6.2	4.0	3.1	4.8	4.7
75 +	6.6	2.0	6.2	4.4	4.2
%	100.0	100.0	100.0	100.0	100.0
No. of Persons	242	996	227	4595	6060

Source: IEG/CIDA Ageing Survey (2002).

Figure 3.3.a

Age Distribution of Respondents by Socio-economic Groups

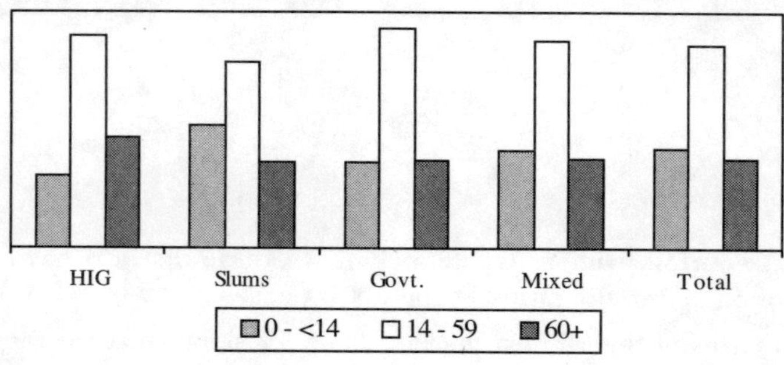

Source: IEG/CIDA Ageing Survey (2002).

Religious Composition

Distributed by religion, the largest share of the sample population is constituted by the Hindus (83 per cent). The next highest are the Sikhs with a share of 8.1 per cent followed by the Muslims (5.9 per cent), Christians (2.4 per cent) and others (0.7). [9] This distribution is however vitiated at the district level. At least in two districts—the North and New Delhi—there are no respondents from the Sikh community (Table 3.8a). The same can be noticed for Christians in New Delhi. At the aggregate level, however, our distribution matches closely with the National Family Health Survey (NFHS), conducted in

---

9. Others comprising mostly by Jains.

1998-99 for Delhi. This can be noticed from Figure 3.3b. Despite some marginal differences for Sikhs and Muslims, both the distributions are fairly close to each other. A distribution of these communities by different stratum or social group is given in Table 3.8b. As is the case, Hindus dominate in all the four strata with the highest share in the high-income groups. Next to Hindus in the HIG category are the Sikhs (4.5 per cent) followed by a very small fraction of the Muslims (2.2 per cent). Slum dwellers are however shown to have a significant proportion of Muslims (12.7 per cent).

Table 3.8a

Religious Composition 14+ Sample Population

Percentage

Districts	Hindus	Muslims	Sikhs	Christians	Others	Row Total
1. North-West	88.0	2.7	6.6	0.4	2.2	100.0
2. North	74.4	22.6	0.0	3.0	0.0	100.0
3. North-East	69.0	12.2	15.3	3.4	0.0	100.0
4. East	83.0	4.4	11.2	0.8	0.5	100.0
5. New Delhi	96.2	3.8	0.0	0.0	0.0	100.0
6. Central	73.6	13.2	10.2	3.0	0.0	100.0
7. West	79.2	2.2	16.7	0.9	1.0	100.0
8. South-West	92.7	2.3	1.3	3.6	0.0	100.0
9. South	80.4	7.0	6.8	5.6	0.2	100.0
Total	**82.9**	**5.9**	**8.1**	**2.4**	**0.7**	**100.0**

Source: IEG/CIDA Ageing Survey (2002).

Figure 3.3b

Distribution of Sample Population by Religion: Comparison of NFHS and IEG/CIDA Ageing Survey

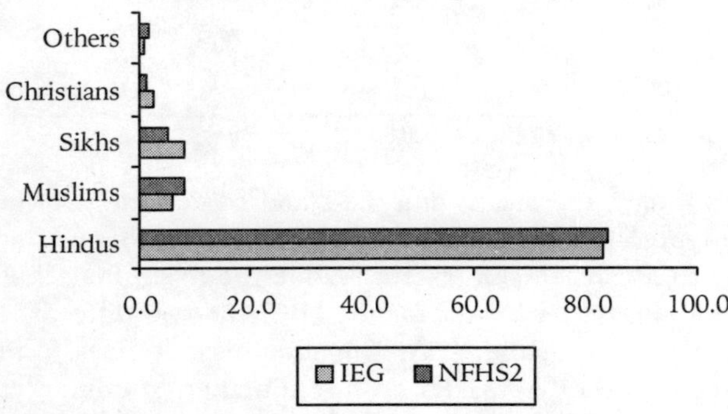

Source: Delhi NFHS (1998-99) and IEG/CIDA Ageing Survey (2002).

Table 3.8b

Religion-wise Distribution of Sample Population in
Each Stratum: 14+ Persons

Percentage

Religions	HIG	Slum	Govt.	Mixed	Total
Hindus	93.4	82.5	82.6	82.3	82.9
Muslims	2.0	12.7	2.3	5.1	5.9
Sikh	4.5	2.2	7.3	9.6	8.1
Christian	0.0	2.6	7.8	2.2	2.4
Others	0.0	0.0	0.0	0.9	0.7
Col. Total	100.0	100.0	100.0	100.0	100.0

Source: IEG/CIDA Ageing Survey (2002).

Size of Sample Households

Two forms of computation are made to judge the variations in size of the sample households. One is to make an assessment about the stratum-wise differences in mean household size, and the second to test the significance of these differences statistically. The usual 'F' and 't' tests were applied.

Table 3.9a

Mean Household Size: Total and by Socio-economic Groups (All Ages)

Social Groups	Number of Households	Average Household Size		Number of Persons in a Household	
		Mean	Std. Dev.	Minimum	Maximum
HIG	48	5.042	1.879	2	10
Slum	163	6.110	2.833	1	30
Govt.	41	5.537	1.206	3	9
Mixed	767	5.991	2.264	2	21
Total	1019	5.947	2.325	1	30

Source: IEG/CIDA Ageing Survey (2002).

Interestingly, the means and the standard deviations of household size computed separately for all the four socio-economic groups do not vary to a considerable extent. While the mean household size is largest for slums and lowest for the HIG, the two differ by a margin of just one person (Table 3.9a). This difference declines further when compared to other non-HIG groups. Further, it compares almost identically with the mixed category of the households. Mean household size at the aggregated level is worked out to be 5.9, which is marginally higher than the NFHS (1998-99).[10]

Does this imply that the differences in socio-economic status have no major implications for the household size in a cosmopolitan city like Delhi? Or does the mean household size for four different stratums remain statistically the same? An F-test was applied to draw certain inferences.[11] The values are given in Table 3.9b.

Table 3.9b

F-Statistic to Test the Equality in Mean Household Size across Strata (All Ages)

Number of Observations	Degrees of Freedom (DF)	Root MSE	F-value	Prob. > F
1019	3	2.317	3.23	0.0217

Source: Estimated on the basis of IEG/CIDA Ageing Survey (2002).

Though significant only at the 5 per cent level, the F-value clearly suggests similarities in average household size across the four socio-economic groups under consideration. Given this, we attempted to go further and tried to identify the pair of stratums with or without any significant differences in the underlying context. The results, using the two-sample t-test, are shown in Table 3.9c. As expected, the HIG turns out to be significantly different from the slums and the mixed income households. They however conform to those residing in the public apartments. The mixed income households, on the other hand, compare well with the slum settlers. In sum, these results underline the fact that the average households in Delhi are in two size classes, and both are not far apart.

---

10. It turns out to be 5.3 in the Delhi NFHS (1998-99), p. 19.

11. Analysis of variance basically relies on the assumption that the samples are drawn from normal populations, and that each of these populations has the same variance (σ^2). In case of smaller samples like the HIG and those drawn from the government colonies, this assumption bears considerable significance.

Table 3.9c

Paired Comparison of Stratum-wise Means:
Average Household Size (All Ages)

Pair-wise Observations	Mean	Degrees of Freedom (DF)	t-values	Standard Error
HIG vs. Slums: H_0 = Mean (HIG) – Mean (Slums) = Diff. = 0				
HIG = 48	5.042	115.9	(-) 3.050**	0.271
Slums = 163	6.110			0.222
HIG vs. Govt.: H_0 = Mean (HIG) – Mean (Govt.) = Diff. = 0				
HIG = 48	5.042	81.1	(-) 1.500	0.271
Govt. = 41	5.537			0.188
HIG vs. Mixed: H_0 = Mean (HIG) – Mean (Mixed) = Diff. = 0				
HIG = 48	5.042	55.9	(-) 3.351**	0.271
Mixed = 767	5.991			0.082
Govt. vs. Mixed: H_0 = Mean (Govt.) – Mean (Mixed) = Diff. = 0				
Govt. = 41	5.537	56.4	(-) 2.212*	0.188
Mixed = 767	5.991			0.081
Govt. vs. Slums: H_0 = Mean (Govt.) – Mean (Slums) = Diff. = 0				
Govt. = 41	6.110	154.5	1.972*	0.222
Slums = 163	5.537			0.188
Slums vs. Mixed: H_0 = Mean (Slums) – Mean (Mixed) = Diff. = 0				
Slums = 163	6.110	208.1	0.506	0.222
Mixed = 767	5.991			0.082

Source: Estimated on the basis of IEG/CIDA Ageing Survey (2002).
** Significant at the 1 per cent level. * Significant at the 5 per cent level.

Composition of Households

Generational characteristics of the households are given in Table 3.10. We notice that the share of multi-generational households in Delhi is still very high, although a change is apparently in sight—especially among the higher income households. It can be noticed that the share of two-generation households (i.e., without grand children) is highest among the high-income category (over 35 per cent) followed by households with members employed in the government

(19.5 per cent). In contrast, the remaining two stratums are mostly multi-generational—though a good proportion of them in both the categories are bi-generational too. Households with no children or grand children (i.e., single generation households) are very few in number (Table 3.10).

Table 3.10

Single and Multi-generation Households: Distribution by Strata

Stratums	Composition of Households							
	Single Generation Households		Two Generation Households (no grand children)		Multi Generation Households (with grand children)		Total Households	
	Number	%	Number	%	Number	%	Number	%
HIG	-	-	17	35.4	31	64.6	48	100.0
Slums	2	1.2	27	16.6	134	82.2	163	100.0
Government	-	-	8	19.5	33	80.8	41	100.0
Mixed	2	0.3	126	16.4	639	83.3	767	100.0
Combined	4	0.4	178	17.5	837	82.1	1019	100.0

Source: IEG/CIDA Ageing Survey (2002).

Marital Status

Marital status of the sample population is given in Tables 3.11a and 3.11b—the former for the entire sample, and the latter by stratum. Three points are more revealing from Table 3.11a. One, the shares of currently married males and females are almost equal in our sample. Second, the share of widows in the sample population is far higher than that of widowers (widows 20.2 per cent, widowers 5.9). And lastly, divorcees and separated men outnumber the women—although marginally. All these are nevertheless on expected lines.

A stratum wise distribution of marital status in Table 3.11b reveals that the share of currently married is highest among the high-income category. This is true for both the genders. Somewhat striking, but those widowed or divorced are more in households with public sector employment. The slum dwellers and those drawn from mixed income localities come next. Another striking point to notice from this table is the lower share of the unmarried among the HIG.

Table 3.11a

Sample Population by Marital Status: 14+ Males and Females

Characteristics	Sex-wise Marital Status (%)		
	Male	*Female*	*Total*
Currently Married	64.1	64.3	64.2
Separated	1.2	0.4	0.8
Widowed	5.9	20.2	13.0
Divorced	0.7	0.4	0.5
Never Married	28.1	14.7	21.4
Total	**2259**	**2266**	**4525**

Source: IEG/CIDA Ageing Survey (2002).

Table 3.11b

Marital Status of Sample Population by Sex and Socio-economic Stratums: 14+ Ages

Percentage

Marital Status	Males					Females				
	HIG	*Slums*	*Govt.*	*Mixed*	*Total*	*HIG*	*Slums*	*Govt.*	*Mixed*	*Total*
Married	67.7	66.7	57.5	63.8	64.1	67.8	62.8	64.3	64.5	64.3
Separated	2.0	1.5	0.0	1.2	1.2	0.0	0.6	0.0	0.5	0.4
Widowed	4.0	4.1	6.4	6.3	5.9	19.1	20.8	23.8	19.9	20.2
Divorced	0.0	1.8	1.1	0.5	0.7	0.0	0.0	0.0	0.5	0.4
Unmarried	26.3	26.0	35.1	28.3	28.1	13.1	15.9	11.9	14.6	14.7
Column	99	339	94	1727	2259	99	347	84	1736	2266
Total	**100.0**	**100.0**	**100.0**	**100.0**	**100.0**	**100.0**	**100.0**	**100.0**	**100.0**	**100.0**

Source: IEG/CIDA Ageing Survey (2002).

We also tried to compare the marital status of the aged and the non-aged. These are highlighted through the pie charts in Figures 3.4a and 3.4b. The most visible difference between the two categories relates to the share of widows. Aged in 60+ age brackets are found suffering with this problem to a much larger extent. At the policy level, it implies that India is not only moving towards accelerating growth in ageing, it also suffers from a very high share of ageing widows—requiring specific policy initiatives to ensure their well-being.

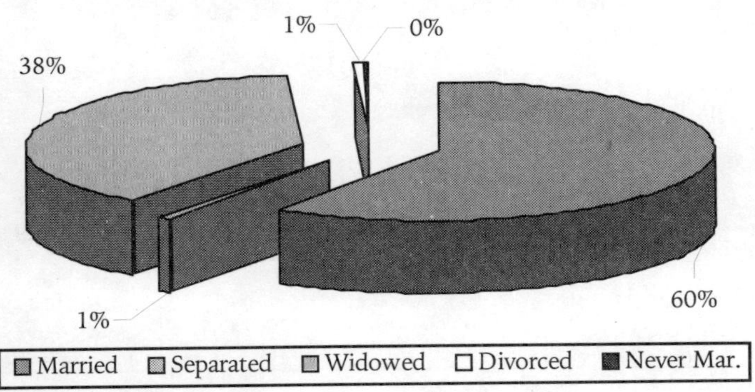

Figure 3.4a

Marital Status of the Elderly Respondents

Source: IEG/CIDA Ageing Survey (2002).

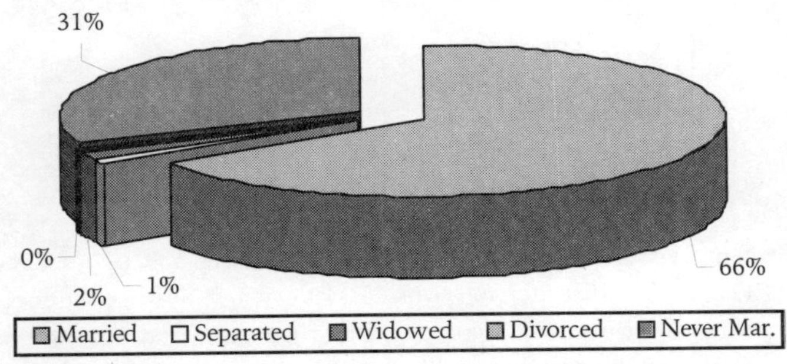

Figure 3.4b

Marital Status of the Non-elderly Respondents

Source: IEG/CIDA Ageing Survey (2002).

Literacy Level

Table 3.12a and its appended figure (Fig. 3.5) suggest that the share of educated population in our sample is significantly large. This is evident from the combined shares of matriculate, secondary and post-secondary including graduates. Putting them together, these three represent over two-thirds of the sample population. Another 9.6 per cent are those with primary level education. The remaining 24 per cent are either illiterate or without any formal schooling. For our analysis, a higher share of educated persons ensures the considered views of the respondents on several complex issues including altruism in familial transfers, reforms and income security issues, old age planning, preference in expenditure pattern, and so on.

Table 3.12a

Literacy Level of Responding Households: 14+ person

Literacy Level	Persons	(%)
Illiterate	953	21.05
Literate (No formal education)	142	3.14
Primary	436	9.64
Matriculate	1377	30.43
Secondary	641	14.17
Secondary+	976	21.57
Total	**4525**	**100.00**

Source: IEG/CIDA Ageing Survey (2002).

Figure 3.5

Literacy Level of Responding Households(%)

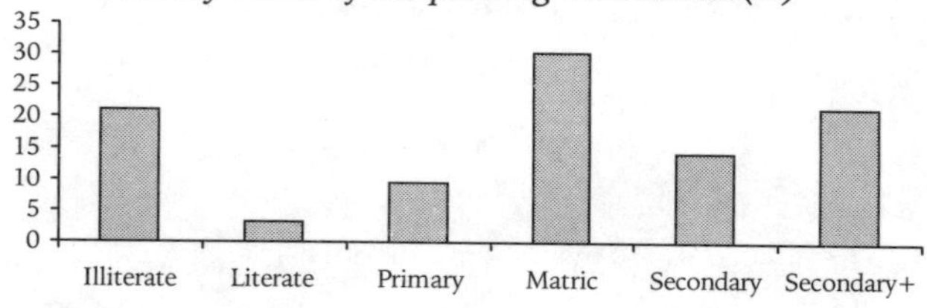

*Source:*IEG/CIDA Ageing Survey (2002).

Stratum-wise literacy level is shown in Table 3.12b. As expected, the HIG has no illiterate persons, and very few without any formal education. More than half of this stratum comprises persons with post-secondary education.

Table 3.12b

Stratum-wise Literacy Level: 14+ Population

Literacy Level	Strata (%)				
	HIG	Slums	Govt.	Mixed	Total
Illiterate	0.0	52.3	16.3	16.3	21.1
Literate	0.5	7.1	3.4	2.5	3.1
Primary	6.1	11.5	8.4	9.5	9.6
Matriculation	21.2	22.0	22.5	33.0	30.4
Secondary	15.2	3.6	19.7	15.9	14.2
Secondary+	57.1	3.4	29.8	22.7	21.6
Total	**100.0**	**100.0**	**100.0**	**100.0**	**100.0**

Source: IEG/CIDA Ageing Survey (2002).

In contrast, slum dwellers comprised the most illiterates. However, respondents from the mixed and the government colonies were no exceptions, and a good share of them was illiterate (Table 3.12b). Further investigation however revealed that many of them were in higher age groups.

Table 3.12c

Distribution of Sample Aged by Sex and Literacy Level

Sex	Illiterate	Literate	Primary	Matriculate	Secondary	Secondary+	Total
Males	27.7	32.1	40.9	64.4	74.7	77.7	44.6
Females	72.3	68.0	59.1	35.6	25.3	22.3	55.5
Total M+F	**588**	**78**	**230**	**320**	**75**	**94**	**1385**

Source: IEG/CIDA Ageing Survey (2002).

Educational statuses of the responding aged are given in Table 3.12c. Following the over-all situation in the country, this table also reveals large-scale illiteracy among the aged. Women are especially at a disadvantage with very few of them educated up to the secondary or higher levels. In addition, their share declines with each successive increase in the educational ladder (Figure 3.6).

Figure 3.6

Sex-wise Differentials in Educational Level: 60+

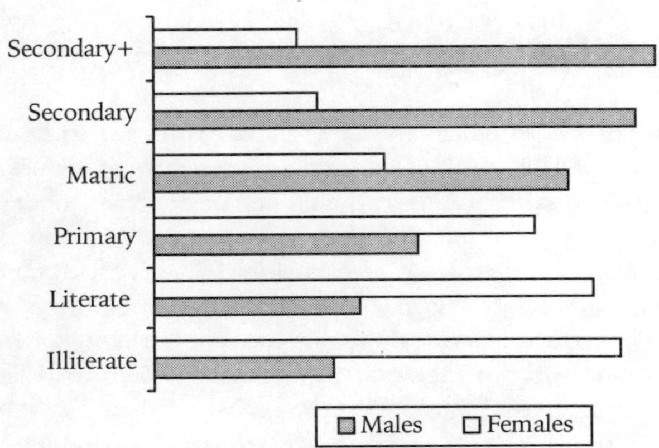

Source: IEG/CIDA Ageing Survey (2002).

Employment Status of Respondents

Work status of the population in question is analysed at two levels. First, we distribute the entire 14+ population into working and non-working categories with all non-labour market participants including housewives, students, voluntarily unemployed, sick, frail and retired are treated as non-workers. The workers, on the other hand, are those engaged in income generating activities either in organised or informal economies. These workers are further classified into eight major occupation divisions following the recent National Classification of Occupation (NCO). Workers are also categorised as those below and above 60 years of age.

Working and Non-working Members in the Sample Households

We notice from Table 3.13a that the overall working population in our sample is merely 36.4 per cent with the remaining 63.6 per cent as non-working dependents. This suggests that every working person in our sample is supporting over 1.74 persons of different age groups.

Table 3.13a

Work Status of the Sample Population: 14+ Ages

Work Status	Male		Female		Total	
	Number	*%*	*Number*	*%*	*Number*	*%*
Working	1389	61.5	260	11.5	1649	36.4
Non-Working	870	38.5	2006	88.5	2876	63.6
Total	**2259**	**100.0**	**2266**	**100.0**	**4525**	**100.0**

Source: IEG/CIDA Ageing Survey (2002).

Women workers in our sample population turn out to be merely 11.5 per cent of the total (Table 3.13a), revealing low levels of economic participation among the women. In contrast, males with 61.5 per cent are economically more active. An extension of this distribution by age and stratum reveals slum females as economically more active. Table 3.13b suggests that about a fifth of these women are engaged in earning activities. Pitiable though, but a higher fraction of the slum elderly, both men and women, are shown to have been working till later ages (Table 3.13b). For most of them, working till later years in life is not by choice but a strategy to cope with hard times and lack of social security provisioning.

Table 3.13b

*Works Status of Sample Elderly and Non-Elderly by
Sex and Stratums: 14+ Population*

Percentage

Broad Age Categories	HIG		Slums		Government		Mixed	
	Working	Non-working	Working	Non-working	Working	Non-working	Working	Non-working
Males								
Elderly	39.4	60.6	47.5	52.5	22.7	77.3	21.6	78.4
Non-Elderly	77.3	22.7	79.6	20.4	69.4	30.6	73.7	26.3
Total	**64.7**	**35.4**	**70.2**	**29.8**	**58.5**	**41.5**	**59.8**	**40.2**
Females								
Elderly	0.0	100.0	23.1	76.9	3.5	96.6	2.9	97.1
Non-Elderly	10.9	89.1	18.7	81.3	16.4	83.6	13.6	86.4
Total	**7.1**	**92.9**	**20.2**	**79.8**	**11.9**	**88.1**	**10.0**	**90.0**

Source: IEG/CIDA Ageing Survey (2002).

Elderly working women from the non-slum strata are much fewer, and none of them are from the HIG. As against this, elderly men from the higher income categories are far more active, and going by this criterion they are second only to their slum counterparts. All these details and differentials may lead to a specific observation—old age work is more a phenomenon of poverty and economic insecurity, particularly in the case of women.

Occupational Classification of Economically Active Members

Workers from all the four stratums were further classified into eight major occupation divisions (Figure 3.7). We notice from this distribution that the workers in better quality occupations do not come from the slums. The slum households are mostly engaged in low-paid menial employment as production workers, venders (clubbed here with sales workers) or to a limited extent transport workers. Similarly, they are also engaged in farming, fishing or fish vending. To a large extent, mixed category households are engaged in the transport business including owners of small auto workshops and related activities. In addition, they are also employed as professionals or sales and clerical workers. Similarly, many of the government households are engaged in professional activities or engaged in administration and low level blue-collar office work.

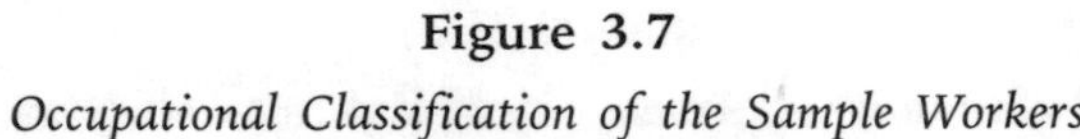

Figure 3.7

Occupational Classification of the Sample Workers

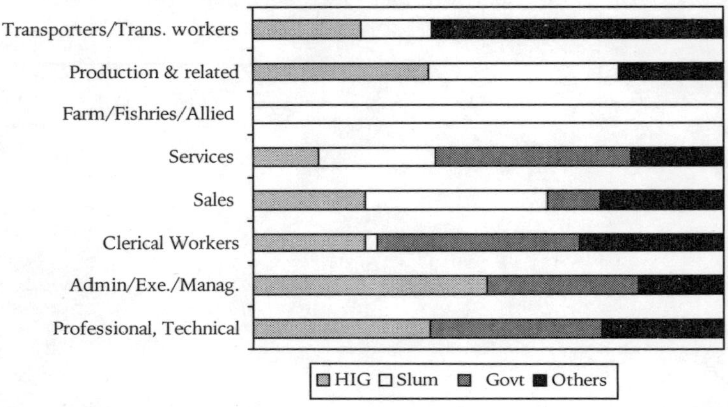

Source: IEG/CIDA Ageing Survey (2002).

Standard of Living Index (SLI)

The SLI is constructed as a proxy to capture the living standard of individual households using an ownership criterion of a range of items comprising major consumer durables, assets and houses for non-commercial purposes.[12] While constructing this index, we have *a priori* divided these assets into two broader categories, namely,

- Tangible items, and

- consumer durables including certain income generating assets and services.

Tangible items basically include residential houses with qualitative details (e.g., *kutcha, pucca* or *semi-pucca*) and toilet facilities. Under the consumer items, different types of assets that help to improve the income or comfort level of a household are considered. In all, 12 such

---

12. For decades, social scientists have been using social surveys to study poverty, deprivation and health outcomes in many developing and developed countries including India. Most of these surveys have shown that certain groups of population are likely to suffer more from multiple deprivation and poor health conditions than the rest. This led to large-scale experimentation socio in construction of the SLIs and their methodologies. Often four different methods are used to derive these indices: (i) possession weighting, (ii) proportionate possession weighting, (iii) opinion weighting, and (iv) proportionate opinion weighting. Following Townsend (1979), we relied on the possession weighting method implying households with the highest score on this index would be the wealthiest (also see, DFID, 2003; Nolan and Whelan, 1996; Gordon *et al.*, 2000, etc.).

items were considered in the survey (Table 3.14a). This table also ranks the assets on the basis of their notional market value in order to score them individually.

The allocation of these scores was made keeping in mind that every owner household of a specific item scores the point assigned in Table 3.14a. It may be noted that there is unidirectional relationship between the notional price or value of a commodity and the score. In other words, the higher the notional price of a commodity, the higher is the score assigned to it (Figure 3.8). We finally summed up the points scored by individual households and obtained the levels of living score for all the four socio-economic groups under consideration. Table3.14b presents these average values and their standard deviations (also see Figure 3.9).

Table 3.14a

Item-wise Scores: SLI

Assets & Consumer Durables	Scores*
Goods and Services	
1. Truck/van/heavy vehicle	12
2. Automobile/Car	11
3. Two wheeler	10
4. Computer (Desktop)	10
5. Refrigerator	9
6. Television	9
7. Telephone	8
8. Sewing Machine	7
9. Table Fan	6
10. Bicycle	5
11. Banking & other facilities (combined)	5
12. Radio	4
Tangible Assets (House)	
1. *Pucca* house	3
2. *Semi-kutcha* house	2
3. *Kutcha* house	1
4. Inside and flush toilet	3
5. Inside and dry toilet	2
6. No toilet inside the house	1

Source: IEG/CIDA Ageing Survey (2002).

Note: Higher the notional price of the asset, higher is the score point.

Figure 3.8

Scores Assigned to Individual Commodities: SLI

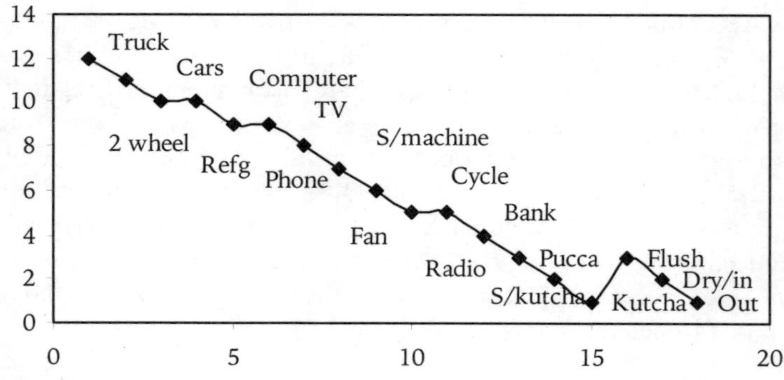

Source: IEG/CIDA Ageing Survey (2002).

Table 3.14b

Mean SLI by Stratums

Stratums	Observations	Mean	Std. Dev.	Min.	Max.
HIG	48	55.6	10.15	30	88
Slums	163	17.4	10.08	1	55
Government Colony	41	40.6	12.51	3	59
Mixed	767	41.1	11.38	2	90

Source: Constructed on the basis of the scores given in Table 3.14a.

Figure 3.9

Stratum-wise Mean SLI Values

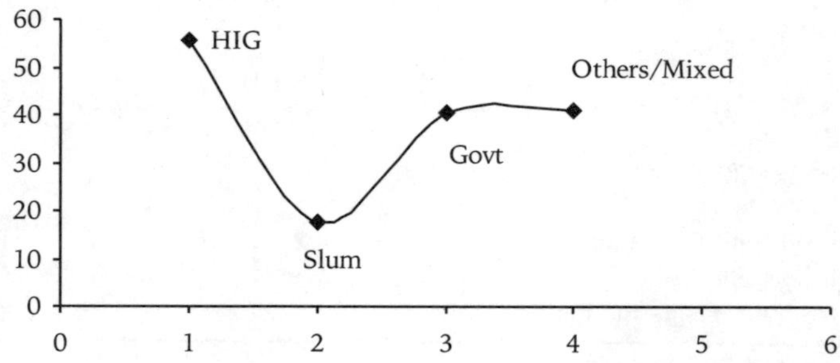

Source: Based on Table 3.14b.

4

Socio-Economic Issues of the Aged

4.1. Introduction

Using data from the survey of households and their co-residing older respondents, this chapter attempts to highlight a few of the socio-economic issues of the aged considered central in the ongoing debate on ageing world over including India.

One of the basic issues for discussion in this chapter relates to income sources of the aged. To be more precise, a few important income sources of the older persons have been identified besides their own labour or familial support. Similarly, the expenditure pattern was analysed to derive an ordinal list of items perceived by each responding person as most essential for their survival. This analysis was conducted in support of our previous discussion on old age poverty and its non-conformity with the existing norms used to generate poverty indices in the literature.

The second issue relates to their preferred living arrangements—especially in a joint family set-up. In this context, an interesting point for them to comment was their choice between the sons and the daughters—if at all they need to co-reside. An attempt was also made to ascertain their views for staying in an old age home. Some results regarding their views on grand parenting will also be presented.

Finally, we will briefly discuss about their views on the current interest rate regime. The issue under examination here is: does the persistent decline in interest yield on small savings make the aged vulnerable? Besides, we also tried to analyse some information about the savings and the saving instruments used by the sample elderly for their old age income security.

Yet another issue to be discussed at some length relates to their functional health—which often starts deteriorating without reaching senescence. To enable this analysis, we looked more closely into the questions of functional impairments, disabilities and large-scale dependence in basic activities of daily living (ADL). We also generate a disability-dependence index to assess their help requirements, and the likely pressure it might generate on the caregivers. A part of this analysis has also been devoted to suggest public health initiatives to prevent sickness and improve the health conditions of the old.

4.2. Income Sources of the Aged: Transfer Income *versus* Own Source Income

The discussion on old age poverty in India and many other developing countries remained scanty for a variety of reasons. One of them perhaps is the large-scale lifetime poverty in most of the developing world including India—leaving many to believe that age has little to do with poverty generating processes.[1] And yet references to ageing have been made in mainstream economic literature—often in the context of gender related intra-family distributional biases (Agarwal, 1990). In addition, a few suggestions have also been made by analysts to distribute people below the poverty line by their age categories to judge the age-specific poverty differentials, and derive poverty alleviation strategies accordingly (Visaria, 1980). While this analysis may not be able to offer any useful insight on most of the issues mentioned above, an attempt is however made to examine the major income sources of the sample aged. These sources are divided into two categories: (i) own source income, and (ii) transfer income. Arguably, larger the share of those relying on transfers, greater would be the prevalence of old age poverty.

A total of eleven earning sources were considered in both the categories. These are:

1. Own Source Income (self and spouse combined)

- income from work,
- employers' pension,
- shared family business,
- interest earnings,

---

1. Another reason for the neglect of this important issue in most developing countries is the general premise that unlike investments in children or youth, programmes aimed to reduce old age poverty may have limited social pay-off with smaller effects on growth or over-all poverty reductions. This notion of human capital theory was however refuted in several recent studies. For an interesting review of these details, see Barrientos (2002).

- rental income and
- income from agricultural sources.

2. Transfer Income
- financial help received from children,
- financial help received from other relatives,
- social security payments by the Centre and states (i.e., destitute pension),
- other public help programmes like 'Annapurna,' and
- NGO support.

A distribution of sample elderly by their income sources is presented below. A related exercise examining implications of old age dependencies on per capita monthly consumption expenditure (PCMCE) of the observed households has also been made. We postulate that the households with non-earning elderly dependents may have lower PCMCE than those where the aged have their own income sources.

Earning Sources

Earning sources of the elderly respondents were computed in two ways. First, we tried to identify the persons with no or grossly inadequate own source income (Table 4.1a). Obviously, these persons would be relying on transfers. Another table, i.e., Table 4.1b, which shows the earning sources in a matrix form, follows this. The diagonals in Table 4.1b represent the persons with a single source of income. The off-diagonals, on the other hand, indicate persons with multiple income sources.[2]

Out of a total of 909 persons with no independent earning, Table 4.1a reveals that 541 (or about three-fifths) are completely dependent on transfers. Of these, over 83 per cent relied on children or relatives, and another 16 per cent on destitute pension. The share of NGOs is apparently negligible. Another interesting observation from this table relates to a good number of persons drawing destitute pension along with their own earning sources. Even in certain cases

---

2. Numbers reported in Tables 4.1a and 4.1b may not match with the previous tables because of a few multiple earning cases.

there are multiple income sources as reported by the pensioners (see column 4, Table 4.1a). It amounts to violation of eligibility norms set for the destitute pension scheme by the government.

Table 4.1a

Older Persons Depending on Transfers Cross Classified by Financial Security Index (FSI) Values

FSI Values	Transfer Sources				
	Children	Relatives	Destitute Pension	NGOs	Total Persons
0	434	18	87	2	541
1	269	12	50	0	331
2	23	1	12	0	36
3	1	0	0	0	1
Total	727	31	149	2	909

Source: IEG/CIDA Ageing Survey.

Table 4.1b displays persons with own source earnings by single or multiple outlets. As noted, the diagonally shown numbers suggest persons drawing income from one source. The remaining cells indicate multiple sources. Two income sources appear to be more common: one is the post-retirement employers' pension followed by work income. Business income applies to only a very small proportion of respondents. Similarly, reliance on annuities is also very uncommon.

Table 4.1b

Non-family Income Sources: 60+ Persons (Respondents & Spouses Combined)

Non-family Income Sources	Work Income	Employers Pension	Business Income	Annuity Income	Income from Real estate	Farm Income
Work	186	20	5	0	0	0
Emp. Pension	20	193	9	8	0	2
Business Income	5	9	25	1	0	1
Annuity	0	8	1	17	0	0
Real Estate	0	0	0	0	1	0
Farm Income	0	2	1	0	0	10
Total Number	211	232	41	26	1	13

Source: IEG/CIDA Ageing Survey.

As a whole, these details lead to two inferences: one, very high economic dependence of older persons as proxied by the transfer income, and two, earnings from work and employers' pension remain two major non-family income sources for the aged. The latter would however be waning with pension reforms and decelerating employment in the organised sector.

4.3. Dependency Burden and Level of Household Expenditure

What does the dependency burden—or inter-generational support transfers—mean to individual households? Obviously, it may mean different things to different households. In this analysis, however, we considered this issue from a limited perspective of reduced per capita household consumption expenditure.[3] Or, in other words, we premised that the households with completely dependent older persons might be having lower per capita expenditure than the households where the older co-residents are financially independent —fully or partially. To justify this argument, we made an attempt to compute the per capita household expenditure with and without a dependent elderly. The FSI values were used to make these computations. We observe from Table 4.2 that the dependencies, especially the financial status of the dependents—did affect the consumption level of a household. For example, the consumption level in Table 4.2 increases with every upward movement in the FSI values —that is from Rs. 1191 of households supporting aged with zero FSI to Rs. 1313 when the FSI increases to the next level and so on. It therefore substantiates our argument implying that old age support has a cost to the households. In addition, this cost may mean far more to the lower income households.

4.4. Expenditure Preferences by the Aged

One of the issues relating to old age poverty in Chapter 1 was to draw a basket of goods and services relevant for the aged. It was argued that the persons of higher ages are likely to differ from others in terms of their basic requirements. To test for the validity to this argument, we tried to come up with a basket of eight expenditure

---

3. It may however imply certain equity in intra-household consumption expenditure. In many cases, however it may not be true.

items, assuming that they mostly surrogate for the basic needs of the older adults. The sample elderly were then asked to rank these items according to their self-perceived needs. Most of these results confirm our earlier argument implying asymmetric nature of basic needs. Also, these results help to impute differences in the combination of goods and services required by the aged.

Table 4.2

Household Consumption Expenditure and FSI Values of Older Persons

Burden of Support Households Supporting Older Persons with:	Household Consumption Expenditure According to FSI				
	No. of Observations	*Mean Consumption (Rs.)*	*Standard Deviation*	*Minimum Expenditure (Rs.)*	*Maximum Expenditure (Rs.)*
0 FSI Value	909	1190.9	658.3	500.0	5000.0
1 FSI Value	432	1312.7	897.9	500.0	11000.0
2 FSI Value	43	1647.8	814.4	500.0	3350.0
3 FSI Value	1	3466.7	0.0	3466.7	3466.7

Source: IEG/CIDA Ageing Survey.

The exercise presented below is conducted at three levels. One is of course for the entire sample. At the subsequent levels, attempts were also made to make assessments about the differences amongst the elderly themselves – particularly after controlling their age, gender and stratum. We begin by listing the expenditure items considered for this analysis.

The following expenditure items were considered:

Health Expenditure

(1) doctors' fee/consultation charges,

(2) expenses on medicines,

(3) diagnostic check-up/medical examination,

Expenditure on Basic Needs

(4) food,

(5) housing/shelter,

(6) clothing,

Items of Psycho-emotional Satisfaction

(7) entertainment,

(8) socio-religious events/responsibilities, and

(9) any other.

The results, based on ranks assigned to each of these items by the elderly respondents, are presented below. These ranks suggest the relative position of each expenditure item for the old.

Expenditure Priorities of the Aged

We first describe the results at the aggregate level. The disaggregated results showing intra-aged differentials follow next.

Table 4.3 presents the views obtained from the entire sample. We notice from this table that food was the most preferred item for a very large majority of the responding old. A total of 87.4 per cent (see figures in italics) reported food as their number one priority. Immediately after food however is health care—especially medicines. This is true for about a third of those responding to this question. Housing and clothing are yet other important items, though in many cases these are ranked at lower level.

Table 4.3

Expenditure Priorities: 60+ Persons

Percentage

Expenditure Items	Rank Orders								
	1	*2*	*3*	*4*	*5*	*6*	*7*	*8*	*9*
Doctors' fee	0.3	3.0	11.2	6.8	20.3	46.1	7.0	5.6	6.9
Medicine	7.7	*32.5*	13.4	23.0	10.8	6.6	4.9	0.9	6.9
Med. Check-up	2.7	6.3	4.3	*30.8*	*31.8*	16.1	6.4	1.6	10.3
Food	*87.4*	6.9	2.9	2.3	0.2	0.4	0.0	0.1	0.0
Housing	1.5	29.3	*39.6*	7.9	7.8	13.1	0.1	0.5	0.0
Clothing	0.3	21.4	27.9	26.9	16.5	5.5	1.0	0.4	3.4
Entertainment	0.1	0.4	0.0	0.4	1.2	5.6	*41.7*	*51.5*	34.5
Relig. & Social	0.0	0.3	0.6	1.9	11.4	6.7	39.0	39.3	37.9
Total N	1011	1020	1014	1011	1006	1006	1005	981	29

Source: IEG/CIDA Ageing Survey.

Going by these responses, a mix of five major goods and services appear to constitute the bulk of old age consumption requirements in urban areas. On a descending priority scale, these include:

1. food,

2. health care (including medicine, diagnostic check-up and doctors' fee),

3. housing,

4. clothing, and

5. socio-religious services followed by some entertainment requirements including reading materials like newspapers, magazines, etc.

Figure 4.1

Expenditure Priorities by 60+ Persons Priority Scales:
Highest = 1 & Lowest = 9

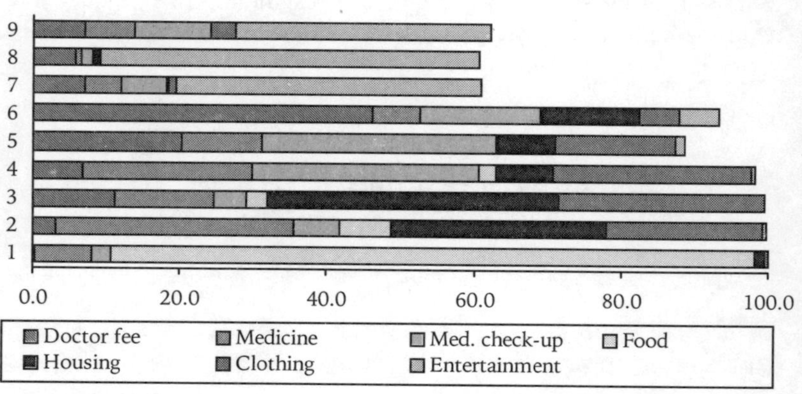

Source: IEG/CIDA Ageing Survey (Table 3.24a).

Figure 4.1 further clarifies these priorities and their rank orders. These results may as well reveal that even a modest upward fluctuation in the price of these basic items may significantly erode elderly welfare, and cause a big fraction of the older population to suffer from more severe poverty and escalating cost of health care. This may especially be true for those with lower FSI values with no or inadequate income security. It may also increase the dependency cost incurred by the care providers.

Expenditure Priorities by Sex and Socio-economic Characteristics of the Aged

As the results provided in Table 4.3 (Figure 4.1) didn't consider the intra-aged differences in their expenditure priorities, some more exercises were conducted by controlling the age, sex and socio-economic categories of the responding aged. A Chi^2 test was also applied to account for the differentiating effects of these factors on their expenditure preferences.

Stratum-wise results are highlighted in Table 4.4a, b and c. For the sake of brevity, we present here the first three most critical items chosen in order of priority by people of each stratum.[4] Interestingly, food was the top priority for most of the high and middle-income respondents (i.e., 93.6 per cent from the HIG, and 91 per cent from the mixed income categories). In contrast, the bulk of those from the other two stratums (slums and government) cited medicine as their first priority. It obviously makes an interesting observation and amounts to suggest that the aged of different socio-economic stratum do not conform mutually in terms of their expenditure priorities. This happens despite food being placed as the highest priority item for all the four socio-economic groups. Chi-square results also confirm these differences. As expected, some of the low-income respondents—who also suffer from poor health standards and multiple diseases—rank medical expenses over the rest. However, it needs to be further investigated with a bigger sample both from the rural and the urban areas.

Similar differences arise for the second and the third priorities as well. While medicine is reported as the second most preferred item by a large fraction of respondents in each of the four strata (Table 4.4b), a part of the HIG and mixed income respondents have chosen shelter as the next priority. Like-wise, the third choice also remained divided between housing and clothing. The chi-square tests also confirm these differences. The results also indicate the socio-economic status as one of the differentiating factors in expenditure priorities.

---

4. For more detailed results, see Appendix Table 4.1.

Table 4.4

Expenditure Priorities of 60+ by Stratums

(a) First Priority

Percentage

Expenditure Items	Stratum-wise Expenditure Priorities (Total N = 1011)			
	HIG	*Slums*	*Govt.*	*Mixed*
Cloth	0.0	0.0	0.0	0.4
Doc. Fee	0.0	0.6	0.0	0.0
Entertainment	0.0	0.0	0.0	0.1
Food	93.6	74.5	70.7	90.9
Housing	0.0	5.0	2.4	0.5
Med. Check-up	4.3	3.7	9.8	1.8
Medicine	2.1	16.2	14.6	5.9
Others	0.0	0.0	0.0	0.1
Multiple Choice*	0.0	0.0	2.4	0.1
Total %	100.0	100.0	100.0	100.0
Stratum-wise N	47	161	41	762

Chi^2 (24) = 78.4   P-value = 0.000

(b) Second Priority

Percentage

Expenditure Items	Stratum-wise Expenditure Priorities (Total N = 1020)			
	HIG	*Slums*	*Govt.*	*Mixed*
Cloth	27.7	3.8	2.4	26.0
Doc. Fee	0.0	10.6	12.2	1.1
Food	4.3	10.0	4.9	6.6
Housing	36.2	31.9	24.4	28.8
Medical Check-up	2.1	3.1	4.9	7.4
Medicine	29.8	40.6	48.8	30.0
Religious Exp.	0.0	0.0	2.4	0.1
Multiple Choice*	0.0	0.0	0.0	0.1
Total %	100.0	100.0	100.0	100.0
Stratum-wise N	47	166	42	765

Chi^2 (21) = 121.7   P-value = 0.000

(c) Third Priority

Percentage

Expenditure Items	Stratum-wise Expenditure Priorities (Total N = 1014)			
	HIG	*Slums*	*Govt.*	*Mixed*
Cloth	31.9	29.4	22.5	27.3
Doc. Fee	4.3	20.6	20.0	8.5
Entertainment	0.0	0.0	0.0	0.4
Food	2.1	6.9	7.5	1.8
Housing	44.7	18.1	35.0	44.0
Med. Check-up	2.1	10.6	7.5	3.0
Medicine	14.9	10.0	5.0	14.3
Religious Exp.	0.0	0.6	0.0	0.7
Multiple Choice*	0.0	3.7	2.5	0.0
Total %	100.0	100.0	100.0	100.0
Stratum-wise N	47	166	41	760

$Chi^2 (21) = 142.4$ P-value $= 0.000$

Source: IEG/CIDA Ageing Survey (2002).

Note: * Fraction of respondents assigning equal rank to a set of expenditure items. To illustrate, a small fraction of respondents, mostly from slums or other low-income areas, considered doctor's fee and cloth or doctor's fee and housing as the same in terms of their expenditure priorities.

Table 4.5

Sex-wise Expenditure Priorities of 60+

(a) First Priority

Percentage

Expenditure Items	Sex-wise Expenditure Priorities (Total N = 1011)	
	Male	*Female*
Cloth	0.21	0.37
Doc. Fee	0.0	0.19
Entertainment	0.21	0.0
Food	88.42	86.89
Housing	2.32	0.37
Med. Check-up	1.89	3.18
Medicine	6.32	8.99
Others	0.21	0.0
Multiple Choice*	0.42	0.0
Total %	100.0	100.0
Sex-wise N	477	534

$Chi^2 (8) = 17.0$ P-value $= 0.030$

(b) Second Priority

Percentage

Expenditure Items	Sex-wise Expenditure Priorities (Total N = 1020)	
	Male	*Female*
Cloth	20.1	22.9
Doc. Fee	2.1	3.8
Food	6.5	7.3
Housing	34.4	25.0
Medical Check-up	5.2	7.3
Medicine	31.5	33.3
Relig. Exp.	0.21	0.19
Multiple Choice*	0.0	0.2
Total %	100.0	100.0
Sex-wise N	478	542
	Chi^2 (7) = 14.0	P-value = 0.053

(c) Third Priority

Percentage

Expenditure Items	Sex-wise Expenditure Priorities (Total N = 1014)	
	Male	*Female*
Cloth	32.1	23.6
Doc. Fee	9.0	12.2
Entertainment	0.4	0.2
Food	2.7	3.0
Housing	37.8	41.1
Med. Check-up	4.4	4.3
Medicine	12.2	14.3
Relig. Exp.	0.2	0.9
Multiple Choice*	1.0	0.4
Total %	100.0	100.0
Sex-wise N	477	537
	Chi^2 (13) = 18.6	P-value = 0.137

Source: IEG/CIDA Ageing Survey (2002).

Note: * Fraction of respondents assigning equal rank to a set of expenditure items. To illustrate, a small fraction of respondents, mostly from slums or other low-income areas, considered doctor's fee and cloth or doctor's fee and housing as the same in terms of their expenditure priorities.

The sex-wise results are also presented in a similar format.[5] Most of these results did follow the expected line. For example, food remains the biggest choice for more than four-fifths of responding men and women (Tables 4.5a, b and c). This is however not the case at subsequent stages. The second preference, for instance, includes three different expenditure items—housing, medicine and clothing. Further, while some of these priorities remain common between the two genders, they differ in magnitude. To be more precise, a large percentage of the males (over 34 per cent) concurred in favour of housing as their second choice. In contrast, females reported medicine as their second choice (Table 4.5b). Gender dissimilarities are also noted in the third choice (Table 4.5c), suggesting that the stratum is not the only differentiating factor in prioritisation of consumption needs.

Unexpectedly, but an extension of this analysis on the basis of two age categories—i.e., 60-69 and 70+—doesn't add much, and both the age categories follow a similar pattern in their choice of different expenditure items.

To sum up, three broad observations follow from these exercises. One: in a hierarchy of eight different expenditure items, medicine often competes with food in priority—especially for many of those from low-income households. Two: food, medicine, housing, clothing and certain socio-religious expenses are ranked as the five basic expenditure items by most of the aged surveyed. This, therefore, implies that any upward movement in prices of these commodities and services need to be monitored for the welfare of the elderly. Three, expenditure priorities of the aged differ by sex and socio-economic stratums. Further, these results also underline the need for more elaborate studies on this important issue.

4.5. Preference in Living Arrangements

For some years now, a significant body of literature on ageing has already been devoted to the living arrangements of older persons, especially in developing countries (Sokolovsky, 2001; Lamb, 2000; Hashimoto, 1991; Martin, 1990). While much of this literature

---

5. More detailed results are given in Appendix Table A-4.2.

signifies the primacy of multi-generational family living in most of these countries, it also reveals instances of growing neglect in elderly care. Such instances are also found to be true for India (Lamb, 2000; Martin, 1990 and Biswas, 1985).

Seldom however has an attempt been made to find the changes in residential preference of the aged themselves—especially in response to declining family values and growing instances of neglect. Nor has there been an attempt to gauge the sense of insecurity among the aged without a surviving child. To fill some of this void, we tried to elicit views in the survey on both these issues. The following questions were asked:

1. Will the aged prefer?

    * living alone,

    * living alone but close to the children,

    * rotate residence among children, and

    * living with any one of the children.

2. Will the aged feel more secured if they have?

    * more number of children, or

    * one or two children may also suffice.

3. Do childless aged feel more vulnerable?

Their responses are presented below. A Pearson Chi^2 test is applied to check for the affects of gender and socio-economic status on their responses.

Living Alone versus Co-residing

Table 4.6a summarises the living preferences by the elderly respondents. Somewhat surprising, we observe from this table that a majority of them (over 51 per cent) did not prefer to reside with their children. Though they preferred to live near them. Devoid of any such option, they want to keep shifting from one child to another (up to 35 per cent). Only 11 per cent of them favoured staying with children. Staying alone was the least preferred choice. Clearly, therefore, while a majority of the urban aged may not be willing to live in a joint family system, they are also averse to the idea of living far from children and relatives.

Table 4.6a

Choice in Living Arrangements: 60+ Persons

Options	N	Per cent
1. Stay alone	31	3.05
2. Stay alone but close to children	520	51.08
3. Rotate residence among children	356	34.97
4. With son or daughter	111	10.9
Total Number	1018	100

Source: IEG/CIDA Survey (2002).

Do these preferences vary across different socio-economic stratums? Table 4.6b goes into this question. It is clear from this table that the people of different strata differ quite significantly on this issue. For example, a much larger fraction of the HIG elderly (67 per cent) preferred living alone, though in the vicinity of their children. Next to the HIG are those from the mixed category. More than half of these respondents have agreed with their HIG counterparts. In contrast, more than 57 per cent of the slum respondents, and about 49 per cent of those from the government colonies have opted for joint living with children. Most of them would however like to keep rotating residence at their will. Despite some of these differences in views, the results clearly reveal that co-residing with a single child is fast losing acceptability among the older people. Also, staying alone is more a choice of those with higher economic means. Yet another observation stemming from these results may relate to the single child family. Since most parents may like rotating residence, it is clear that the slogan of single child family may not be acceptable to the lower income strata.

Male-female perceptions on this issue are presented in Table 4.6c. Interestingly, there are no major differentials between the males and females on this crucial issue. Almost an equal share of both the sexes preferred living alone, though closer to children. A more or less similar distribution follows for all other patterns of living. As a whole, therefore, it suggests that the gender is not the differentiating factor in the choice about living arrangements.

Table 4.6b

Choice in Living Arrangements by the Aged: Stratum-wise Distribution

Percentage

Stratums	Options				N
	Stay Alone	Stay Alone but Close to Children	Rotate Residence among Children	With Children: Son or Daughter?	
HIG	4.2	66.7	29.2	0.0	48
Slums	8.6	32.5	57.7	1.2	163
Government	0.0	48.8	48.8	2.4	41
Mixed	2.0	54.2	29.8	14.1	766
Total	3.1	51.1	35.0	10.9	1018

Chi^2 (9): 97.380   P- value: 0.000

Source: IEG/CIDA Survey (2002).

Table 4.6c

Choice in Living Arrangements by the Aged: Sex-wise Distribution

Percentage

Stratums	Options				N
	Stay Alone	Stay Alone but Close to Children	Rotate Residence among Children	With Children: Son or Daughter?	
Male	2.91	50.31	34.51	12.27	481
Female	3.17	51.77	35.38	9.68	537
Total	3.05	51.08	34.97	10.9	1018

Chi^2 (3): 1.767   P-value: 0.622

Source: IEG/CIDA Survey (2002).

Family Size and Sense of Protection among the Elders

In a traditional set up, risk-bearing capacity of families was usually considered as linked with the family size, especially the number of male children. Not entirely in the context of this discussion, but Cain (1981, 1985a and 1985b) has noted the significance of larger families with several children as an effective insurance mechanism for families in rural areas of South Asia. He has particularly drawn this observation on the basis of his studies for India and Bangladesh. Based on this, and also drawing upon the popular notion that the aged with larger family size feel better protected, we asked our 60+ respondents to check on the following: (i) whether or not a larger family with several children helps to bring a greater sense of security among them, and (ii) do the childless parents feel more vulnerable? Their responses are summarised in Tables 4.7a, 4.7b and 4.7c; the last two tables bifurcate responses by stratum and gender, respectively.

Table 4.7a does not fully support the traditional viewpoint that a large number of children essentially help parents to feel more secure in their old age. Size-wise, for instance, more than 60 per cent of the total respondents have disagreed with the idea. They felt that even fewer children might also help to derive the same feeling. But another 30 per cent have responded in favour of larger family size with a large number of children. In effect, it appears that this particular notion is currently in transition with a majority realising that a bigger family size with too many children or grand children may not necessarily make old age more secure. This is further evident from responses on childlessness and the feeling of vulnerability. Only little over six per cent of the respondents has agreed with this idea. Does this suggest that inter-generational living has started losing its traditional appeal in societies like India? In addition, how do the rural elderly feel on some of these issues? Both the questions are indeed significant and deserve further examination with data from rural areas.

Table 4.7a

Family Size & Sense of Protection: 60+ Persons

Options	Number	Percentage
Feeling more secure with:		
1. Many Children	310	30.63
2. Few Children	638	63.04
3. Are Childless Vulnerable?	61	6.03
4. Don't Know	3	0.3
Total	1012	100.0

Source: IEG/CIDA Survey (2002).

Table 4.7b

Family Size and Sense of Protection: Distribution of 60+ by Stratums

Options	Stratums (%)				Percentage
	HIG	*Slums*	*Govt.*	*Mixed*	
Feeling more secure with:					
1. Many Children	27.08	34.57	39.02	29.57	30.63
2. Few Children	62.5	59.26	56.1	64.26	63.04
3. Are Childless Vulnerable?	8.33	6.17	2.44	6.04	6.03
4. Don't Know	2.08	0	2.44	0.13	0.3
Total	100.0	100.0	100.0	100.0	100.0
N	48	162	41	761	1012

Chi^2 (9): 17.1   P-value: 0.047

Source: IEG/CIDA Survey (2002).

Table 4.7c

Family Size and Sense of Protection: Sex-wise Distribution of 60+

Options	Male	Female	Percentage
Feeling more secure with:			
1. Many Children	33.89	27.72	30.63
2. Few Children	57.95	67.6	63.04
3. Are Childless Vulnerable?	7.95	4.31	6.03
4. Don't Know	0.21	0.37	0.3
Total	100	100	100
N	478	534	1012

Chi^2 (3): 12.7   P-value: 0.005

Source: IEG/CIDA Survey (2002).

Extending this analysis by taking into consideration the stratums or sex doesn't significantly add to the overall results (Tables 4.7b and c, respectively). While some modest variations may be noticed across these groupings, the over all inferences do not change. Nevertheless, two responses need to be mentioned.

One is relating to the elderly from the slums. A good majority of them—i.e., over 59 per cent—have agreed with the modern perception implying that even fewer number of children are good enough to feel secure. It also reveals that the size of family, and especially the number of children, is losing its relevance across the board.

Relating to female respondents. Like their male counterparts, they also agreed that old age security is not essentially linked with the number of children. Not only that, women have outnumbered men in endorsing this viewpoint (Table 4.7c).

Summing-up

Some of the preceding results, *inter alia,* led to draw two significant observations. First, a large proportion of the urban aged seems to be losing interest in co-residing with children or relatives. They would however like to stay in their vicinity. And, if they were at all required to live with children, they would prefer rotating residence. Second, too many children are not considered essential by parents to feel more secure. The definition of small or big was, however, not elicited in the survey.

4.6. Views of the Elderly on Declining Returns to Savings

After issues relating to the living arrangements, we now move to another important concern of the ageing population in the country—namely, the soft interest rate regime currently pursued by the government. Often, two arguments are made in favour of this regime: one, it helps minimising the debt repayment burden on public borrowings, and two, it would accelerate investment, promote GDP growth, and cut down the capital cost of production—necessary conditions to become trade competitive in the global market. A third argument in this context follows from the low rate of inflation both nationally and internationally. A higher interest payment to savings may, therefore, make the real rate of interest out of sync.

Without disagreeing with any of these arguments, there are two important questions that need to be examined. First, how does this regime affect the persons of higher ages who often rely on interest earnings for their survival? Or, in other words, does the decline in interest earnings make the aged vulnerable—especially those relying on accumulated savings? This question essentially draws its justification from the fast emerging societal changes including depletions in non-market support institutions,[6] smaller family size, growing role of the market and almost complete lack of social safety net for the aged.

---

6. Some of the related details of this particular question have already been described earlier in Chapter 1.

The second question basically stems from the argument that justifies reduction in deposit rates to match the low inflationary situation in the economy. Attempting to go into this question may need a discussion on many wider issues including the nature of inflation itself, its measurement, the basket of goods and services going into these measurements, and the compatibility of these goods and services to those required by the older persons. While an attempt will be made in the rest of this analysis to make a few observations on both these questions, the one relating to the inflation mediated decline in interest rates will be examined later in the study.

Does Interest Rate Decline Make the Elderly Vulnerable?

Two methods may be used to judge the linkages between the declining interest earnings and old age vulnerability. One is to analyse changes in pre and post decline consumption expenditure of the households run by the elderly, and the second may be to seek their views on this critical issue. This analysis relies on the latter, and attempt has been made to impute vulnerabilities based on the responses to the following three questions:

(i) Do you agree with the soft interest rates regime?

(ii) Do you feel that the interest cut would make the elderly more vulnerable?

(iii) While working, did you save for your old age; and if yes, name the instruments of saving?

The last question was asked purposely to ascertain the awareness among the older persons about the major instruments of old age savings. We also premised that the lack of proper understanding among investors about different saving instruments (e.g., bank deposits, public provident fund, LIC annuities and other upcoming pension plans, etc.), their advantages and disadvantages, and differentials in earning might cause them to suffer from lower yields.

Soft Interest Rate Regime

Table 4.8 summarises the over all responses into four broad categories. The first two relate to those agreeing or disagreeing with this regime, and the remaining two comprise persons who either don't fully understand these complex issues or may not be able to link interest rate policies with old age vulnerabilities. We observe that over a third of the total respondents fall into the last two categories without a categorical yes or no. Many of them were females. More than two-fifths of the respondents (42.5 per cent) disagreed with the idea of soft interest rate policy and, therefore, expressed their dissatisfaction with this regime. Interestingly, however, almost a fourth of them (23.3 per cent) favoured reductions in deposit rates.

Table 4.8

Responses on Soft Interest Rate Regime

Do you Agree with Soft Interest Rate Regime?	Respondents	Percentage
Yes	237	23.3
No	433	42.5
Don't know	294	28.9
No idea	55	5.4
Total	1019	100.0

Source: IEG/CIDA Ageing Survey.

Given the somewhat inconclusive nature of responses obtained on this very important question—roughly 43 per cent disagreed with the current interest rate policies, 23 per cent were in agreement and over 35 per cent did not give a specific answer—we tried to check whether the socio-economic background has anything to do with these hung responses. Table 4.9 gives these details. While there appears to be some support in favour of a low interest regime from the mixed and higher income respondents, a large percentage (56.3 per cent HIG, and 37.4 per cent mixed households) also opposed this policy. Largely, slum and government respondents have either disagreed with the soft interest rate regime or expressed their inability to answer this question. We also notice that the socio-economic background doesn't turn out to be a very decisive factor in approving or disapproving this policy. Rather, it mostly appears to be a need-based response. For example, those seeking loans for personal use or guided by the business interest may opt in favour of low interest rates, and vice versa. And yet, it may be noticed that barring the mixed income category, majority of respondents from the remaining three categories disagreed with the current interest rate regime. Even about 56 per cent of the slum elderly, who may not be frequent depositors or users of pension plans, opposed this policy.

Table 4.9

Stratum-wise Responses to Soft Interest Rate Regime

Percentage

Do you Agree with Soft Interest Rate Regime?	Stratum				Total
	HIG	Slum	Govt.	Mixed	
Yes	31.3	4.3	9.8	27.5	23.3
No	56.3	55.8	68.3	37.4	42.5
Don't Know	8.3	34.4	14.6	29.7	28.9
No idea	4.2	5.5	7.3	5.4	5.4
Total N	48	163	41	767	1019
%	100.0	100.0	100.0	100.0	100.0

Pearson chi^2 (9) = 67.947	P Value = 0.000

Source: IEG/CIDA Ageing Survey (2002).

Declining Interest Rate and Vulnerabilities among the Aged

To what extent does the aged really feel insecure or vulnerable due to the ongoing decline in interest earning? Apparently, not many,—if judged from Figure 4.2. Only a fourth of the responding aged felt vulnerable as a result of these declines. The remaining 75 per cent either did not have specific views or did not feel threatened because of this. This result, and especially the expression of indifference about this whole issue, is perhaps an indication that the

Figure 4.2

Do the Elderly Feel Vulnerable Due to Interest Rate Cuts?

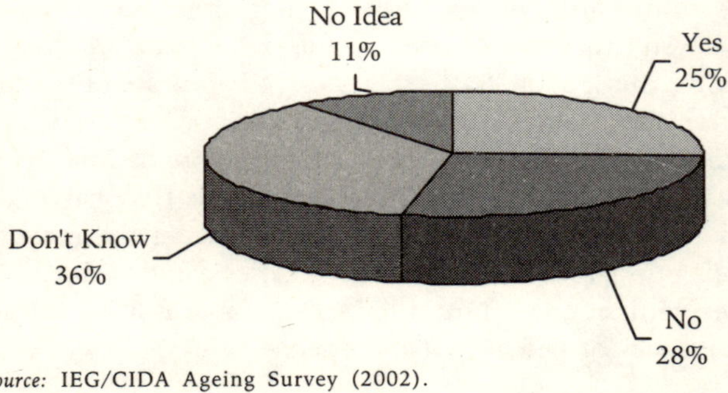

Source: IEG/CIDA Ageing Survey (2002).

concept of planned ageing, as judged by old age saving, is yet to fully evolve in the country. Simultaneously, however, this result also indicates that the old age saving has started gaining at least some credence.

Stratum-wise distribution of these respondents is given in Table 4.10. A point to be noticed from this table is the contrasting sense of perception on this issue between the HIG and the slum respondents. The highest share of those feeling insecure due to the declining rate of interest (i.e., 50 per cent of their total) comes from the HIG. In contrast, merely 10 per cent of the slum dwellers share this perception. The reason is obvious: unlike the slum dwellers, a large number of the high-income aged would have to forego their interest earnings with each successive decline in the deposit rate.

Table 4.10

Vulnerability Due to Interest Rate Decline: Stratum-wise Distribution of Responses

Percentage

Feeling vulnerable due to cut in interest rate?	Stratums				Total
	HIG	Slum	Govt.	Mixed	
Yes	50.0	9.8	26.8	27.1	25.4
No	27.1	32.5	46.3	26.1	28.0
Don't Know	12.5	42.3	17.1	37.3	36.1
No idea	10.4	15.3	9.8	9.5	10.5
Total N	48	163	41	767	1019
%	100.0	100.0	100.0	100.0	100.0

Pearson chi^2 (9) = 53.001　　　　P Value = 0.000

Source: IEG/CIDA Ageing Survey (2002).

Instruments of Old Age Savings

Finally, to obtain further insight about the share of actual losers due to the declining rate of interest, we tried to seek information from the respondents about the following: (i) have they ever saved for their old age, and (ii) if yes, the instruments of saving. These responses are shown in Table 4.11. Two interesting observations follow from this table: first, the share of those who saved for their old age is very small, that is, merely 17 per cent of the total. The second interesting point to be noticed from this table is the reliance on bank deposits as the major instrument of old age saving. Of the total 169 savers, 129 or 76 per cent have saved in a bank deposit. Another 20 per cent contributed to the provident funds (PF/PPF).[7] Those who opted for the specialised old age saving plans or annuities were as low as 3.6 per cent of the total. From the policy angle, a high dependence on bank deposits as the old age saving instrument implies that any fluctuation in the bank rate would affect very high proportions of the elderly depositors.

Table 4.11

Persons with Old Age Savings and their Savings Instruments

Did you save for the old age?	No. of Respondents	Percentage
Yes	169	17.0
No	823	83.0
Total N	992	100.0
Those saved: Instruments of saving		
PF	23	13.6
PPF	11	6.5
Bank Deposits/Fixed Deposits	129	76.3
Pension Plans/Annuities	6	3.6
Total Savers	169	100.0

Source: IEG/CIDA Ageing Survey.

4.7. Concluding Observations

On the whole, three major observations emerge from these results. One, is the reliance on family support by a majority of the poor and lower middle-income aged. Hence, soft interest rate policy remains a moot issue for many of them. Against this, the high-income groups do consider this issue as important for their later life.

---

7. The public provident fund (PPF) is a long term saving instrument administered by the State Bank of India, and can be opted by anybody including employed, self-employed or even a casual worker.

Two, old age savings are still in their infancy, and largely confined to the high or the middle-income aged. Three, those who reportedly saved for their old age, have largely relied on bank deposits. Therefore, even minor changes in deposit rates will have implications for them. The non-bank old age schemes are apparently less known, and therefore, need greater publicity.

Appendix Table A-4.1

Stratum-wise Differentials in Expenditure Preferences by the Elderly Respondents

Percentage

Rank	Doctors Fee				Ranks	Medicine			
	HIG	Slum	Govt.	Mixed		HIG	Slum	Govt.	Mixed
1	0.0	0.6	2.4	0.1	1	2.1	16.2	14.6	5.9
2	0.0	10.6	14.6	1.1	2	29.8	40.4	48.8	30.4
3	4.3	24.4	19.5	8.5	3	14.9	9.9	7.3	14.4
4	2.1	7.5	7.3	6.9	4	29.8	24.2	17.1	22.6
5	31.9	20.6	17.1	19.5	5	19.2	8.7	9.8	10.7
6	55.3	28.8	29.3	49.7	6	4.3	0.6	0.0	8.3
7	2.1	1.3	0.0	8.8	7	0.0	0.0	0.0	6.4
8	4.3	6.3	9.8	5.1	8	0.0	0.0	0.0	1.2
9	0.0	0.0	0.0	0.3	9	0.0	0.0	2.4	0.1
Total	100.0	100.0	100.0	100.0	Total	100.0	100.0	100.0	100.0
N	47	164	41	765	N	47	161	41	764

Chi^2 (24) = 140.73   Pr = 0.000   Chi^2 (24) = 83.91   Pr = 0.000

Rank	Medical/Diagnostic Check-up				Ranks	Food			
	HIG	Slum	Govt.	Mixed		HIG	Slum	Govt.	Mixed
1	4.3	3.8	9.8	2.0	1	93.6	75.0	70.7	90.3
2	2.1	3.1	4.9	7.3	2	4.3	10.0	4.9	6.5
3	2.1	10.7	7.3	3.0	3	2.1	6.9	7.3	1.8
4	29.8	28.3	24.4	31.7	4	0.0	7.5	12.2	0.8
5	31.9	20.8	19.5	34.6	5	0.0	0.6	0.0	0.1
6	23.4	18.2	19.5	14.9	6	0.0	0.0	4.9	0.3
7	4.3	11.3	12.2	5.1	7	-	-	-	-
8	2.1	2.5	2.4	1.3	8	0.0	0.0	0.0	0.1
9	0.0	1.3	0.0	0.1	9	-	-	-	-
Total	100.0	100.0	100.0	100.0	Total	100.0	100.0	100.0	100.0
N	47	159	41	764	N	47	160	41	765

Chi^2 (24) = 66.72   Pr = 0.000   Chi^2 (18) = 92.70   Pr = 0.000

Contd. ...

Contd. ...

Rank	Housing				Ranks	Clothing			
	HIG	*Slum*	*Govt.*	*Mixed*		*HIG*	*Slum*	*Govt.*	*Mixed*
1	0.0	5.0	4.9	0.7	1	0.0	0.0	0.0	0.4
2	36.2	31.9	24.4	28.9	2	27.7	3.8	2.4	25.9
3	44.7	20.0	34.2	43.9	3	31.9	31.3	24.4	27.2
4	10.6	10.0	7.3	7.3	4	27.7	22.5	31.7	27.5
5	6.4	16.3	19.5	5.4	5	6.4	23.1	17.1	15.6
6	2.1	16.3	9.8	13.2	6	6.4	16.9	22.0	2.1
7	0.0	0.6	0.0	0.0	7	0.0	1.9	2.4	0.8
8	0.0	0.0	0.0	0.7	8	0.0	0.6	0.0	0.4
9	-	-	-	-	9	0.0	0.0	0.0	0.1
Total	100.0	100.0	100.0	100.0	Total	100.0	100.0	100.0	100.0
N	47	160	41	764	N	47	160	41	764

Chi^2 (21) = 84.42   Pr = 0.000   Chi^2 (24) = 128.17   Pr = 0.000

Rank	Entertainment				Ranks	Socio-Religious Expenses			
	HIG	*Slum*	*Govt.*	*Mixed*		*HIG*	*Slum*	*Govt.*	*Mixed*
1	0.0	0.0	0.0	0.1	1	-	-	-	-
2	-	-	-	-	2	0.0	0.0	2.4	0.3
3	0.0	0.6	0.0	0.4	3	0.0	0.6	0.0	0.7
4	0.0	0.0	0.0	0.5	4	0.0	0.6	2.4	2.3
5	0.0	0.6	7.3	1.1	5	4.4	5.8	4.9	13.5
6	2.1	6.9	0.0	5.8	6	6.5	12.2	14.6	5.2
7	44.7	58.8	43.9	37.5	7	50.0	26.3	36.6	41.4
8	53.2	31.3	48.8	53.7	8	39.1	51.9	36.6	36.0
9	0.0	1.9	0.0	0.9	9	0.0	2.6	2.4	0.8
Total	100.0	100.0	100.0	100.0	Total	100.0	100.0	100.0	100.0
N	47	160	41	763	N	46	156	41	756

Chi^2 (21) = 50.43   Pr = 0.000   Chi^2 (21) = 56.77   Pr = 0.000

Source: IEG/CIDA Ageing Survey

   - Indicates no response.

Note: The sample size (N) in this table may not necessarily match with Table 4.3 because of the exclusions of certain multi-choice responses.

Appendix Table A-4.2

Sex-wise Differentials in Expenditure Preferences by the Elderly

Rank	Doctor's Fee		Rank	Medicine		Rank	Med./Diag. Check-up	
	Male	*Female*		*Male*	*Female*		*Male*	*Female*
1	0.4	0.2	1	6.3	9.0	1	2.1	3.2
2	2.3	3.7	2	31.9	33.4	2	5.3	7.3
3	10.1	12.3	3	12.2	14.6	3	4.4	4.3
4	6.5	7.1	4	26.2	20.2	4	29.0	32.3
5	24.5	16.3	5	11.3	10.3	5	29.2	33.8
6	44.0	47.5	6	6.7	6.3	6	20.4	12.2
7	7.3	6.5	7	4.6	5.0	7	7.1	5.6
8	4.6	6.2	8	0.8	0.9	8	2.3	0.9
9	0.2	0.2	9	0.0	0.4	9	0.2	0.4
Total	100.0	100.0	Total	100.0	100.0	Total	100.0	100.0
N	477	535	N	477	536	N	476	535

Chi² (8) = 14.0 Pr. = 0.082 Chi² (8) = 9.83.0 Pr. = 0.277 Chi² (8) = 20.20 Pr. = 0.010

Rank	Food		Rank	Housing		Rank	Clothing	
	Male	*Female*		*Male*	*Female*		*Male*	*Female*
1	87.9	86.7	1	2.7	0.4	1	0.2	0.4
2	6.5	7.3	2	34.4	25.2	2	20.1	22.8
3	2.7	3.0	3	38.2	41.1	3	32.7	23.7
4	1.9	2.6	4	6.5	9.2	4	26.8	26.9
5	0.4	0.0	5	6.3	9.0	5	13.6	18.9
6	0.4	0.4	6	11.3	14.6	6	5.2	5.6
8	0.2	0.0	7	0.0	0.2	7	1.1	0.9
Total	100.0	100.0	8	0.6	0.4	8	0.2	0.6
N	478	535	Total	100.0	100.0	9	0.0	0.2
			N	477	535	Total	100.0	100.0
						N	477	535

Chi² (6) = 4.31 Pr. = 0.635 Chi² (6) = 25.0 Pr. = 0.001 Chi² (8) = 14.33 Pr. = 0.074

Rank	Entertainment		Rank	Socio-Religious Expenses	
	Male	*Female*		*Male*	*Female*
1	0.2	0.0	2	0.2	0.4
2	0.4	0.4	3	0.2	1.0
3	0.4	0.4	4	2.3	1.5
4	1.7	0.8	5	12.1	11.0
5	4.8	6.2	6	7.2	6.3
6	37.7	44.8	7	42.0	36.8
7	54.1	46.3	8	35.2	41.8
8	0.6	1.3	9	0.9	1.3
9	100.0	100.0	Total	100.0	100.0
Total	477	534	N	472	527
N	0.2	0.0			

Chi² (7) = 11.09 Pr. = 014 Chi² (7) = 8.91 Pr. = 0.250

Source: IEG/CIDA Ageing Survey.

5

Ageing, Functional Limitations and Public Health

5.1. Introduction

A great deal of our earlier discussion has already shown that India is fast catching up with other graying societies with a rapid growth in the size of its ageing population (see Chapter 1). Two major contributory factors to this direction are: (i) a progressive decline in fertility and mortality, and (ii) added life span with increased survival chances,—especially at the later end of the life cycle. These changes, and especially the added life span, have however been mired by the high prevalence of chronic diseases that affect more than half of the country's older population (Tables 1.7 and 2.4). Such a situation, coupled with large-scale poverty and the poor financial status of the old is likely to pose many serious socio-medical issues, both for families and the country. One of the more critical may indeed be the growing frailty, senescence[1] and functional dependencies of older persons in their basic activities of daily living (ADL)[2]—constraining the caregivers both in terms of time and money. This aspect has almost been completely overlooked by analysts focusing on health and ageing in India.[3] This analysis is therefore attempted to provide some empirical evidence on this very critical issue.[4] Three broader issues are examined in the order as they are presented below. These are:

---

1. Senescence is defined as (non-disease based) physiological changes of ageing like poor reflexes, sensory decline or loss of skeletal muscle causing frailty, poor endurance and functional disabilities. Also, senescent changes can be accelerated in the presence of diseases. The process of ageing in India is currently mired in disease-linked senescence.

2. Albert *et al.* (2002) present an interesting discussion on the three pathways to disability in the Editorial of the *American Journal of Public Health*. We will describe these pathways in greater detail later.

3. A recent study by Raju (2002) has tried to examine the health status of the urban elderly and the attendant socio-medical issues. The study has, however, not been directed to investigate ADL limitations or support requirements of the sick and functionally dependent.

4. Some of the results presented here have been published in the *Asia-Pacific Population Journal* (Alam and Mukherjee, 2005).

1. Prevalence of ADL limitations among the sample aged caused by physical and sensory impairments, cross-classified by gender and four socio-economic categories. We may also try to identify the most frequent ADL dependencies and their gender differentials.

2. Some of the socio-economic causal risk factors in ADL disabilities.

3. The linkages between the ADL dependencies and public health measures.

The need for public health initiatives have been highlighted by describing three major pathways of old age frailties and functional dependence involving (a) physiological or senescent changes in an individual due to the age factor, (b) non-senescent changes owing to the morbidity or poor health stock, and (c) poor living environment of the older persons. As most of the disabilities reported in our sample are owing to poor health conditions (i.e., pathway b), we outlined a set of preventive measures for administration by the public health institutions. We also posit that in a country like India with very high old age poverty, public health and its involvement in managing the health issues of the ageing population is the only cost-effective solution. It may as well help the country to meet its objectives of healthy and active ageing.

5.2 ADL Limitations and Support Needs

ADL Disabilities: A Conceptual Note

Conceptually, old age disability is a complex phenomenon that manifests itself in many ways, and takes a much longer time period to evolve (Manton and Stallard, 1994). Further, its definition is subject to environmental and socio-economic conditions of individuals. At a more simplistic level, however, it refers to the ability of older adults to perform such basic activities as eating, dressing, cooking, bathing, walking and climbing stairs, etc. Under this paradigm, an individual can be described as disabled if his/her personal capabilities fall short of what is actually demanded in a particular environment or family set-up. When people are unable to perform their basic and self-maintaining tasks, they become dependent on others—either formally (i.e., paid support) or informally (i.e., unpaid family support). The former is yet to evolve in India.

Despite problems in conceptualisation, measuring disabilities is important because of its association with decreased functional autonomy and increased demand for long-term care (LTC). Besides, its usefulness in making assessments about morbidity, mortality and certain health care needs is obvious. For instance, a few of the oft quoted studies by Mor, Wilcox and Hiris (1994), Severson, Smith, Tangalos, *et al.* (1994), etc., have shown that the ADL difficulties can as well be used to derive estimates about the need for nursing home or hospital care. Similarly, an increasing number of long-term care policies are now relying on ADL disabilities as a trigger for paying benefits to those covered against these risks (Van and Johnson, 1989).

As further refinements, attempts have also been made in literature to assess the hierarchy by which the loss of functional abilities progresses across a set of activities required by individuals for their self-maintenance.[5] We have however refrained to postulate any such hierarchies in this exercise, and have attempted to analyse the extent of disabilities and support requirements as drawn from the survey under reference.

World Health Organisation (WHO) Model of Disability

WHO presented an International Classification of Impairment Disability, and Handicap (ICIDH) to catalogue the functional limitations suffered on account of physiological impairments and poor health. The model was subsequently revised in 2001 to explore further the relationship between functioning, disability and health (WHO, 2001).

An interesting feature of the ICF (2001) was that it allowed survival to be partitioned according to the functional status of the aged (Albert, 2004). The exercise presented below is largely drawn on the basis of this partitioning assumption with two additional premises, namely, (i) frailty precedes disability, so that people reach frailty before disability; and (ii) states of disability precede mortality. With

---

5. Katz *et al.* (1963) have, for example, developed a hierarchy for a set of daily functions including bathing, dressing, using toilet, transferring, feeding, continence, etc. Theoretically, this ordering was justified on the consideration that generally people lose abilities and become disabled in a manner opposite to the order in which primary biological and physiological functions are acquired (Dunlop, Hughes and Manheim, 1997).

high incidence of chronic and multiple diseases in India, the later life years for many are turning into a painful process with high risks of functional dependencies. As a further clarification, Figure 5.1 illustrates a hypothetical partitioning survival curve for India underlining the basic argument that frailty (shown with a thin broken line)—followed by disabilities (thick broken line),—worsen the quality life for many in the later years.

Figure 5.1

Partitioning Survival to Catalogue Functional Status:
A Hypothetical Diagram

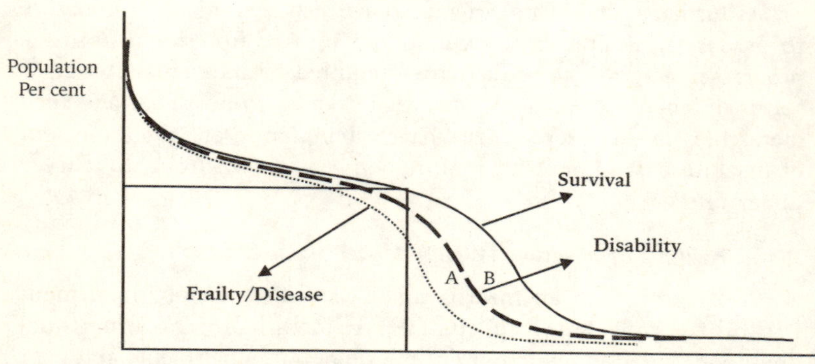

Source: Based on Modified WHO Model cited in Albert (2004).

Note: The length of the individual's survival, separated by A and B in Figure 5.1, suggests the onset of disease, eventually converting into disabilities at an age covered under B. Once set in, these disabilities are expected to persist till the end. Public health may arguably be geared to prevent both these conditions.

ADL Difficulties: Nature and Measurement

As was noted, this analysis is an attempt to examine ADL difficulties based on the two health domains: physical and sensory. In all 11 basic tasks, nine physiological and two sensory, were considered at the time of the survey, and respondents were asked to furnish details about their difficulties in performing them. They were also requested to provide corresponding details about: (a) the need for assistance in their disability domains, and (b) the availability of this assistance (Appendix A-Table 5.1). Following this, non-availability of support may be considered as the unmet assistance for the disabled.

The ADL difficulties considered for this analysis are as below:[6]

(i) Physical Domain:

> (1) Eating, (2) Dressing, (3) Bathing, (4) Walking indoors (say going to bath room), (5) Outdoor walk (say for daily shopping), (6) Cooking or Home cleaning, (7) Climbing stairs, (8) Combing of hair, and (9) Getting-up from a sitting position.

(ii) Sensory Domain:

> (1) Hearing losses (or limitations of the auditory system), and
>
> (2) Vision impairments.

Using these domains and their listed tasks, we attempted to index the functional capabilities (FCI) of the aged into the following:

(a) Functionally normal: No difficulty/No help (ND/NH).

(b) Disabled with unmet assistance: Difficulty/No help (D/NH).

(c) Assisted disabled: Difficulty/Help (D/H).

(d) Exceptional cases: No difficulty/Help (ND/H).

Those without any major functional problem or help requirement (ND/NH) in both the health domains are considered healthy with better health stock. Similarly, there may be instances where people receive help even without any functional problem. Such persons may however be very few in number and does not, therefore, affect the results. The problem group would therefore be the persons falling into the 'second' and the 'third' categories—i.e., D/NH and D/H. Especially, those falling into the D/NH may give an idea about the unmet assistance and their magnitude of the problems. In addition, these capability indices (FCIs) may also be collated further to make an account of persons with no, single and multiple disabilities. These details and especially the number of persons with multiple difficulties may help to get an idea of the quality of survival in later years (Figure 5.2), and the need for preventive measures through public health initiatives leading to a decline in the level of disabilities. These results may also suggest the need for long-term care measures in the country.

---

6. In addition to these, there may be many more disabilities caused by cognitive, psychological or other forms of impairments.

ADL Disabilities: The Results

Table 5.1 helps to profile: (i) the ADL dependence of the older persons in both the respective health domains, and (ii) the assistance they need in their self-maintenance. Clearly, there is revealing evidence from this table of wide-ranging disabilities in all the eleven activities under reference. Two other significant points of concern from this table may be the spread and the magnitude of the disabilities facing the aged. For example, the disabilities—and therefore the need for assistance—are present even in modest activities like eating, dressing, combing or bathing. However, the share of those reporting dependence for these activities are much less and do not exceed 3 to 5 per cent of the total sample. To illustrate, the lowest dependence (about 2.5 per cent) is found in combing followed by dressing (4.2 per cent), bathing, dressing (3.8 per cent) and eating (5.3). Conversely, the remaining five physical activities suggest much greater prevalence of functional impairment, resulting in large-scale dependence on caregivers. It appears from these results that the most

Table 5.1

Physical Status of the Old: Persons with ADL Impairments and Availability of Filial Support

Daily Activities (ADL)	Categories Suggesting Physical Status and Support Availability: (%)				
	ND/NH	D/NH	D/H	ND/H	N
Physical					
Eating	93.3	1.3	5.3	0.1	1004
Dressing	94.1	1.7	4.2	0.0	1004
Bathing	93.9	2.0	3.8	0.3	1003
ID Walk	71.2	9.6	19.2	0.0	1003
OD Walk	41.4	19.3	39.1	0.1	999
Cooking/Cleaning	53.5	13.2	33.2	0.1	873
Climbing stair	20.0	19.3	60.6	0.1	999
Combing	96.5	0.8	2.5	0.2	1003
Getting-up	22.2	24.4	53.2	0.2	1001
Sensory					
Reading	83.9	2.4	13.6	10.0	997
Hearing	77.7	15.6	6.7	0.2	1001

Source: IEG/CIDA Ageing Survey (2002).

Figure 5.2

ADL Assistance to Physically Impaired: Availability and Non-availability

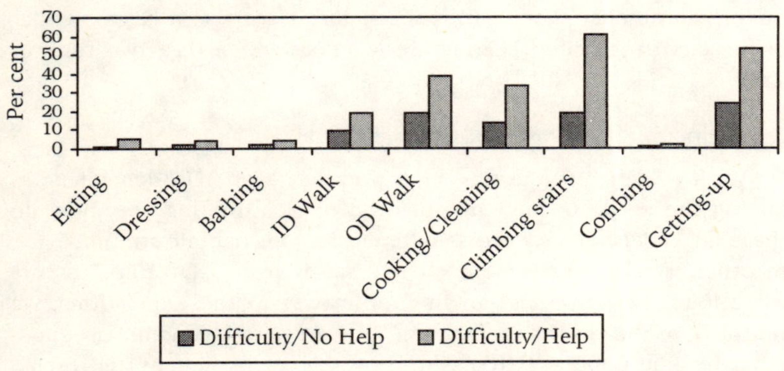

Source: Based on Table 5.1 (columns 3rd and 4th).

difficult task for the old is climbing the stairs with as high as 80 per cent dependencies. Getting-up from a sitting position is another difficult task for more than three-fourths of the respondents. Moreover, it also generates high level of dependencies. Walking outside the house and cooking or cleaning are the two other difficult activities for a very large fraction of the sample elderly (Table 5.1).

Unmet Assistance to ADL Impaired Old

Another issue of considerable significance perhaps is the lack of assistance to a large percentage of those functionally impaired. Figure 5.2, for example, shows a great deal of unmet assistance to the respondents with problems in climbing stairs. This problem is also severe for persons unable to move out for various self-maintenance works or who are not comfortable in getting-up from a sitting position. Many of those unable to cook or clean are also without assistance. Alongside, Figure 5.2 also depicts the share of older persons who receive assistance their daily activities. Interestingly, the shares of those enjoying family assistance are always higher. This is particularly true for the activities requiring greater lower extremity efforts such as getting-up from bed or chair, outdoor walk or climbing stairs.

As was expected, persons receiving help without any difficulty are very few in number and, therefore, we refrain to make any comment (column 5 of Table 5.1).

In case of sensory impairments, persons with hearing losses in our sample outnumber those with poor vision. Here also a large number of those with impaired hearing are left unattended (last two rows of Table 5.1).

Distribution of ADL Impairments by Stratum

With evidence suggesting high prevalence of ADL dependencies among the aged, an obvious question to examine may be: how do these dependencies vary across different socio-economic stratums? Or, in other words, do the poor elderly suffer from ADL impairments more than the non-poor? To find an answer to these questions, we redistribute the results in Table 5.1 by four socio-economic groups— High Income Groups (HIG), slum dwellers, government and mixed category households. These distributions are given in Tables 5.2a, 5.2b, and 5.2c. Given very few cases of the ND/H, we dropped this category altogether from further analysis.

Table 5.2a

Stratum-wise Distribution of Persons with ND/NH

Percentage

ADL Type	HIG	Slum	Government	Mixed
		Physical		
Eating	97.9	83.3	95.1	95.1
Dressing	100.0	91.4	92.7	94.4
Bathing	91.7	93.8	95.1	94.0
ID Walk	81.3	75.3	82.9	69.0
OD Walk	55.3	47.5	43.9	39.1
Cooking/Cleaning	54.1	76.7	72.5	46.5
Climbing Stairs	33.3	31.5	22.0	16.6
Combing	97.9	93.8	97.6	96.9
Getting-up	27.1	20.4	12.2	22.8
		Sensory		
Reading	89.6	82.4	78.0	84.1
Hearing	72.9	79.0	87.8	77.0

Table 5.2b

Stratum-wise Distribution of Persons with D/NH

Percentage

ADL Type	HIG	Slum	Govt.	Mixed
		Physical		
Eating	2.1	3.1	0.0	0.9
Dressing	0.0	0.6	2.4	2.0
Bathing	6.3	0.0	0.0	2.3
ID Walk	12.5	3.1	2.4	11.2
OD Walk	27.7	11.1	24.4	20.3
Cooking/Cleaning	10.8	5.0	5.0	15.9
Climbing Stairs	27.1	22.2	17.1	18.3
Combing	0.0	1.2	2.4	0.7
Getting-up	39.6	16.0	14.6	25.7
		Sensory		
Reading	0.0	2.5	0.0	2.7
Hearing	5.4	15.4	7.3	7.8

Table 5.2c

Stratum-wise Distribution of Persons with D/H

Percentage

ADL Type	HIG	Slum	Govt.	Mixed
		Physical		
Eating	0.0	13.6	4.9	4.9
Dressing	0.0	8.0	4.9	4.9
Bathing	0.0	6.2	4.9	4.9
ID Walk	6.3	21.6	14.6	14.6
OD Walk	17.0	41.4	31.7	31.7
Cooking/Cleaning	35.1	18.2	22.5	22.5
Climbing Stairs	39.6	46.3	61.0	61.0
Combing	0.0	4.3	0.0	0.0
Getting-up	33.3	63.0	73.2	73.2
		Sensory		
Reading	10.4	14.5	22.0	13.2
Hearing	21.6	4.9	5.1	15.1

Source: IEG/CIDA Ageing Survey (2002).

Table 5.2a suggests that the HIG elderly are functionally more competent in most of their day-to-day activities—implying a positive effect of income on functional competence. This table, for instance, reveals that the HIG with ND/NH have the highest share in activities involving eating, dressing, out door walk, climbing stairs, combing, getting-up from a sitting position, reading barring hearing (Table 5.2a). Next to HIG are the mixed income households. In contrast, more of the slum elderly reported themselves competent in cooking and cleaning.

Despite positive income effect on functional health, HIG people did report severe impairments in activities needing to go outdoors, cooking or cleaning, climbing stairs, getting-up from a sitting position and hearing (Table 5.2a). They particularly face difficulty in using stairs (67 per cent dependent), getting-up from sitting position (73 per cent) and hearing (27 per cent dependence). As a bottom line, therefore, while income may prove as a safeguard against certain health conditions or disabilities, it remains ineffective in many others.

Another source of vulnerability for the aged from high and mixed income categories is the lack of assistance. This is clearly borne out from the figures in Table 5.2b. However, given their smaller family size and high incidence of out migration, these results may not be very surprising.

Despite their serious health disadvantages, the low-income slum elderly are more comfortable in terms of family provided support provisioning (Table 5.2c). Does it mean that the family size or the number of children, *inter alia*, serve to minimise the risks of unmet assistance in situations of frailty and ADL dependence? Apparently yes, but a more definitive answer requires further analysis.

Gender and ADL Disabilities

Gender differentials in the underlying context may be noted from Table 5.3. In line with general expectations, ADL impaired women outnumber men in a big way. In addition, barring cooking or cleaning, it's true for all the activities under consideration in both the health domains (see the first two columns of Table 5.3). To illustrate, the share of handicapped women is especially higher in activities requiring more physical strength such as climbing stairs (86 per cent women are impaired and needing help) followed by tasks requiring getting-up from a sitting position (85 per cent impaired) and going-out for various household activities (65 per cent dependence). Even cooking or home cleaning was found to be difficult for more than half of the sample women. Also, a third of the women were not able to hear properly. In comparison, men were found to be less impaired, though a good majority of them expressed serious difficulties in activities requiring use of lower extremities including climbing stairs (73 per cent), getting-up from bed or a sitting position (69 per cent) or going out for shopping and other routine work (49 per cent).

Table 5.3

Gender-wise Distribution of Sample Elderly by ADL Competence

Percentage

Nature of ADL	ND/NH		D/NH		D/H		N	
	Male	*Female*	*Male*	*Female*	*Male*	*Female*	*Male**	*Female**
Physical								
Eating	95.5	91.4	1.1	1.5	3.2	7.1	470	533
Dressing	96.2	92.3	0.8	2.4	3.0	5.3	471	533
Bathing	95.3	92.7	1.5	2.4	3.2	4.3	471	534
ID Walk	78.5	64.7	7.9	11.1	13.6	24.2	470	533
OD Walk	51.2	33.4	21.7	17.1	27.2	49.3	471	532
Cooking/ Cleaning	66.2	43.7	15.3	11.5	18.2	44.7	378	494
Climb. Stairs	27.1	13.7	25.0	14.3	47.9	71.8	468	530
Combing	97.5	95.7	0.6	0.9	1.7	3.2	470	531
Getting-up	30.4	14.9	30.9	18.6	38.7	66.1	470	529
Sensory								
Reading	86.1	81.8	1.5	3.2	12.4	14.8	469	527
Hearing	30.4	66.7	20	24.7	10.4	8.6	470	531

Source: IEG/CIDA Ageing Survey (2002).

Note: * ND/H not included.

Gender differentials are shown to be particularly higher in tasks involving:

Lower extremity limitation

- climbing stairs,
- getting-up from sitting positions,
- out-door walk, and
- Cooking and cleaning.

These gender differentials are further highlighted in Figure 5.3, exhibiting very high shares of women with severe constraints in performing all the four high strength activities noted above. The extent of women's disability is particularly higher in climbing stairs. Getting up from a sitting position is equally difficult for those who find it difficult to climb stairs. Not only that, more than half of them reported disability in cooking for themselves or cleaning the place they live.

Figure 5.3

*Gender-wise Differentials in Performance of
Four Most Critical ADL Functions*

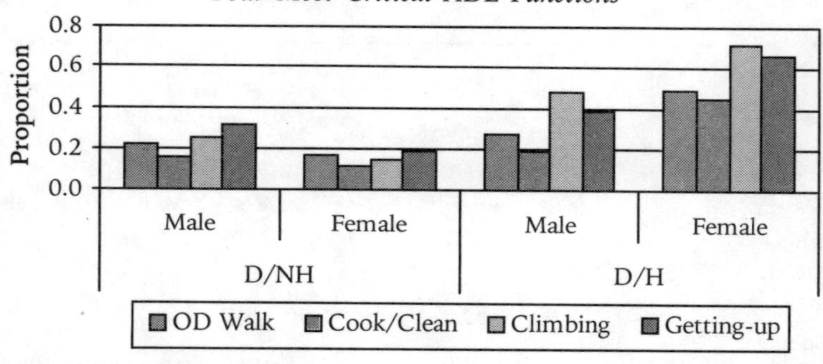

Source: IEG/CIDA Ageing Survey.

Women are not only the worst victims of ADL impairments; they are also short of assistance. While a majority of them are still assisted by families or relatives; the share of those lacking this assistance is also significantly large. This is clearly borne out by the D/NH columns representing the unmet assistance in Table 5.3 (Figure 5.3). Given these, and keeping the fast emerging socio-economic and demographic changes in perspective, the ageing scenario and the need for elderly care in India are apparently fraught with many serious issues. How far the care institutions like old age homes and other specialised centers —both within the public and NGO domains—fill some of this void needs to be examined.

Persons with Multiple ADL Limitations

Given the level of ADL limitations and support required by the disabled, care giving on informal basis may turn out to be a very difficult and time-consuming activity in India—with implicit risks of increasing neglect by the family members. But this is not all, and the problem may complicate further if the disabilities are functionally more constraining and cause multiple impairments. The need for assistance in such situations would in all likelihood be more pervasive. Given this, we tried to compute the number of persons in our sample with and without multiple ADL limitations. This would enable us to get an idea about the burden of dependence imposed on families/siblings if the disabilities follow the pattern emerging from this survey.

Table 5.4 gives a three-way disability status of the sample aged by gender. These are: (i) no disability, (ii) single disability, and (iii) multiple disabilities. In many respects, these results conform to those presented earlier. For instance, this table also suggests that women are in a more pitiable situation. Further, while the share of those with no difficulties is much less for both the genders (hardly over a third of their total sample size) the ADL efficient men outnumber the women. However, the more significant observations arising from this exercise relate to the sex-wise break-up of persons with multiple impairments. Three points merit special attention:

Table 5.4

Distribution of Persons with Single and Multiple ADL Limitations

Number of Disabilities	Gender (%)		N
	Male	Female	
No disability	35.98	34.38	35.09
1 disability	8.59	4.95	6.57
2 disabilities	17.02	10.94	13.65
3 or more disabilities	38.41	49.74	44.69
Column total	617	768	1385

Source: IEG/CIDA Ageing Survey.

Note: Column totals in this table may not compare with Tables 5.1 or 5.3 because of the differences in response formats.

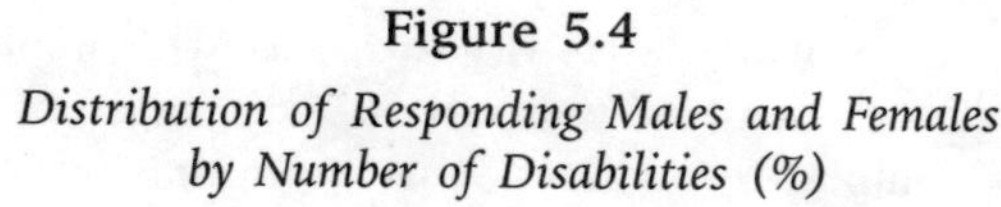

Figure 5.4

*Distribution of Responding Males and Females
by Number of Disabilities (%)*

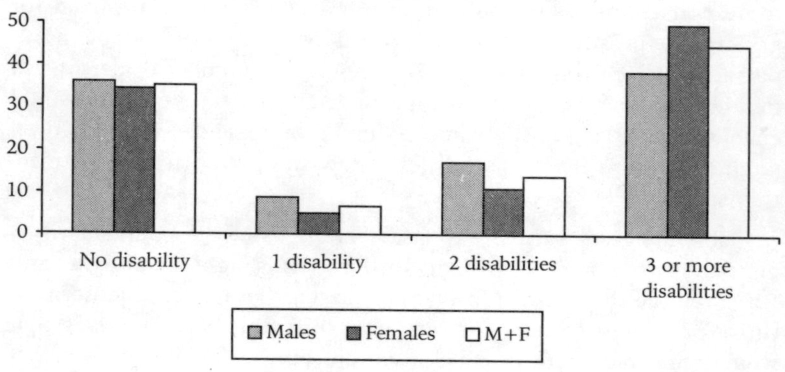

Source: Based on Table 5.4.

(i)   The share of males and females suffering from two or more disabilities is considerably higher than those reporting no or single disability.

(ii)   Compared to men, women suffer from a greater number of disabilities (Figure 5.4).

(iii)   About half of the responding females (49.7 per cent) are reported to suffer from three or more disabilities. This share is however much lesser for the males (38.4 per cent).

Many policy issues arise from these results. One is the quality of survival at the later end of the life span—especially when the later-end life span is increasing with time (i.e., area covered under B in Figure 5.1). Another is the gender dimension of disabilities. Particularly, women with their multiple disabilities may ultimately drop below the threshold of physical, sensory or cognitive capacities and, as a result, need more intense and regular care. Could families make the required care available informally? This is indeed a big issue and needs to be examined with more specific details. Yet another important issue relates to the ongoing debate on healthy ageing. With large-scale occurrence of functional disabilities and chronic diseases, especially among the females, the whole idea of healthy or active ageing needs to be revisited. Simultaneously, this is now the time to re-think the whole concept of health from the viewpoint of ageing and functional capabilities. As a first step, however, what is required is to look into some of the causal risk factors associated with functional impairments. Further, how can public health be geared to bring down the current level of disabilities is another issue of wider public concern. We will take-up these issues below in the same order.

5.3. Risk Factors in ADL Disabilities

As we move to search for more insights into disabilities in various health domains, an obvious issue would be to identify some of their causal factors. Two methods may be followed. The first would be to adopt a more medically oriented approach with a study of a prospective cohort and its requisite details including lifelong health behaviours. Such an approach has however seldom been applied by analysts. Even gerontological research cohorts usually begin from age 55 and above (Albert, 2004). The other is to use socio-economic proxy measures and capture the likely risk factors. This analysis relies on the latter with host of socio-economic and health indicators to assess the possible risks of ADL disabilities among the aged. We begin by a brief discussion of the model, especially the details about the set of variables chosen for the analysis. This would be followed by the results.

Description of the Model

The exercise is based on the Delhi survey and is designed to identify a set of socio-economic and health factors with associated risks of physical disabilities among the aged, forcing them to rely on others for their self-maintenance. An implicit hypothesis of this analysis is that the low-income and financially dependent men and women (especially women) or those with a sedentary life style may have greater risks of suffering from ADL impairments. The necessary details of the model including the set of explanatory variables are presented in Box 5.1. Given the multiple and discrete nature of our dependent variable (i.e., 0-3 disabilities), a count data model is employed for this analysis. Methodologically, the count model usually rely on the Poisson regression where each y_i is drawn from a Poisson distribution with parameter λ_i, which is related to the explanatory variables X_i. A serious drawback of the model, as already explained, lies with the assumption that its conditional mean and variance are equal. In reality, and especially in situations of over dispersions like in the present case, this is highly unlikely.[7] In order to overcome this difficulty, a Negative Binomial Model—which by formulation has a cross-sectional heterogeneity—has been suggested in literature (Green, 2002). The Poisson model is generalized by introducing an individual, unobserved effect into the conditional mean (i.e., $\ln \lambda_I = X'_I \beta + \varepsilon$). This leads to a difference in the conditional mean and conditional variance. We have therefore tried to follow this procedure in the exercise reported below.

Box 5.1

Description of Model to Estimate the Risks of Disabilities

Estimation Model	Dependent Variable	Independent Variables
Count Data Regression (Negative Binomial)	ADL Disability Index (0-3) as shown in Table 5.4	(i) Initial Health Stock (ii) Standard of Living Index (iii) Habit Index (iv) Age (v) Age Square (vi) Sex

---

Construction of Variables

Details of the variables used in this exercise are presented below. In addition, Appendix Table 5.2 presents the descriptive statistics of all the variables under reference.

ADL Disability Index (0-3): A composite disability index was generated with out going into activity specific disabilities to identify the range of persons with no disabilities to those having a maximum of three or more disabilities (see Table 5.4).

Income Status (Standard of Living Index): The income of an individual is proxied by the standard of living indices (SLI). These indices were constructed by taking into consideration the asset holdings of an individual household, where the assets were scored on the basis of their notional market price (see the SLI given in Table 3.14 and related details). Finally, we aggregated these overall scores for every sample household and assigned them to each household member.

---

7. For a more comprehensive discussions on these issues, see Cameron and Trivedi (1986), Grootendrost (2002), etc.

Initial Health Stock Index (1-4): Often health and disabilities are inversely related—that is, healthier an individual the less likely she/he would suffer from disability. In order to capture this effect we have tried to develop a health index on the basis of the number of disease(s) suffered by an individual over a reference period of past one-year from the date of the survey. We asked our respondents to report if they suffer from any of the diseases shown in Appendix Table 5.3. A scrutiny of this data suggested that in no case an individual in our sample was suffering from more than four diseases. Accordingly, we have indexed them on a scale of 1 to 4. An individual suffering from 1 disease is considered healthier (and scored 1) than those suffering from a larger number of diseases.[8]

Habit Index (0-2): Healthy habits will also make an individual lesser prone to disabilities. In our survey, we tried to capture this effect by considering the life style of an individual i.e., whether or not the person goes for a walk or mediates. Also, in order to capture the effect of regularity or irregularity, we have further segregated the respondents into three broad categories: (i) those regular in their routine (almost 5 days a week), (ii) those not so regular, and (iii) those without any exercise or meditation regime. Those with regularity in their habit got the highest index value (i.e., 2) followed by the remaining two with 1 and 0, respectively. We however finally dropped meditation from our estimations to avoid co-linearity between this and the exercising habit.

Gender: This variable was considered in a binary format with 1 assigned to males, and 0 otherwise.

Respondent's age: Persons aged 60 and over. Age^2 was used to make assessments about certain non-linearity (e.g., a kind of parabolic relationship) between the age and number of disabilities.

Estimation Results

In line with general expectations, Table 5.5 shows that the number of diseases, or the health stock of an individual, is the most potent risk factor in ADL disabilities. An individual with multiple diseases is far more likely to suffer from disabilities than the one with better health. This brings to the forefront an important issue now raised in more recent gerontological literature linking the health status in

---

8. We have however failed to consider the nature and the gravity of these diseases.

younger ages—say during the first 50 years of life—to that of the later life span. As most of the existing gerontological research has relied on higher age cohorts, the linkages between the earlier and the later age health stocks are not very evident (Albert, 2004). This may particularly be important for low-income countries like India where the burden of diseases is considerably high among the children and younger people (World Bank, 1993). With the possibilities of such linkages being strong (Table 5.5), there is clearly a need to probe this issue further with more scientifically drawn samples and larger database.

Another interesting result arising from this analysis is the significance of life style, particularly the habit of regular exercising. Our estimates in Table 5.5 suggest that persons with regular walking practices are likely to escape the risks of physical disabilities to a certain degree. The coefficient of habit index is statistically significant at the 1 per cent level with a negative sign, implying greater risks for those with sedentary life style. Another important factor with a higher-level of statistical significance is the income status. Persons with higher SLI values are less likely to suffer disabilities in the physical domain. Gender is another risk factor with women being at the receiving end. It adds to our earlier findings showing women outnumbering the men in various forms of ADL impairments. Age is yet another factor adding to the disability risks. However, these risks may decline with age.

Table 5.5

Risk Factors in ADL Disabilities: CDM Results
Dependent Variable, ADL Disability
(Number of Observations = 959)

Variables	Coefficients	St. Error	z	P>|z|
Constant	-2.566077	1.716195	-1.495	0.135
Health stock index	.1204281**	.0218977	5.500	0.000
Habit index	-.0655843**	.0256563	-2.556	0.011
Age	.0836547	0478117	1.750	0.080
Age^2	-.0005061	.0003298	-1.534	0.125
Sex	-.0916575*	.0462358	-1.982	0.047
Income status	-.0035207**	.0015761	-2.234	0.025

Log likelihood = - 14739751

** Statistically significant at 1 per cent level.

* Statistically significant at 5 per cent level.

While the set of results presented in this chapter may not be conclusive, they are indeed informative and may prove helpful in evolving certain public health responses to the health needs of the ageing population. It may however be noted that the r^2 in our model is low. While this is not very unusual for a cross-sectional exercise, it mostly indicates the relevance of unaccounted factors. In our context, it seems to suggest that the risks of disabilities cannot be fully explained by using the socio-economic factors alone. Further medico-environmental inputs and related details could also be used to capture overtime changes[9] in biomarkers of ageing.

5.4. Ageing, Functional Disabilities and Public Health

Currently, India is in the middle of several transitions. These transitions are perhaps more clearly discernible in three important spheres of life: economic, demographic and epidemiological. At the economic level, for instance, India is aggressively pursuing market reforms and aiming at gradual privatisation of major health and non-health services. This was however brought about without developing a credible social safety net for the vulnerable segments of population including the aged. At the demographic level, India is by and large out of the high fertility-mortality syndrome with major gains in terms of added life span and a reduction in high age deaths.[10] Epidemiologically also, India is now far from the early twentieth century phases of contagious, poverty driven and vector born diseases. The demographic and epidemiological transitions were obviously the results of an improvement in the living standards and sustained public health measures with better sanitation, supply of potable water and a high rate of vaccinations to prevent childhood diseases.

Despite most of these improvements, the results obtained clearly bring out the poor health conditions of the aged with high prevalence of co-morbid conditions followed by multiple ADL disabilities. With the increasing role of the market, growing cost of medical care,

---

9. These changes generally apply to indicators of respiratory and cardiac functions, walking speed, working memory, visual reaction time, gait speed, sensory discrimination, etc. (Albert, 2004).

10. A temporal comparison would however reveal that the rate of decline remains very low during the past few years (see, for example, the reports of Sample Registration System for 1980, 1991 and 1998, published by the Registrar General of India).

persistent poverty, poor quality of health care in the government sector, lack of social health insurance and the degenerating nature of old age diseases it may be easily premised that a majority of the aged in India are running out of options. With time, they may even loose family care as the result of various socio-cultural and economic changes. This is indeed a situation that needs to be seriously examined with more relevant statistical details.

We now examine two specific issues: (i) the pathways of ADL disabilities, and (ii) their likely public health responses. We posit that an understanding of these two issues is important for the reason that a larger fraction of the disabilities reported in our survey was not simply age determined.[11] Rather, they were caused by frailty, medical conditions (Appendix Table A-5.3) and sedentary life style. Given this, a preventive route with public health measures may well be adopted.

Figure 5.5 is drawn on the assumption that the pathways of disabilities follow three major routes: (i) age-determined senescence, (ii) general or disease related frailties, and (iii) lack of supportive environment (Albert, Im and Raveis, 2002). Pathway A in Figure 5.5, for example, illustrates the direct effects of age-based changes in individuals leading to true senescence, severe weaknesses, poor endurance capacities, lack of body resistance, memory loss, and run down physical and mental conditions. Thus, age determined physiological changes might leave the aged in a situation where they may have to rely on external support for their self-maintenance.

Path B, on the other hand, is directly an outcome of various ailments and frailties—a situation reported by more than half of our sample aged. Appendix Table A-5.3 clearly brings out the same. The environmental conditions of individuals, pathway C in Figure 5.5, may also be a reason and lead to severe disabilities if allowed to persist unchecked for a longer duration. Especially, the lack of a supportive environment—a case represented by D/NH in Tables 5.1 to 5.3—is likely to converge into full-blown disabilities. This may especially be true for the older women. Medical psychiatrists and geriatricians have already started recognising that an improper atmosphere or poor inter-

---

11. Geriatricians often distinguish between the "age related" and the "age determined" changes in human life. Also, they argue that the true senescent changes result from the late life declines in physiological reserves (Albert, 2004).

Figure 5.5

Pathways of Frailty and Functional Incapacitations

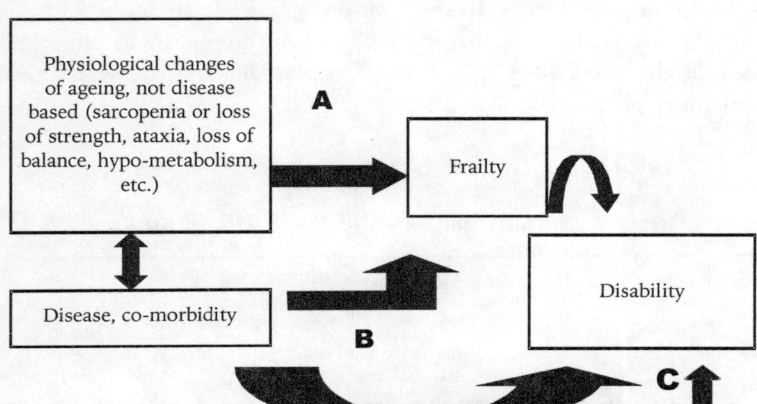

Source: Albert, Im, and Raveis, 2002.

generational bonding may worsen disabilities among people who are otherwise the same in frailty or medical conditions.

Of these three pathways, the roles of B and C are turning out to be the most potent causal factors in Indian conditions. And, for a majority of ageing Indians, getting away from these conditions seems difficult without strong and concerted efforts by the major stakeholders including the families, the community, the NGOs and above all, the government. At the government level, perhaps public health strategies offer a low cost and economically viable window by sensitising people against the risks associated with pathways B and C. We briefly discuss these strategies below.

Role of Public Health in Preventing Disabilities

What role can be played by the public health agencies in: (i) altering the pathways of disabilities, and (ii) preventing or forestalling people from falling sick? A recent study by Albert (2004) has tried to look into these issues at a much broader level. One of the many significant contributions of this study is the identification of a set of public health goals for four different categories of the older people: (i) robust (like ND/NH in Tables 5.1 to 5.3),

(ii) demented with serious cognitive impairments, (iii) persons in late ages (or older old), and (iv) frail. These goals are summarised in Table 5.6 with an emphasis on the prevention of frailties among the robust, and improvements in the living conditions of the frail by helping them to minimise their day-to-day responsibilities, helping them save their remaining physiologic abilities.

Table 5.6

Ageing Experiences and Goals of Public Health Strategies

Type of Older Persons	*Goals of Public Health*
Robust	Prevention of frailty and disability
Demented	Prevention of excess morbidity, and excellent custodial care
Late Stage of Life (old old)	Reduction of isolation, maximisation of choice
Frail	Environmental modification to reduce task demand; rehabilitation to increase capacity by developing spared abilities

Source: Albert (2004).

The study further argues to change the pathways of ageing by sensitising people to improve their post-fifties' life span through enhanced habits of cognitive engagement, physical exercise, balanced diet, no smoking or tobacco chewing, and frequent health screenings. The study also recommends providing mineral supplementations to the more aged (or older old) with a view to forestall decay in their bone mass. Similarly, statins or aspirins may also be provided as part of public health measures to control cholesterol deposition among people and consequent decrease in cases of cardiac death.

The maximum emphasis was given in the study to avoid pathway B—the biggest reason for disabilities, especially in India. Sensitisation to follow good life practices including cutting down in terms of sedentary habits along with measures to reduce the risks of diabetes, dementia, stroke, heart disease, respiratory problems, joint pain, early tooth decay, etc.

The third pathway, that is, unsupportive environment, may be another critical factor and needs special attention in countries where family based support is the mainstay for physically or mentally impaired old. Understanding the social context of ageing may therefore be significant to devise ways for creating a more amenable atmosphere for the growing number of aged.

5.5. Concluding Observations

To conclude, two observations from this analysis may bear significance at the policy level. One is the poor quality of survival due to a high prevalence of disabilities in later life years. And the second relates to the fact that in most cases the functional disabilities are not age determined. These are rather the outcome of gender or health related factors—disease, frailties, life style, etc. It is therefore advisable to follow a public health route to prevent disabilities by: (i) creating awareness among people about the need for preserving their health stock to ensure healthy ageing, (ii) setting up public health goals for different segments of the older population—robust, frail, demented and old old, and (iii) encouraging drug supplementation activities to ensure primary preventions of several complex conditions. Also, there is need for further studies on these issues of vital concern.

Appendix Table A-5.1

Because of Health Problems, Do You have Difficulty in Performing the Following Activities?

Nature of Activities	Self		Spouse	
	Nature of Difficulty Do you have difficulty in performing on your own?	Extent of Help Do you need help from some one to perform this activity?	Nature of Difficulty Do you have difficulty in performing on your own, without help?	Extent of Help Do you need help from some one to perform this activity?
1. Eating	No 1 Sometimes 2 A Lot 3	Never 1 Sometimes 2 Always 3	No 1 Sometimes 2 A Lot 3	Never 1 Sometimes 2 Always 3
2. Dressing	No 1 Sometimes 2 A Lot 3	Never 1 Sometimes 2 Always 3	No 1 Sometimes 2 A Lot 3	Never 1 Sometimes 2 Always 3
3. Bathing	No 1 Sometimes 2 A Lot 3	Never 1 Sometimes 2 Always 3	No 1 Sometimes 2 A Lot 3	Never 1 Sometimes 2 Always 3
4. Indoor Walking (say for toileting etc)	No 1 Sometimes 2 A Lot 3	Never 1 Sometimes 2 Always 3	No 1 Sometimes 2 A Lot 3	Never 1 Sometimes 2 Always 3
5. Outdoor Walking (says for shopping etc.)	No 1 Sometimes 2 A Lot 3	Never 1 Sometimes 2 Always 3	No 1 Sometimes 2 A Lot 3	Never 1 Sometimes 2 Always 3
6. House Cleaning/ Cooking	No 1 Sometimes 2 A Lot 3	Never 1 Sometimes 2 Always 3	No 1 Sometimes 2 A Lot 3	Never 1 Sometimes 2 Always 3
7. Climbing Stairs	No 1 Sometimes 2 A Lot 3	Never 1 Sometimes 2 Always 3	No 1 Sometimes 2 A Lot 3	Never 1 Sometimes 2 Always 3
8. Getting-up	No 1 Sometimes 2 A Lot 3	Never 1 Sometimes 2 Always 3	No 1 Sometimes 2 A Lot 3	Never 1 Sometimes 2 Always 3
9. Combing	No 1 Sometimes 2 A Lot 3	Never 1 Sometimes 2 Always 3	No 1 Sometimes 2 A Lot 3	Never 1 Sometimes 2 Always 3
10. Reading	No 1 Sometimes 2 A Lot 3	Never 1 Sometimes 2 Always 3	No 1 Sometimes 2 A Lot 3	Never 1 Sometimes 2 Always 3
11. Hearing	No 1 Sometimes 2 A Lot 3	Never 1 Sometimes 2 Always 3	No 1 Sometimes 2 A Lot 3	Never 1 Sometimes 2 Always 3

Appendix Table A-5.2

Descriptive Statistic of Variables used in Table 5.5

Variable	Observations	Mean	Std. Dev.	Min.	Max.
Disability index	1385	1.644043	1.331454	0	3
Habit index	1019	1.030422	0.918088	0	2
Age^2	1385	4685.678	971.6838	3600	9801
Age	1385	68.11986	6.737658	60	99
Gender	1385	0.445487	0.497199	0	1
Health stock index	959	2.573514	1.028085	1	4
Std. of living index	1385	38.16029	14.62455	1	90

Appendix Table A-5.3

Disease-Disability Matrix

Diseases	Disability Index				Col.%
	0	1	2	3	
1. Poor vision/Cataract/Other eye impairment	31.7	34.1	19.5	14.6	4.28
2. Lung problem/Respiratory Problem/Asthma	7.7	23.1	15.4	53.8	1.36
3. Tuberculosis/Other chronic fever	33.3	33.3	33.3	0.0	0.31
4. Diarrhea/Gastroenteritis/ Stomach Ulcer	33.3	66.7	0.0	0.0	0.31
5. Skin Disease	33.3	33.3	0.0	33.3	0.31
6. Angina/Chest Pain/Cardiac problem	5.9	5.9	11.8	76.5	1.77
7. High BP	19.4	9.7	19.4	51.6	3.23
8. Arthritis/Rheumatism/Joint pain	3.9	5.2	10.4	80.5	8.03
9. Back Pain/Slip disc	8.3	4.2	25.0	62.5	2.50
10. Neurological or Mental Problems (Depression)	50.0	0.0	0.0	50.0	0.21
11. Cancer (of any form)	0.0	0.0	0.0	100.0	0.10
12. Dementia/Alzheimer	0.0	0.0	0.0	0.0	0.00
13. Frailty/General weakness/Run down condition	7.9	10.2	24.4	57.5	0.10
14. Injury & related disabilities	0.0	0.0	0.0	100.0	52.97
15. Burn & related disabilities	0.0	0.0	100.0	0.0	0.73
16. Diabetes & other problems like Prostate/Dental, etc	2.7	6.6	21.2	69.5	0.21
Row Total	76	97	208	578	959
Row %	7.9	10.1	21.7	60.3	100.0

Source: IEG/CIDA Ageing Survey.

6

Caring for the Aged and Planning for Self-Ageing: Views of Younger Adults

6.1. Introduction

How do the non-elderly perceive the following:

(i) need to plan for their own ageing, and

(ii) caring for their ageing dependents?

These questions arose in the preceding discussion on two important considerations. One was the cost of care. We argued that the monetary cost of elderly care—especially the health related expenses—is likely to increase with growing privatisation and health sector reforms in the country. As a result, it may not be easier for many to endure the cost of elderly care. Or, going by micro economic reasoning, the utility function of caregiver declines with increase in the cost of services and consumables utilised by the dependent elderly.[1] Another consideration in raising this issue was the growing need for planned ageing. As public provisioning for the aged in India is far from satisfactory, there is a growing consensus in favour of self-help and contributions towards annuities or other deposit-linked

---

1. Some of the recent attempts to derive an estimable model of co-residence postulates two utility functions, one for the care provider (Uc), and another for the aged (Ua). Each would depend on levels of consumption, c, a set of various services, h, and a pair of coefficients, A and B, capturing preferences for joint living arrangement for the aged and care provider. In addition, there is a utility function that applies when they choose to live together. This is a weighted average of (Uc) and (Ua), where the weight is a parameter è chosen jointly by the caregiver and the care seeker. This parameter also reflects their bargaining process However, knowledge of the particular value of è chosen by the two if they both decide to live together is not necessary to infer their preferences for the shared living arrangements. All that is needed is that there be a set of possible values of è such that, in each case, both are better off living together than living apart (Kotlikoff and Morris, 1990). A more recent extension of this model is to involve multiple pairs—i.e., more than one care giving child and the elderly parent (Logan, Hoff and Newton, 1999).

income security plans for old age. A big question may however be the general awareness among the non-aged about these issues and plans.

This chapter therefore attempts to investigate some of these issues with focus on:

- Motivational factors for the non-aged in elderly care.

- Altruism in care providing.

- Non-elderly views on self-ageing—especially their health and income security aspects.

6.2. Factors Contributing towards Care for the Elderly

Being a society embedded in deep-rooted values and traditions, caring for the aged in India was considered as one of the biggest moral responsibilities of individuals and families. This applies universally across the country irrespective of caste, religion or ethnicity. Large-scale adherence to this responsibility, which proved to be the biggest insurance mechanism against fatalities, old age and other providential risks, has led public institutions to escape from a major role in social security provisioning. Despite growing contradictions, this role of the family is assumed to continue by the makers of the National Policy on Older Persons (January 1999).

With ongoing changes in family composition, and gradual erosion in values, many of these traditions are now increasingly at stake. Even though not conclusively, a few similar observations did emerge from some of our earlier econometric exercises on living arrangements of the older women in chapter 2. To probe further into some of these crucial though unsettled issues, we have asked our non-elderly respondents:

1. Is caring for the aged a burden to them?

2. Why should the younger siblings (or family members) be responsible for caring for the aged? Is it their:

   - social obligations?

   - religious and moral responsibility? Or,

   - in return for the care they received when young and non-earning.

Interestingly, an overwhelming majority (92 per cent) of these respondents denied that caring for the aged is a burden. It may however not be less surprising to notice that eight per cent of the respondents have felt that caring for their aged is becoming burdensome. Males exceeded females in holding this view (Table 6.1a). While such respondents are numerically few, it dispels the notion that the family system in India is impregnable and would remain so in future as well. One may smell a change from these results. Tables 6.1b and c, distributing those agreeing with this question by stratum and educational level, substantiates our argument. Clearly a majority of those agreeing with the question come from a non-slum background with higher levels of education.

Figure 6.1

Is Caring for the Aged a Burden?

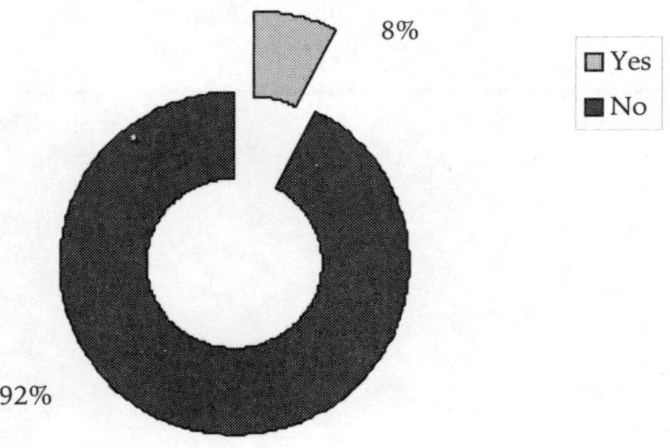

Source: IEG/CIDA Ageing Survey (2002).

Table 6.1a

Is Caring for the Aged a Burden? Sex-wise Responses (Respondents in 15-59 Ages)

Is Caring for the elderly a burden?	Male Respondents		Female Respondents		Total Respondents	
	No.	%	No.	%	No.	%
Yes	55	68.8%	25	31.2%	80	100.0%
No	511	54.7%	424	45.3%	934	100.0%

Source: IEG/CIDA Ageing Survey (2002).

Table 6.1b

Is Caring for the Elderly a Burden? Stratum-wise Responses of Persons Aged 15-59

Is Caring for the elderly a burden?	HIG		Slums		Government		Mixed		Total Respondents	
	No.	%	No.	%	No.	%	No.	%	No.	%
Yes	4	8.70	17	10.56	3	7.32	56	7.30	80	7.88
No	42	91.30	144	89.40	38	92.70	711	92.70	935	92.12
Total	46	100.0	161	100.0	41	100.0	767	100.0	1015	100.0

Source: IEG/CIDA Ageing Survey (2002).

Table 6.1c

Is Caring for the Elderly a Burden? Education-wise Responses of Persons Aged 15-59 years

Caring for elderly a burden?	Illiterate	Literate	Education up to 8th Standard	Matriculate	Higher-Secondary	Graduate & Post-graduate	Total Respondents (N=1015)
Yes	8	7	15	15	18	17	80
%	10.0	8.8	18.8	18.8	22.5	21.3	100.0
No	93	14	173	168	168	319	935
%	10.0	1.5	18.5	18.0	18.0	34.1	100.0
Total	101	21	188	183	186	336	1015
%	10.0	2.1	18.5	18.0	18.3	33.1	100.0

Source: IEG/CIDA Ageing Survey (2002).

Caring for the Aged: Some Non-pecuniary Motivational Factors

Reverting to the preceding three derivers towards the cause of elderly care, we observe from Figure 6.2 that a combination of socio-religious and moral factors does actually help at the motivational level. Among the three, the most potent motivational factor for supporting the aged is religion combined with the sense of strong moral values. While social responsibilities are also significant for about three-fourths of the respondents, a sense of religion appears to work better. In other words, religious institutions and leaders of various faiths may play a significant role in inculcating pro-elderly sentiments among the young.

Figure 6.2

Motivational Factors in Caring for the Old

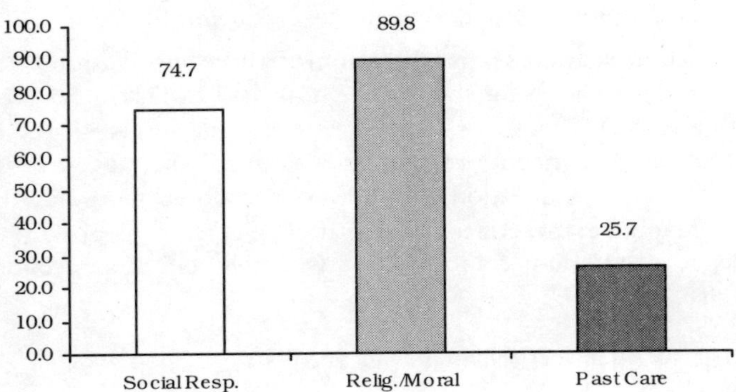

Source: IEG/CIDA Ageing Survey (2002).

Care giving to parents and older relatives owing to their past contributions did not evoke a very favourable response from the younger persons. Although a quarter of them did find that as an important motivational factor.

Figure 6.3

Elderly Care as Socio-Moral and Religious Responsibility: Distribution of 15-59 Persons by Stratum

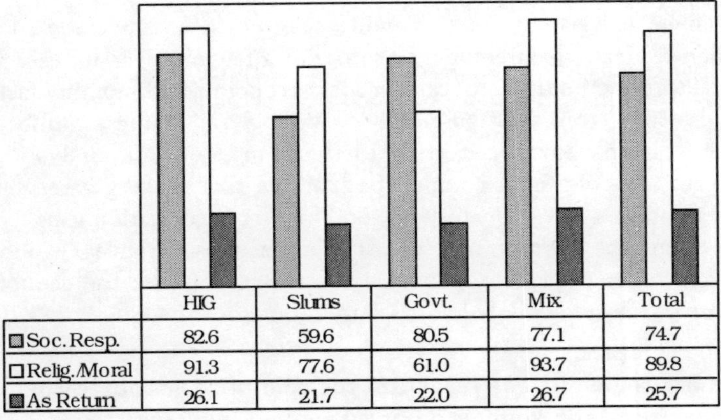

	HIG	Slums	Govt.	Mix	Total
☐ Soc. Resp.	82.6	59.6	80.5	77.1	74.7
☐ Relig./Moral	91.3	77.6	61.0	93.7	89.8
■ As Return	26.1	21.7	22.0	26.7	25.7

Source: IEG/CIDA Ageing Survey (2002).

Notwithstanding the role of socio-religious or moral factors in caring for the aged, Figure 6.2 also reveals that over ten per cent of the respondents did not believe in most of these values, and recognised the cost of elderly care as a growing financial burden.

Stratum-wise cross-classification of three motivational factors responsible in caring for the aged is furnished in Figure 6.3 (also see its Data table). From this table, it is clear that larger shares of the HIG and mixed income respondents support their aged on moral considerations. A question may however be posed here: how far are these responses practised in real life? We tried to provide some evidence on this important question with the help of an econometric exercise.

Support to the Elders: Non-religious Factors

Religious and socio-moral values are significant in drawing filial support and co-residential living arrangements for a large number of the aged in our sample. However, two questions of serious concern for policy makers are: (i) how long can these values be at work or be relied upon? This question draws its justification in the context of growing fragility of various traditional values and institutions. And (ii) what other factors—other than the religiosity and socio-moral values—may really help to improve the chances of intergenerational bonding and support transfers in the underlying context? These questions are increasingly asked in most of the literature on this subject, though without a robust or clear-cut answer (Palloni, 2001 and Gwatkin, 2000).

Given the paucity of this genre of literature, especially in the Indian context, we attempted to carry out a few multivariate exercises to capture the influence of certain socio-economic and morality factors on transfers from the non-elderly to the elderly. While a number of specifications have been tried in the course of this analysis, we present in Table 6.2 a couple of equations that make greater sense along with better explanatory power. The first specification uses moral values and the SLI scores as the major explanatory variables, while the second relies on a host of non-SLI factors to capture the economic status of the non-elderly and its implications for the elderly care (see Box 6.1).

Both the equations reconfirm the role of socio-moral values in predisposing the younger family members towards the aged. We

---

Box 6.1

Variables Used for Estimation in Table 6.2

Model: Binary Probit

Explained Variable (Binary):

Mentally prepared for taking responsibility of the elderly alone = 1; 0 Otherwise

Explanatory Variables:

MR Dummy: Aged as moral-religious responsibility = 1, otherwise 0;

WHHM/THHM: Ratio of working to non-working household members;

PCMCE: Per capita monthly consumption expenditure;

SLI: Standard of living scores (Table 3.14a);

HK & BS: House keeping and baby-sitting dummy. Those willing to do these = 1, otherwise 0;

EDU: Education levels (Table 3.12a);

Age: Non-elderly aged 14-59;

Sex Dummy: Male = 1, Female = 0

WORKC: working as casual worker = 1, self-employed = 2, and wage earners = 3.

Table 6.2

Factors Motivating Young to Old Transfers: Probit Results
Dependent Variable: Non-aged Prepared to Take Responsibility of the Aged

Explanatory Variables	Coefficients	Std. Error	$Z(b-\hat{a})/S_b$
Equation 1: (Number of Observations 1012)			
Constant	1.375	0.495	2.779
MR Dummy	0.580**	0.188	3.084
WHHM/THHM	- 0.120	0.452	- 0. 266
PCMCE	0.0004**	0.0002	2.716
SLI	- 0.017**	0.006	- 2.942
Log likelihood = -205520			
Equation 2: (Number of Observations 542)			
Constant	2.160	0.834	2.590
MR Dummy	0.687**	0.237	2.894
HK & BS Dummy	- 0.252	0.218	- 1.159
EDU	- 0.025@	0.017	- 1.425
WHHM/THHM	- 0.892@	0.552	- 1.616
Age	- 0.018@	0.012	- 1.529
Sex Dummy	- 0.678@	0.460	- 1.474
WORKCS	0.082	0.151	0.545
PCMCE	0.0005*	0.0002	2.278
Log likelihood = -109.4559			

Source: IEG/CIDA Ageing Survey (2002).

Note: ** statistically significant at 1 per cent, * significant at 5 per cent, @ significant at 10 per cent levels.

notice that the MR dummy remains highly significant in both the equations. A similar relationship holds for the per capita monthly consumption expenditure (PCMCE) as well. We notice from Table 6.2 (equation 1) that households with higher PCMCE are likely to be more supportive, and help the aged better. Surprisingly, however, the SLI scores—also a proxy to determine the economic strength of households—failed to yield the expected relationship. As an alternative, we used a few of its surrogates in the other specification.

The specification used in equation 2 (Table 6.2) revalidates our earlier perception relating to fast growing changes in traditional values with repercussions for the ageing population in India and many other societies with similar conditions. To be specific, while both the MR dummy and the PCMCE in this equation retain their original sign and remain statistically significant, the remaining variables—especially education, age, sex and share of working to non-working household members—brook a sense of non-traditionalism. All of them have also become significant at the 10 per cent level with negative signs, implying that decisions about caring for the aged may be guided by several other considerations beside socio-moral values.

A negative sign attached with the age factor in equation 2, for instance, indicates that persons in higher age brackets might less likely to take the responsibilities of their elderly. Possibly they feel uncomfortable with these responsibilities as they themselves are ageing and going to join the same rank. Similar relationships hold with the EDU and the WHHM/THHM. More of education and more of economic participation make elderly care less probable (equation 2, Table 6.2).

Perhaps the most interesting result arising from equation 2 relates to the respondents' sex. The sex dummy used in this equation raises doubts about the care-providing role of male siblings. In other words, it validates the general perception that females—especially daughters—are likely to prove more dependable in caring for ageing parents.

These results need further substantiation for two specific reasons: (i) low explanatory powers of the equations—amounting to exclusion of certain important variable/s, and also the fact that care giving in many societies like India is governed by subjective characteristics of an individual, and (ii) limited sample size with non-representation of the rural population.

6.3. Saving for Retirement and Planned Ageing

Faced with the growing need to reform the public funded social security system all over the world, emerging views on ageing in India have been to work towards the goal of planned ageing. An aspect of this was to persuade more and more younger adults to join individually contributed old age plans with benefits in the form of annuities or coverage of post-retirement health risks.

While this sounds logical, there are at least two major demand side issues in the underlying context that need scrutiny. One: do the non-aged—especially those from the low-income strata—realise the need for planned ageing to cover age related insecurities? And, if so, do they know or find it worth consideration to going for self-contributory income (or health) security plans? In addition, there are certain operational issues. One of the more pertinent relates to the pension fund management (i.e., public *versus* private fund managers),[2] and its regulatory system.

Though not very exhaustively, some of these issues are highlighted here using data emanating from the household survey under reference. The non-elderly respondents were asked to give their opinion regarding:

i.   planned ageing to minimise the old age income and health insecurities. And,

ii. self-contributory old age plans marketed by public and private financial institutions.

The bivariate frequency distributions presented in the following tables offer some useful insights about views held by respondents from different socio-economic segments. Table 6.3a, for example, suggests a much greater acceptance among the respondents about the need for secured ageing. It may be noticed that three-quarters of the total respondents agree with the need for old age planning. Only one quarter of them either showed ignorance or felt to the contrary. This is indeed an interesting finding with considerable significance both for planning bodies and those interested in ageing issues. However, would the same hold true for rural areas? This analysis unfortunately fails to provide any such clue. In addition, there are differences in perceptions as—well, and a large proportion of low-income people do not see the

---

2. Further discussion on recent changes in pension plans and strategies will be presented in Chapter 7.

need for planned ageing. These differences are clearly borne out from Table 6.3b. To be precise, the disagreement with the idea of planned ageing is shown to be highest among slum dwellers. In addition, a fifth of those from the mixed colonies also did not support this idea. Apparently, therefore, this concept still remains in the domain of those with higher education and income. A substantial fraction of the population from the lower income stratum held a contrary view. Sex of the respondents makes little difference to these views (Table 6.3c).

Table 6.3a

Need to Plan for Old Age: Persons Aged 15-59

Responses	N	%
Agreed to go for planned ageing	761	75.0
Disagreed with the idea of planned ageing	254	25.0
Total Respondents	**1015**	**100.0**

Source: IEG/CIDA Aging Survey (2002).

Table 6.3b

Need to Plan for Old Age: Responses of 15-59 Persons from Different Strata

Stratums	Agreed with Planned Ageing		No Need for such a Plan	
	N	%	N	%
HIG	43	935	3	6.5
Slums	80	49.7	81	50.3
Government	28	68.3	13	31.7
Mixed	610	79.5	157	20.5
Total N	**761**	**75.0**	**254**	**25.0**

Person Chi^2 (3)   = 72.7176   P-value = 0.000

Source: IEG/CIDA Ageing Survey (2002).

What other support mechanism (or institution) can help the aged better if planned ageing is not an agreed choice for about a quarter of the sample respondents? The respondents' views were sought on four types of care giving institutions, namely: (i) family, (ii) relatives, (iii) government, and (iv) family and government combined. A large share of respondents from slums considered government as the basic institution to provide old age security. A third of HIG respondents

Table 6.3c

Need to Plan for Old Age: Sex-wise Responses (Persons Aged 15-59)

Sex	Planed Ageing: Agreed		Planed Ageing: Disagreed		Total	
	N	%	N	%	N	%
Male	421	55.3	145	57.1	566	55.8
Female	340	44.7	109	42.9	449	44.2
Total	**761**	**100.0**	**254**	**100.0**	**1015**	**100.0**
	Pearson	Chi^2 (1) =	0.240	P-value = 0.624		

Source: IEG/CIDA Ageing Survey (2002).

also endorsed this view. Families came in only after government, and were supported overwhelmingly by mixed income people. These results also reveal socio-economic characteristics as an important decisive factor in planning for old age (Table 6.3d).

Table 6.3d

Institutions Responsible for Caring the Old: Responses of Persons Disagreeing with Planned Ageing (> 60)

Institution Type	Respondents by Socio-economic Categories			
	HIG	Slums	Govt.	Mixed
Government	33.3	40.7	23.1	8.9
Family	0.0	28.4	38.5	83.4
Relatives	0.0	1.2	0.0	1.3
Family & Government	66.7	24.7	38.5	3.8
No Idea	0.0	4.9	0.0	2.5
Total N	**3**	**81**	**13**	**157**
	Pearson Chi^2 (12) = 28.72		P-value = 0.050	

Source: IEG/CIDA Ageing Survey (2002).

Knowledge about Old Age Saving Instruments

In traditional settings with families as the basic care providers, knowledge about health or income security plans for the old age was often confined to a few privileged and more educated people. While in recent years there may be some changes in perception, these are not well documented in available literature. Table 6.4a is an attempt in this direction, and helps to provide an idea about the size of those in each stratum who knew about some of these plans or *vice versa*.

As was expected, the high-income stratum has the highest percentage of respondents who knew about old age saving schemes including all the pros and cons. Slum respondents are least aware of such schemes. As a whole, however, this knowledge seems to have already trickled through a large proportion of those interviewed. Again, rural people are not included here.

Table 6.4a

Knowledge of Old Age Saving Plans: Stratum-wise Responses
(Persons in 15-59 Ages)

Stratums	Knowledge About the Old Age Plans		
	Yes (%)	No (%)	Total N
HIG	87.0	13.0	46
Slums	28.0	72.0	161
Government	78.1	21.9	41
Mixed	82.8	17.2	767
Total	**74.1**	**25.9**	**1015**
Pearson chi^2 (3) = 213.08		P-value = 0.000	

Source: IEG/CIDA Ageing Survey (2002).
Note: N= No. of Population Sample.

Regarding differentials by stratum, this table reconfirms the earlier result that income and socio-economic background play an important role in making people aware and realise about the need for planned and secured ageing.

Finally, we tried to find out from the respondents about the major fund managing agencies in the public and private sectors and their old age plans. We also attempted to make some queries about a few non-government organisations (NGOs) and whether or not the respondents knew about them even vaguely. The results are shown in Table 6.4b.

Two observations stemming from this table warrant special attention. One is the poor response from the slum dwellers. And the reasons may not be difficult to discern. The other observation relates to the popularity and outreach of the publicly governed Life Insurance Corporation (LIC) of India. We notice from the table that a large proportion of respondents from every stratum knew about LIC and its schemes. This is however not true for Unit-Trust of India (UTI)—another equally reputed Government financial institution. UTI seems to be a much lesser known entity. The PPF and the privately managed financial institutions, on the other hand, fared considerably better and surpassed UTI on this count. NGOs are apparently the least known entity. It ought to be noted that barring a few very big NGOs like Self Employed Women's Association (SEWA), most of these organisations don't often run worthwhile savings plans (Figure 6.4). The chi^2 test reveals significant differences across the four socio-economic strata.

Table 6.4b

Knowledge of Fund Management Agencies: Stratums-wise Responses (Persons in 15-59 Ages)

Stratums	Percentage Distribution of Persons Knowing About					Number of Respondents (N)
	PPF[1]	LIC[2]	UTI[3]	Private[4]	NGO[5]	
HIG	85.0	100.0	77.5	80.0	52.5	40
Slums	20.0	68.9	8.9	6.7	22.2	45
Govt.	50.0	93.8	15.6	28.1	12.5	32
Mixed	68.2	96.1	44.7	47.2	28.0	635
Total	65.4	94.6	43.1	45.7	28.3	752
Pearson χ^2	53.33	62.65	51.32	51.18	16.31	
P-values	0.000	0.000	0.000	0.000	0.001	

Source: IEG/CIDA Ageing Survey (2002).

Note: 1. Public Provident Fund (PPF). 2. Life Insurance Corporation (LIC) of India. 3. Unit Trust of India (UTI). 4. Private fund managers like the ICICI. 5. Non-government Organisations like the SEWA.

Figure 6.4

Knowledge of Fund Managing Institutions: Inter-Stratum Comparison (Persons in 15-59 Ages)

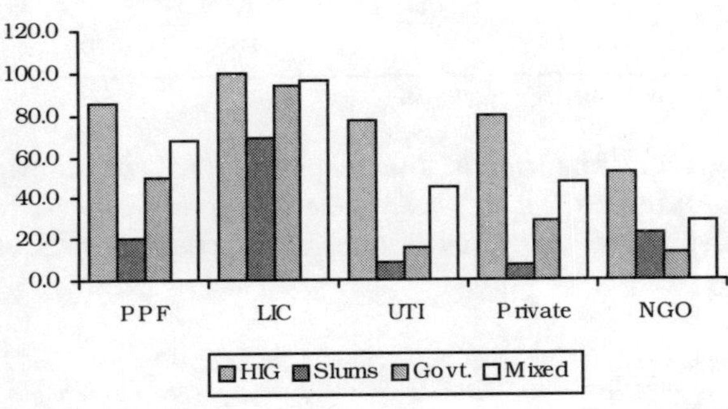

Source: IEG/CIDA Ageing Survey (2002).

Declining Interest Rate Regime: Would it Make Old Age Difficult?

Ever since the current phase of liberalisation in the early 1990s, India has increasingly been on the path of soft interest rate regime. Two reasons are mostly given to justify this regime. One was to bring down the capital cost to ensure the country's industrial competitiveness in the global market. Another was drawn from declining (point-to-point) inflation based on the manufacturers' price indices (i.e., WPI). Without going into the merits of these reasons,[3] there is now a growing realisation in certain segments of the population on the adverse ramifications of this regime—especially if the aged are made to rely on accumulated savings without a publicly funded social security pillar in the country. In order to judge the validity of these arguments, we raised the question of declining interest rate regime with both our respondents—namely the aged and the non-aged. The responses obtained from the latter are summarised in Table 6.5a.

Table 6.5a

Views on Declining Interest Rate and Ageing: Persons Aged 15-59

Will the Declining Interest Rate Affect Aged Adversely?	HIG	Stratum-wise Responses Slums	Govt.	Mixed	Row Total
Yes	97.8	59.6	90.2	87.7	83.8
No	0.0	14.9	7.3	8.9	9.4
No idea	0.0	11.2	0.0	0.0	1.7
Don't know	2.2	14.3	2.4	3.4	5.1
Column Total	46	161	41	767	1015

Pearson chi^2 (9) = 152.24   P-value = 0.000

Source: IEG/CIDA Ageing Survey (2002).

Clearly, a big majority of the respondents have identified the adverse fallouts of the soft interest rate regime—especially in the absence of social security provisioning in the country. This view was

---

3. A more detailed discussion on ageing and the declining returns to saving is attempted in Chapter 7.

held by as many as 84 per cent of the total respondents in the survey (Table 6.5a, see last column). There are however certain variations in responses across the social groups. Especially, in the case of a large number of the slum respondents who had certain clarity problems on this issue. Consequently, over two-fifths of them have either disagreed or failed to react meaningfully on this question. As almost the entire stratum belonged to low-income people with the bulk of them without proper education, this was not very unexpected. But the remaining three strata mostly agreed with the insensitivity of the policy makers towards the income security aspects of ageing persons.

Figure 6.5

Declining Interest Rate and Ageing: Responses of 15-59 Persons (Stratum-wise Comparison)

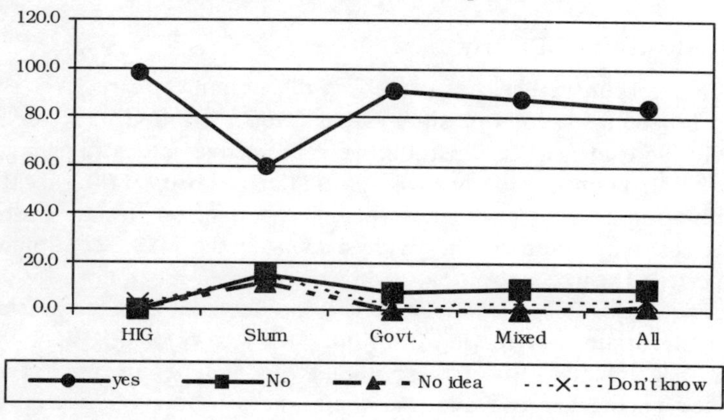

Source: Table 6.5a.

Bringing the gender dimension of this core issue into focus, we notice that most of the women respondents have concurred with this viewpoint. This is clearly emerging from Table 6.5b that shows a larger number of women agreeing about the adverse effects of the declining rate of interest on old age income security.

Despite certain variations, it is clear from these results (especially from Tables 6.5a and b) that the pattern of continuing decline in interest on savings is a cause for worry for a large proportion of the people. Further, it worries even those who are yet to face retirement—irrespective of their gender or socio-economic group affiliations.

Table 6.5b

Impact of Declining Interest Rate: Sex-wise Responses
(Persons Aged 15-59)

Nature of Response	Sex-wise Distribution (%)		Combined
	Males	*Female*	*(M+F)*
Adverse Impact: Yes	83.5	84.1	83.8
Adverse Impact: No	10.1	8.5	9.4
No Idea	2.5	0.9	1.8
Don't Know	3.9	6.5	5.0
Column Total (Number)	**565**	**447**	**1012**
%	100.0	100.0	100.0

Pearson Chi^2 (3) 10.125   P-value 0.038

Source: IEG/CIDA Ageing Survey (2002).

6.4. Altruism in Elderly Care

To a certain extent, our preceding discussion on caring for the aged by younger adults or siblings has remained mired in a lack of conclusive evidence. To illustrate, we come across issues implying a lack of altruism in elderly care—particularly those relating to the living arrangements of elderly women. A few of our binary probit exercises, employing country-wide data from the NSS 52nd Round, suggested that women were at higher risks of being left alone by the care providers (Table 2.11). These results, however, later contrasted with the findings stemming from our own survey. Siding with the aged, a good majority of the younger respondents in our survey viewed caring for the aged as their socio-moral and religious responsibilities (see Figures 6.2 and 6.3). Going by these assertions, altruism is likely to stay as a basis in intra-family relationships—at least for some in the country.

Altruism and Rational Exchange Relationship: Basic Concepts

"How selfish so ever man be supposed, there are evidently some principles in his nature which interest him in the fortune of others, and their happiness necessary to him, though he derives nothing from it, except the pleasure of seeing it."

Adam Smith. Cited in Piliavin and Charng (1990, p.27)

Like Smith, several recent studies and theoretical advancements in most areas of the social sciences have agreed with the notion of conformity between altruistically motivated behaviour and the rational choice (Piliavin and Charng, 1990). Economists, and especially those dealing with the intra-household distribution of resources, have particularly used this concept for a long time. We therefore decided to rely in our own brief application of this concept on some of these studies, and the way they have drawn an economic rationale from it.

Economists have brought to bear a number of perspectives to explain why individuals may like to support parents or close family members. One explanation, for example, focuses on the altruistic (or benevolent) behaviour—commonly seen to ensure an intra-family bonding or bonding among descendents and relatives (Becker, 1974, 1991).[4] Another hypothesis, mostly known in literature as the hypothesis of 'generational stake,' argues in favour of support to be directed mainly from the older family members to the younger generations (Bengtson and Schrader, 1982). This hypothesis however allows bi-directional flows as well—with younger generations helping their older parents.

Without going much into these hypotheses, it needs to be mentioned that the tests for altruistically guided resource flows still remain mired by various contradictions and inconclusive empirical findings.[5] Two studies may be cited to exemplify these contradictions.

Supporting the idea of altruistic exchanges, for instance, a study by Hogan, Eggebeen and Clogg (1993) found that, other things being equal, adult children with widowed or infirm parents helped more than those whose parents were not suffering from these conditions. Contradicting this viewpoint, Spitze and Logan (1989) have noted in a study that women's early life investment in care giving and kin keeping activities is a strategy to create obligation in men and children for later assistance and help in old age.

Another competing hypothesis in the context of inter-generational flows relates to the 'exchange relationship.' This hypothesis considers these flows more as a reciprocal process. It also suggests that the exchange may be immediate, circumstantial or may occur over the life

---

4. Becker's model was originally related to the benevolence of parents. There is however no reason why this notion cannot be extended to other family members.

5. For a very comprehensive discussion on some of these issues including data limitations and lack of conclusive support on different perspectives of altruism, see Eggebeen and Davey (1998). More recently, Saad (2005) has tried to examine some of these issues using a set of data from SABE surveys of four Latin American countries.

span (Cox, 1987 and Cox and Rank, 1992). Which of the two—the altruism or the exchange based relationship—is closer to reality is however not very clear from most of the literature available to us.

The inconclusive nature of these hypotheses is further highlighted by our own analysis. As noted, we encounter a lack of altruistic behaviour when it comes to the living arrangements of elderly women (Table 2.11). Our own survey data show that of the adults aged below 60 surveyed, those in the higher age brackets were less likely to take on the responsibilities of their old (equation 2 in Table 6.2). Many others from the same survey however negated these findings as they felt that caring for the aged was their moral responsibility. Given these contradictions, we tried to analyse further the altruism implied in responses made by the younger respondents in our survey. We undertook this exercise by assessing the health care support provided by the younger children and grandchildren to ailing parents (or grand parents) without any tangible assets or earnings. If support is found to be greater in cases where the ailing persons happen to be financially dependent and unsecured, it may be presumed as altruism or benevolence—a situation closer to what has been argued in the study by Hogan, Eggebeen and Clogg (1993).

Hospitalisation of Elderly Dependents and its Financing

Altruistically, health care or such other needs of the aged need not be an outcome of his or her socio-financial status. These principles are however subject to violations as may be noticed from instances cited earlier. To ascertain some of these issues and their magnitude, especially in the Indian context, we tried to work through the following question: Is non-altruism taking over elderly support in India? Or, in other words, do support providers expect something tangible in return for what they do? And if the answer is yes, does it happen routinely? In response to both these questions, we present below the results of a simple exercise based on the household survey in Delhi. Methodologically, this exercise was conducted in two stages, and relates to ageing dependents hospitalised for treatment over a specified reference period.

Financial Security Index (FSI) of the Aged

This exercise was carried out in two stages. First, a FSI was constructed of the sample aged to distinguish between:

(i) completely family dependent with no own source of income (i.e., unsecured), and

(ii) persons with one or more income sources—self and spouse combined.

The following income sources were used to construct the index:[6]

1. earnings through self or spouse's work,

2. employer's pension,

3. income from family business,

4. annuity or investment earnings,

5. income from real estate, and

6. farm income.

Based on these income sources, we tried to construct a FSI of the sample elderly. The range of this index lies from 0 to 6. The maximum value (i.e., 6) will be assigned to persons drawing income from all the six sources listed above. Against this, a minimum index value 0 will be given to persons without income. Financially, such a person will be treated as completely unsecured and family dependent.

FSI Values of the Sample Aged

Table 6.6a gives the distribution of the elderly by their FSI values. One of the most significant points to notice from this table is that two-third share of the elderly were completely unsecured with grave risk of income vulnerability and family dependence. Another 31 per cent have merely one source of income. Persons with two or more sources of earning are simply negligible. We may also notice that nobody in the sample has more than three income sources. Also, the situation worsens for persons aged 70 or more (see the last column of Table 6.6a).

Sample men and women distributed by their FSI values are given in Table 6.6b. This table clearly reveals a strong gender dimension with women turning out to be more financially vulnerable than men. We notice that more than two-thirds of the elderly women do not have any independent source of income. In the case of men, this proportion is simply half of that. In other words, women are likely to remain more critically dependent on familial altruism.

---

6. We do not include destitute pension or support provided by NGOs in this exercise. Both these sources are considered here as out of self or family ambits.

Table 6.6a

Distribution of 60+ and 70+ by FSI: Persons

FSI values	60 Years & more		70 Years & More	
	Number	*%*	*Number*	*%*
0 (no independent income)	909	65.6	380	70.8
1 (income from 1 source)	432	31.2	142	26.4
2 (with two income sources)	43	3.1	14	2.6
3 (with three income sources)	1	0.1	1	0.2
4 (with four income sources)	0	0.0	0	0.0
5 (with five income sources)	0	0.0	0	0.0
6 (with six income sources)	0	0.0	0	0.0
Column Total	**1385**	**100.0**	**537**	**100.0**

Source: IEG/CIDA Ageing Survey (2002).

Table 6.6b

Sex-wise Distribution of 60+ by FSI

FSI Values	Male (%)	Female (%)	N (M+F)
0 (or no independent income)	33.7	66.3	909
1 (persons with one income source)	280	152	432
2 (with two income sources)	30	13	43
3 (with three income sources)	1	0	1
4 (with four income sources)	-	-	-
5 (with five income sources)	-	-	-
6 (with six income sources)	-	-	-
Column Total (%)	**44.5**	**55.5**	**1385**

Source: IEG/CIDA Ageing Survey (2002).

Out-of-Pocket Expenditure on Medical Care

At the second stage of this exercise, we tried to cross tabulate the out-of-pocket financial support provided by the children and grand children on the treatment of older parents or relatives by their FSI rankings.[7] A reference period of 30 days preceding the date of survey was used to collect the expenditure data. One of the objectives of this

---

7. For doing that, we constructed an altruism dummy where the variable takes the value 1 if the children and the grandchildren have supported the cost of hospitalisation or non-ambulatory medical treatment; takes the value 0 otherwise.

analysis was to make an assessment about filial support given to persons with low financial rankings. Lack of support to the financially insecure may be viewed as a contradiction to the socio-moralist stands emanating from Figures 6.2 and 6.3.[8]

Table-6.7a cross-tabulates the health care supports for the aged by their FSI rankings. Out of a total of 1385 sample aged, 669 received these supports over the reference period. About 16 per cent of those medically treated did not receive any support from their families—a majority of them of course had some personal income. The children or grand children supported the rest of them—a big majority without any own-source income. The chi-square test, used to indicate the role of FSI in familial decisions, confirms that children opt to support more unsecured parents.[9] To some extent, this finding appears to coincide with the argument made by Hogan, Eggebeen and Clogg (1993).

Table 6.7a

*Expenditure on Medical Care by Children
and the FSI Rankings of the Old*

Medical Expenditure	Ranking of Aged by Financial Security Index				Row Total
	0	1	2	3	
No Expenditure by Children					
Number (Persons)	36	63	7	0	106
%	8.9	26.6	26.9	0	15.8
Expenditure Supported by Children					
Number (Persons)	369	174	19	1	563
%	91.1	73.4	73.1	100.0	84.2
Column Total	**405**	**237**	**26**	**1**	**669**
%	100.0	100.0	100.0	100.0	100.0
Chi^2 (3) = 37.770			P-value = 0.003		

Source: IEG/CIDA Ageing Survey (2002).

---

8. It may however be noted that many of those failing to meet the cost of parental treatment may themselves be financially weak.

9. A further analysis of this data reveals that over 42 per cent of the total elderly —mostly from the mixed category—have used private medical facilities for their treatment. Apparently, therefore, the altruism shown by the younger adults in caring for the health of their parents has not been very much affected by cost considerations.

Table 6.7b

*Cross-Classification of Expenditure on Medical Care by FSI Values
(Persons Aged < 70 and > 70)*

Medical Expenditure	Age Group: 60-69 FSI Values			Row Total	Age Group: 70 & More FSI Values				Row Total
	0	1	2		0	1	2	3	
No. Expenditure									
Persons	22	45	5	72	14	18	2	0	34
%	9.9	28.0	31.3	18.0	7.7	23.7	20.0	0.0	12.6
Family Expenditure									
Persons	201	116	11	328	168	58	8	1	235
%	90.1	72.1	68.8	82.0	92.3	76.3	80.0	100.0	87.4
Total	223	161	16	400	182	76	10	1	269
%	100.0	100.0	100.0	100.0	100.0	100.0	100.0	100.0	100.0

$Chi^2(2) = 20.700$ P-value = 0.000 $Chi^2(2) = 13.066$ P-value = 0.004

Source: IEG/CIDA Ageing Survey (2002).

Table 6.7c

*Gender-wise Cross-Classification of Expenditure on
Medical Care by FSI Values*

Expenditure	Male FSI (60+)				Row Total
	0	1	2	3	
No Exp. (%)	27.3	65.5	7.3	0.0	55
Family Exp. (%)	50.0	44.0	5.6	0.4	234
Total %	45.7	48.1	5.9	0.3	289

$Chi^2 (3) = 9.750$ P-value = 0.021

Expenditure	Female FSI (60+)				Row Total
	0	1	2	3	
No. Exp. (%)	41.2	52.9	5.9	0	51
Family Exp. (%)	76.6	21.6	1.8	0	329
Total %	71.8	25.8	2.4	0	380

$Chi^2 (2) = 27.620$ P-value = 0.000

Source: IEG/CIDA Ageing Survey (2002).

As a further extension of this analysis, we tried to re-tabulate these results: (i) by gender, and (ii) by the two distinct categories of the aged—namely the young old (60-69) and the old (70+). Results of these exercises are shown in Tables 6.7b and 6.7c, respectively.

These results further substantiate our earlier findings suggesting inverse linkages between the filial support and the FSI rankings of the ailing aged. A big majority of the aged in both the categories – 60-69 and 70+ – are able to receive support from their siblings. The same is true for elderly women. Elderly women are in fact placed better than their male counterparts in this regard. Chi-square results also indicate the same. The children also support a good number of persons with higher FSI ranks can also be noted from these tables.

6.5. Concluding Observations

This chapter was basically devoted to highlight the views of non-elderly persons on a set of issues including the way they foresee their own ageing, and caring for the aged, especially in the current economic regime characterised by decelerating growth of quality employment and informalisation of the labour market. Four specific issues were subjected to empirical scrutiny:

(i)   how far are the non-aged willing to support and look after their old?

(ii) what motivational factors are at work in this direction?

(iii) is there altruism in elderly care? and

(iv) what views were held by the younger adults on planned ageing?

Our results clearly bring out the positive role played by socio-religious and moral factors in motivating people, especially the younger siblings, to help the aged. A very large majority of the responding younger adults, for example, have agreed that caring for the aged is their socio-moral responsibility. This sense of their confessed morality was further tested in our subsequent analysis by probing the cases of hospitalisation required by their elderly family members—both men and women. We observed that the younger siblings have helped in accessing hospitalisation care for their ailing elders, especially women, even if they had no tangible or intangible wealth to bequeath. This leads us to infer that the sense of altruism still exists between the young and the old—that too in a cosmopolitan society like Delhi. Stretching this argument a little further, it implies that the socio-moral institutions, particularly the religious leadership of different faiths, may have a role in fostering the sense of altruism in elderly care. Educational institutions, especially at the elementary level, may also do the same.

In regard to planned ageing, our results are somewhat hazy. It is obvious that the idea of long-term savings to earn post-retirement annuities is still in its infancy and confined mostly to people from higher income households. Further, the knowledge about long-term retirement linked savings instruments is also limited.

7

Public Responses to Old Age Income Security

7.1. Introduction

Responding to fast emerging changes in the age composition and the increasing proportion of ageing population, the central and state governments in India have for the past several years been engaged in drawing up a set of policy initiatives to help older persons. Further, there have been commitments at various national and international fora by the Government to assimilate the aged in the process of development. Internationally, this commitment was particularly more resounding at the time of the Second World Assembly on Ageing in Madrid (Spain) in April 2002.[1] At the national level, apart from some direct measures of protective subsidies and income transfers, the Union Government has also drawn up a NPOP in January 1999.[2] This policy underscores the need for public initiatives in areas of financial security, health care, nutrition, shelter, education, welfare and safety of life and property of the aged. Despite all these commitments, policy initiatives and guidelines, there remain serious physical and financial issues faced by a majority of the aged in India.

This part of the study, however, does not attempt to provide a chronology of what and how much has so far been done in India for the aged in terms of the measures or action plans suggested in various national and international policy pronouncements. The focus here is rather narrowed to basically examine: (i) a few of the public funded income security plans for the aged, (ii) the reformist measures to make these plans fiscally sustainable, and (iii) the efficacy of these reforms against the backdrop of many serious issues including large-scale old age poverty, poor physical and functional health, growing role of the market without a foolproof safety net and so on. While a

---

1. For the key provisions of this conference, see Appendix A-2.1.
2. The NPOP has been summarised in Chapter 1.

few of these issues have already been spelt out in the preceding chapters, it may well be re-emphasised that the additions in the cohort of the aged over the next few decades would mostly comprise the baby boomers of yesteryears—the bulk of them mired in poor life course experiences. Their reliance on subsidies and public transfers is therefore expected to remain higher. Within this perspective, we try to discuss below the two public funded major income security plans for the aged. These are:

1. destitute old age pension as part of the National Social Assistance Scheme (NSAS); and

2. post-retirement income security plans for government employees, suggested reforms and their embedding questions.

In addition, we will also discuss the decline in deposit rates in response to lower inflation levels in the economy, judged on the basis of the wholesale price indices (WPI), which are largely weighed in favour of industrial commodities.[3] Three significant questions are at the root of this discussion. First, does the WPI—used to judge the inflationary conditions in the economy—reflect the prices faced by ordinary consumers in the country? Second, would it be justifiable to assume a semblance between the baskets/weights of commodities used to compute the WPI and the goods and services required by ordinary persons—especially the elderly? The third question relates to the stability in prices and inflationary conditions in the economy. Apparently, there have been considerable variations in the inflationary condition over the past years, causing difficulties to the reliance on savings by the elderly.

7.2. Income Security for the Destitute Elderly: Emerging Issues

Like in many other developing countries, ageing in India is projected to follow an accelerated pace over the coming years (see Table 1.3). The preceding discussion has clearly revealed that a large fraction of this population would continue to face in the coming years many serious issues including financial dependence, poor old age health and impaired functional status. Despite this, public response to

---

3. The weight assigned to the manufactured commodities turns out to be 63.75 per cent in the current wholesale price index (WPI) (see Appendix Table A-7.3b). We will take up this issue later in this discussion.

many of these issues, and especially old age poverty, remains at best elusive.[4]

Constitutionally, the poor—especially the destitute—are the responsibility of the state. The Constitution of India, especially entry 24 in list III of Schedule VII, deals with many of these issues including the welfare of labour, provident fund, maternity benefits, disability and old age pension. Article 41 of the Directive Principles of State Policy reasserts some of these welfare-enhancing roles of the government including social security for the aged.[5] Obligated by these constitutional requirements, the central and state governments have designed a number of contributory and public funded measures for the income security of different social groups. A few of the more significant for our reference include the Workmen's Compensation Act (1923), Payment of Gratuity Act (1972), Maternity Benefit Act (1962), National Social Assistance Programme (1995), Annapurna Programme (1999), Employees' Estate Insurance Scheme (ESIS, 1948), etc. In addition, there are provisions of gratuity, provident fund (PF) and pension plans for employees working in government organisations, public sector undertakings and organised private sector establishments.[6] As we are basically concerned in this discussion with old age income security, we will largely confine ourselves to (i) non-contributory transfer benefits provided to the destitute aged, and (ii) retirement benefits available to the government employees. Some of the reforms suggested recently to make these schemes more sustainable are also discussed.

Plans for the Destitute Elderly by States

Income security for the aged in India is currently designed at two levels. One is the centrally financed national social assistance scheme (NSAS).[7] And the other relates to the welfare activities funded by the

---

4. We will further highlight this argument while discussing the National Old Age Pension Scheme (NOAPS) and the ceiling procedure adopted by the government to put a cap on the size of the beneficiaries.

5. For more specific details, see pages 1 and 2 of the Senior Citizens' Guide by the HelpAge India (2000).

6. For further description of various social security schemes in India and South Asia, see Rajan (2002).

7. Introduced in 1995, the entire NSAS comprises the following three schemes: (i) National Old Age Pension Scheme (NOAPS), (ii) National Family Benefit Scheme (NFBS), and (iii) National Maternal Benefit Scheme (NMBS). We will however focus in this discussion only on the NOAPS.

states themselves (Rajan, 2002; Parikh, 2002 and HelpAge India, 2000). One of these activities also includes the old age pension programmes for the destitute elderly. Owing to the growing fiscal constraints, however, this programme remains largely dented in many states by meagre per capita pension amount.[8] Further, this amount varies from one state to another, raising questions about the underlying factors used to determine the pension amount by the states. In addition, there are signs of administrative mismanagement and limited coverage of the beneficiaries as well (Kumar, 1998; HelpAge India, 2003).

Inter-state Variations in Pension Amount and Qualifying Age

The entitlement age and the per capita pension amount in 15 major states and the NCT of Delhi are given in Table 7.1. Going by these details, three categories of states may be identified: (i) those without their own contributions towards the pension fund such as Andhra Pradesh and Assam,[9] (ii) those paying a very meagre amount of up to Rs. 100, and (iii) those with an amount exceeding Rs. 100. As may be noticed, the number of states with no contributions are only few. All other states contribute at least some amount from their own resources—varying from a minimum of Rs. 25 by Bihar, Karnataka, Orissa and West Bengal to a maximum of Rs. 200 by Gujarat.

Like the pension amount, Table 7.1 also indicates considerable variations in the entitlement age for pension by the states. While a majority of them including Uttar Pradesh, Bihar, Haryana, Delhi, Gujarat, West Bengal and Tamil Nadu decided upon 60 as the cut-off age for both men and women, there are others—Andhra Pradesh, Karnataka, Kerala and Orissa—with age limit raised to 65 years. Yet another group of states (Madhya Pradesh, Maharashtra, Punjab and Rajasthan) follow a differential age criterion with a lower age limit fixed for women beneficiaries (Table 7.1).

---

8. Even though there has been a recent hike in overall contribution by the Centre towards the National Social Assistance Programme, this problem persists.

9. These states are simply relying on the Centre's contribution of Rs.75 per person per month drawn as part of the National Social Assistance Scheme.

Table 7.1

Per Person Contribution Towards Destitute Pension by Major States:
Variations in Pension Amount and Age of Eligibility

States	Per Person Contribution (Rs.)	Minimum Age of Eligibility	
		Male	Female
Andhra Pradesh	0	65	65
Assam	0	65	60
Bihar	25	60	60
Gujarat	200	60	60
Haryana	125	60	60
Karnataka	25	65	65
Kerala	35	65	65
Madhya Pradesh	75	60	50
Maharashtra	175	65	60
Orissa	25	65	65
Punjab	125	65	60
Rajasthan*	125	58	55
Tamil Nadu	125	60	60
Uttar Pradesh	50	60	60
West Bengal	25	60	60
NCT of Delhi**	125	60	60

Source: Rajya Sabha Starred Question Number 422, dated August 22, 2001.

Note: * Rajasthan is contributing Rs. 150 towards the females' pension.

** Currently, Delhi is contributing Rs. 275 per person.

Inter-state Differentials in Per Capita Destitute Pension

A question may be asked here: what is the explanation for differentials in age and pension amount paid by the states? To be precise: does it indicate variations in cost of living? That is, are the costs of living in lower pension states relatively less? Or, does it represent their fiscal health? A similar question arises in the case of the entitlement age. While the received literature on ageing in India has nothing specific to add in answer to these questions, a cursory attempt is made below with the help of a simple regression analysis linking the state's contributions with its financial health, and the level of old age poverty.[10] We postulate that the pension amount is

---

10. Readers are warned that this is merely an illustrative exercise with limited theoretical justification.

expected to remain low in states with (i) higher old age poverty, and (ii) low levels of revenue generation. We argue that the claimants for transfer money in higher poverty states will remain high and, therefore, states will have to reduce the pension amount to accommodate a greater number of beneficiaries. The simple model is described in Box 7.1.

<table>
<tr><td colspan="3" align="center">Box 7.1

Variations in Pension Amount by States: Ordinary Least Square (OLS) Regression</td></tr>
<tr><td>Model</td><td>Dependent Variable</td><td>Explanatory Variables</td></tr>
<tr><td>OLS Regression</td><td>States' per capita pension amount (Table 7.1).</td><td>SF or State's finance (expected sign: positive).Old age poverty, i.e., PCMCE below Rs. 250 (expected sign: negative).</td></tr>
</table>

Data Sources

The data on states' finances (SF) are obtained from the Reserve Bank of India (2002) for 1999-2000 after combining the: (i) total tax revenue, (ii) total non-tax revenue, and (iii) transfer of resources from the Centre including shareable taxes and grants.[11] The market borrowings and loans—gross or net—from the Centre are not included. Similarly, we do not include devolution of resources from the Centre to exclude borrowings, debt and contingent liabilities arising from certain state guarantees.

The share of below poverty older persons is obtained from Table 1.13, and includes persons with PCMCE below Rs. 250.

The per capita pension amount of all the 16 states is given in Table 7.1.

The Results

The estimated coefficients are presented in Table 7.2. Interestingly, the relationship appears to hold for the pension amount and the level of old age poverty in the respective states. The two turn out to be

---

11. See Statements 13, 16 and 18 of State Finances published by the Reserve Bank of India (2002).

inversely related suggesting that a higher share of poor elderly may tend to reduce the per capita pension amount. In contrast, the state's revenue (SF) has nothing significant to do in the underlying context. It may however be noticed that the coefficient yields the expected sign.

Table 7.2

OLS Regression Results Number of Observations 16

Variables	Coefficients	Std. Error	t-statistics
Constant	118.39	41.93	2.882
PCMCE	- 7.78	2.46	- 3.159**
SF	2.07E-10	1.78 E-10	1.160
$R^2 = 0.531$		$\overline{R}^2 = 0.427$	

** Significant at the 1 per cent level.

Programme Management by States: Poor Funding and Underutilised Funds

In addition to inadequate pension amounts and their variations by states, this programme appears to have suffered from poor management as well. This can be noticed from Table 7.3 that, *inter alia*, gives the under-utilisation of the national pension fund allocated to the states. Barring a few instances, this table suggests considerable differences between the allocations and release of funds on the one hand, and the extent of their actual utilisation by states on the other. Despite being less conclusive because of its cross-sectional nature, the figures presented in Table 7.3 clearly reveal the under-utilisation of funds by states as one of the major policy issues for the income security of the aged.

Table 7.3 also suggests very meagre per capita allocation of the pension fund (column 7, Table 7.3). Using state-wise projection of 60+ populations (Registrar General, 1996), we notice that the per capita allocation of the pension fund varies from a minimum of Rs. 1.60 in Gujarat to Rs. 10 in Orissa. At the all-India level, this amount was barely Rs. 6 a month. By any standard, it tends to give an impression that old age income security did not receive the attention it deserved while public finances were being allocated.

Table 7.3

Under-utilisation of Funds by States on Old Age Pension Scheme: 1999-2000

States	Pension Fund (Rs. in Lakh)			Fund Utilisation (%)		60+ Population (in 000)*	Per Capita Allocations (Monthly)
	Allocation (1)	Release (2)	Expenditure (3)	(2)/(1) (4)	(3)/(2) (5)	(6)	(7)
Andhra Pradesh	4361.8	4361.8	2951.1	100.0	67.7	5196	6.99
Assam	827.0	599.9	465.8	72.5	77.6	1359	5.08
Bihar	6877.2	5002.2	4701.4	72.7	94.0	5857	9.78
Gujarat	561.6	250.8	127.3	44.7	50.8	2937	1.59
Haryana	535.8	316.1	169.6	59.0	53.7	1395	3.20
Karnataka	2959.6	2934.5	1679.2	99.2	57.2	3591	6.87
Kerala	1396.3	1054.0	1035.1	75.5	98.2	2969	3.92
Madhya Pradesh	4585.5	4377.4	3330.5	95.5	76.1	5100	7.49
Maharashtra	4158.5	2589.2	1493.0	62.3	57.7	6274	5.53
Orissa	3120.6	2696.2	1887.1	86.4	70.0	2534	10.26
Punjab	386.8	193.4	0.0	50.0	0.0	1703	1.89
Rajasthan	1474.5	1041.4	87.0	70.6	8.4	3250	3.78
Tamil Nadu	3276.0	1886.5	2475.6	57.6	131.2	4912	5.56
Uttar Pradesh	8264.8	5693.4	5645.8	68.9	99.2	10886	6.33
West Bengal	3312.5	2626.5	2138.5	79.3	81.4	4895	5.64
Delhi	249.6	124.8	200.0	50.0	160.3	1127#	1.84
All India	**47623.6**	**36644.5**	**28704.4**	**76.9**	**78.3**	**66673**	**5.95**

Source: Ministry of Rural Development's Annual Report (1999-2000). Figures are provisional.

* Size of 60+ Population is obtained from the projections made by the Technical Group on Population, and relates to the year 1999 (see Registrar General of India, 1996) .

60+ population for Delhi was obtained from the National Family Health Survey (NFHS-2, 1998-99).

Non-Pension Plans to Benefit the Poor Aged

In addition to the destitute pension, there are a few special schemes run by states for poor widows and widowers. One such scheme, for example, is the Sanjay Gandhi Niradhar Anudan Yojna by the Maharashtra Government. Similar schemes are also available in states including Karnataka, West Bengal and Kerala. These plans are restricted to persons without any tangible source of income and include those below 60 as well.

As a food security measure for the poor elderly, the Centre has started running since March 1999 an 'Annapurna Scheme,' which entitles the below poverty aged to get 10 kilogramme of wheat or rice monthly free of cost. Also, there are subsidies provided to the aged while traveling by rail and air. The National Policy on Older Persons (NPOP) has also empowered the aged to seek legal redressal against personal misdemeanour or parental abuse. In pursuance of this, the Central government is currently in the process of introducing suitable legislation to make parental care mandatory for the immediate family and siblings.[12] Most of these schemes however bear no or limited statistical details. We will therefore remain mostly confined to NOAPS in the rest of this discussion.

National Old Age Pension Scheme (NOAPS): Eligibility Criteria and Formula for State-wise Fixation of Target Beneficiaries

The NOAPS, launched on 15 August, 1995, subjects its beneficiaries to satisfy the following three conditions:

1. The beneficiary—male or female—should not be less than 65 years of age,

2. The beneficiary must be destitute[13]—i.e., those with little or no regular means of subsistence from his or her own source of income or through financial support from family members, and

3. The amount of pension for claiming the central assistance by states is Rs.75 per month. States may however contribute

---

12. In pursuance of the provision of Article 41 read with Entry 23 of the Concurrent List (Schedule VII) of the Constitution of India, a model legislation – The Older persons (Maintenance, Care & Protection) Bill, 2005 – is currently under consideration of the Government. One of the thrust areas of the Bill is to promote the maintenance, care and protection of the older persons.

13. States have no or very limited discretion to define destitution.

further and provide higher benefits as per their financial resources as shown in Table 7.1.

NOAPS, a hundred per cent centrally sponsored programme, was designed to ensure the minimum national standard of social assistance. It is also used to provide opportunities for linking social assistance packages to poverty alleviation schemes in the country. Further, the scheme is mostly implemented on the basis of the bottom-up approach by involving panchayats and other local bodies with additional provisions to seek assistance in its management from voluntary agencies.

Despite all these qualities and assured funding, this scheme severely suffers for two reasons: (i) it involves complex administrative procedures and, therefore, proves especially difficult for the illiterates[14], and (ii) the size of programme beneficiaries is capped artificially by using an arbitrary ceiling formula. We briefly describe this formula below.

As was pointed out, NOAPS, a centrally funded scheme, was designed to help the destitute elderly. While doing this, the criterion used to determine destitution remains strictly within the Centre's domain. In addition, the Centre has also imposed a numerical ceiling on the number of state-wise beneficiaries by using a somewhat arbitrary ceiling formula. In effect, this formula serves as a mechanism to keep many destitute outside the programme even if they satisfy the criterion used to define destitution (Dreze, 2003).[15]

The ceiling formula, used by the Centre to decide the size of target beneficiaries in each state, is written as:

Numerical Ceiling = Total Population × Poverty Ratio × proportion of 65 and above × 0. 5

Using the above-mentioned formula, we tried to compute the size of below poverty aged in each of 15 major states, and then compare them with the target beneficiaries of the corresponding states drawn

---

14. For some of these difficulties, see HelpAge India 2003).

15. In a newspaper write-up, Dreze (2003) has noted that 2,421 applications were pending for the old age pension in the Lesliganj Block (Palamu, Jharkhand State) at the time he was visiting the area. "As the quota of 1663 pensions assigned to the block was fully utilised, new pensions are sanctioned only when a former pensioner dies. Assuming a mortality rate of 50 per 1000 among the elderly, this means that a new applicant would have to wait for about 30 years for a pension".

by the Centre.[16] Table 7.4 gives these details. Three major observations emerge from this comparison. One, the ceiling formula

Table 7.4

*Gap between the NOAPS Target Beneficiaries and
Below Poverty Elderly: 1999-00*

Major States	Share of 65+ in Total Population[#] (1)	Below Poverty Population* (2)	Below Poverty 65+ (3)	Half of Below Poverty 65+ (4)	Target Beneficiaries of NOAPS** (5)	Under & Over Coverage$ (6)
Andhra Pradesh	0.0451	14055367	633897	316949	466000	47.0
Assam	0.0343	10362925	355448	177724	84967	-52.2
Bihar	0.038	46469617	1765845	882923	715752	-18.9
Gujarat	0.0397	7481121	297000	148500	63862	-57.0
Haryana	0.0535	2324122	124341	62170	31359	-49.6
Karnataka	0.0468	13267113	620901	310450	195235	-37.1
Kerala	0.0641	4638417	297323	148661	119507	-19.6
Madhya Pradesh	0.0626	29084886	1820714	910357	586400	-35.6
Maharashtra	0.0449	26034839	1168964	584482	70714	-87.9
Orissa	0.0465	16545328	769358	384679	330272	-14.1
Punjab	0.0492	1411050	69424	34712	32859	-5.3
Rajasthan	0.04	10832196	433288	216644	451325	108.3
Tamil Nadu	0.0519	13244180	687373	343686	430300	25.2
Uttar Pradesh	0.0426	55470212	2363031	1181516	940539	-20.4
West Bengal	0.041	25202978	1033322	516661	350810	-32.1
India	0.0448	283408092	12696683	6348341	4980951	-21.5

Note: ** Target Beneficiaries were obtained from the website *www.indiastat.com*

   \# For age specific projection of population, see Report of the Technical Group on Population Projection, Registrar General (1996).

   * Economic Survey (2002-03).

   $ Column 6 is computed as: (col.5 – col.4/col.4) x 100. Values with minus sign represent the extent of under-coverage.

assumes parity between the old age poverty and the general poverty. In reality, however, this may not be the case. Intra-household studies have shown that aged men and women are far more vulnerable and lack bargaining strength—especially in crisis situations (Agarwal, 1990 and Visaria, 1980). The second observation relates to the discriminatory procedure, which is inbuilt in the ceiling formula—

---

16.   The state-wise number of target beneficiaries in 1999-2000 was provided in response to an un-starred Lok Sabha Question (Number 4514, dated 22 August, 2000). See *www.indiastat.com*.

namely, only half of the below poverty aged are considered as worthy for pension benefits. The remaining half is considered as drawing support from one or the other source. This leaves district administrations and Panchayats with considerable leverage for subjective decisions. Thirdly, the number of target beneficiaries falls short of the ceiling population in all the states barring Andhra Pradesh, Tamil Nadu and Rajasthan. This is clearly revealed by Figure 7.1. It suggests the insecurity and pathetic financial condition suffered by the aged in this country.

As a whole, therefore, this discussion strongly suggests the need for evolving a public pillared social assistance system with greater understanding about the interface between ageing and poverty. It also suggests the need for suitable amendments in the ceiling formula with an attempt by the states to bring the entire below poverty aged under the NOAPS umbrella.[17] Attempts may also be made to develop financing strategies to help the destitute elderly.

The Annapurna scheme, yet another centrally funded means tested plan to provide food security to the poor elderly, was initially expected to cover a total of about 660,000 destitute elderly. However, this programme is still in its infancy and confined to only a limited number of states (Rajan, 2002).

Figure 7.1

Gap between the Below Poverty Aged and the NOAPS Target Beneficiaries: 1999-2000

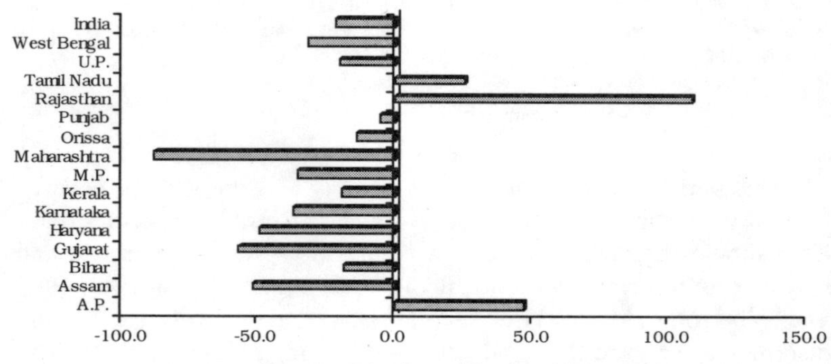

Source: Table 7.4 (col. 6).

---

17. Recently, there have been indications that the Central Government has decided to withdraw the ceiling formula and transfer this entire programme to the states.

7.3. Income Security for Superannuating Employees: Existing Provisions and Proposed Reforms

As part of the income security cover for superannuating employees in major establishments, the Central and State governments in India have been making provisions for two major benefits. These are: (i) an inflation adjusted post-retirement pension cover with benefit rate fixed at around 50 per cent of the terminal wage, and (ii) a contributory provident fund with defined benefits.[18] The former—based on a pay-as-you-go (PAYG) system—has been a scheme solely financed through budgetary allocations by the respective governments. Despite marginally declining public sector employment,[19] the growing burden of pension obligations on government finances has remained a matter of intense debate in recent years.[20] With faster demographic ageing, growing life span, and also because of the restricted investment options with public fund managers, the problem is expected to compound further. As a solution, several measures have been suggested recently with provisions to make the entire pension system a fully paid self-contributory venture, without a defined benefit, and run by private fund managers under the control of an empowered regulatory body. These measures were largely adopted on lines suggested by a team of experts working in the late nineties on *Old Age Social and Income Security Project*, popularly known as project OASIS. There have however been some doubts about these measures, originally borrowed from the pension plan designed decades ago in Latin America by the Peru government.

Project OASIS

Besides questioning the long-term viability of the existing PAYG pension provisions, the debate around retirement and old age income

---

18. About a total of 177 notified industries and classes of establishments covered by the Employees Provident Fund and the Miscellaneous Provision Act (1952), and establishments employing 20 or more workers are mandated to subscribe to the Employees' Provident Fund Scheme, the Employees' Pension Scheme (1995), and the Employees' Deposit Linked Insurance Scheme (1996). For further discussions on these provisionings, see Rajan, Mishra and Sharma (1999), World Bank (2001), etc.

19. Combined employment of the Central and State governments has marginally declined from 10.75 million in 1995 to 10.69 million in 2001 (Economic Survey, 2002-03, Table 3.1).

20. See, for example, Srinivas and Thomas (2003).

security issues has also been evolved to raise concern about the lack of a pension cover for the workforce outside the organised economy. Responding to this debate, the Union Ministry of Social Justice and Empowerment (Government of India) has commissioned a study on old age social and income security (OASIS) to a panel of experts under the leadership of P.K. Dave. The Committee presented its report to the Government in January 2000 with a number of recommendations in line with the Peruvian system. Some of the critical elements of these recommendations are as under:

- A portable individual retirement account (IRA) with a unique number that will stay with the individual through life.

- The individual would save and accumulate assets into this account subject to a minimum of Rs. 100 per contribution and Rs. 500 in total accretions per annum.

- A sound regulatory mechanism to ensure the safety of the accumulated fund.

- Centres for collection of fund with facilities to open, and access details about the IRA in rural and urban areas.

- A centralised record keeping system.

- Multiple fund managers with participation from the private financial institutions as well.

OASIS Recommendations

Three issues undermine the tenacity of the OASIS project and its recommendations:

One, most of the suggested mechanisms in the OASIS committee report relate to future cohorts of the working population. But what will happen to those who are already employed and in their working life span? The authors of this report have failed to address this issue explicitly.

The second issue relates to the whole gamut of pension fund management and its transaction cost incurred by the fund managers. While the Committee has argued in favour of public involvement to provide infrastructural support as means to minimise operational cost, these are mere conjectures. In many Latin American countries with privately managed pension plans, the overall transaction cost turns out to be much higher, impacting the terminal benefits paid to the account holders.

The third major problem may arise with investment policies. Should or shouldn't the fund be invested in high-risk policies such as equities and private bonds? Supposing that the risk bearing funds are capable of yielding a higher terminal yield, what should be the right combination of debt-equity ratio? This question draws relevance on two important considerations: (i) the stock market in India remains volatile, and (ii) the regulatory system in the country—and in many other countries as well—is not completely reliable. Given these, suggestions such as private fund management and equity investments need greater scrutiny. Further, the issue of whether Government will need to bear the contingent liability in case of diminution of investments also remains unanswered. But, given the multi-decade nature of pension investment, this aspect bears serious consideration.

A committee was set-up in 2001 by the Government to evolve a procedure for the implementation of the OASIS project recommendations. Following this, Government has declared in February 2003 its intent to introduce a new pension system in the country—especially for civil servants.

Civil Servants' Pension Provisions: Proposed Reforms

As has been mentioned, the growing escalations in the overall cost of pension obligations have led the Government to consider redesigning the pension system on lines suggested by the OASIS Project Report. In addition, there were two subsequent committees: (i) the Insurance Regulatory and Development Authority Committee (2001), and (ii) the Bhattacharya Committee (2002). These committees were constituted to provide a roadmap for implementation of the framework suggested by the OASIS report. Currently, Government is in the process of implementing this framework for all of its civilian employees.[21]

Pension Reforms

The Union Budget of 2003-04 has proposed the introduction of an earnings related and defined contribution pension system based on: (i) individual retirement account (IRA), (ii) multiple product choice for the account holders, (iii) professional fund managers with

---

21. It was originally proposed to implement the new pension system (NPS) from April 2004. However, its implementation has been delayed by the Ministry of Finance (Government of India) for further scrutiny on suggestions of the Parliamentary Standing Committee.

participation from private financial institutions, (iv) a regulatory authority, and (v) portability through a centralised record keeping system. Government finally approved this scheme on 23 August, 2003. A Pension Fund Regulatory and Development Authority (PFRDA) was also suggested on the lines of many Latin American countries to supervise the functioning of the new pension system and regulate its overall management. It was premised that the inbuilt competitive environment, professional fund management, and widely dispersed investment portfolios would help subscribers to obtain higher terminal yield. In addition, this new system is also expected to contribute with greater aggregate savings, boost overall capital accumulation in the economy and bring rapid development in efficient financial market with easy access to loans for long gestation projects. Government however remains wary of offering any guarantee either in the form of minimum benefit paid to the subscribers or towards the security of their subscriptions.

Pension Reforms–Issues

As it is, underlying the reforms introduced to modify the pay-as-you-go pension system are several questions. This may also affect the multi-decade horizon of the pension investment—especially among those with poor financial literacy. Some of these questions include the following.

- One, India is severely lacking in terms of a multi-pillared income security system for the aged. The World Bank, while suggesting moving away from a completely defined and non-funded pension plan, has favoured systematic reform by pursuing a multi-pillared social security system (World Bank, 1994). The major pillars of this system comprise:

    (i) A mandatory, publicly managed and tax financed social security system

    (ii) A mandatory, pay-as-you-go and privately managed system

    (iii) A voluntary pillar for persons looking for additional security.

The reformist approach adopted by Government in August 2003 completely overlooks this particular aspect of the Bank's suggestion.[22]

---

22. Even the Government has not followed a hybrid scheme, i.e., a combination of defined benefit/defined contribution, suggested by the Bhattacharya Committee (2002) in its report.

- The newly devised pension plan by the Government is relying on an IRA system by which an individual is held responsible for all the necessary investment decisions and their associated risks. While a small fraction of people with understanding about the financial market and its operatives might draw benefits from these provisions, a big majority of low-paid blue-collar employees may suffer disproportionate risks. Such a suggestion as 'default allocation' may not work in Indian conditions.[23] Further, it exposes individuals to too much risk.

- Lack of guarantee about certain minimum return at the time of retirement turns out to be another significant issue for many. It also dilutes the public role. Government may therefore consider providing some minimum cover against investment risks including those of frauds and market volatility. While such guarantees may involve a certain cost for the Government (assuming that guarantees are provided with a cost),[24] it is undeniably important for a large number of employees with limited investment skills or understanding about the capital market complexities. To assume that every single account holder would stay in touch and follow the roadmap provided by the retirement advisors all through their multi-decade work-span is fraught with over simplification.

- The entire change over from the defined benefit to defined contribution pension plan rests on the basic premise that the PFRDA will remain effective and regulate the entire system including six or more PFMs/annuity providers with multiple investment products. Further, the PFRDA is also expected to act as a watchdog against all kinds of fraud, dispute resolutions, implementation of relative return guarantee, standardisation of information about the fund performance, etc. Given the past scams in the financial market, cartels of various market operators,[25] and the ineffective role of the SEBI, the fate of

---

23. Under this provision, accretions of account holders incapable of taking a proper decision would be placed into a scheme that has yielded maximum return in the preceding years.

24. For an interesting discussion on this, see Shah (2003).

25. The Disinvestments Minister had raised this doubt in February 2004 when the minority stakes of the Public Sector Undertakings (PSUs) remained under-subscribed initially for few days. See Aiyar (2004) for an interesting account of this story in his Swaminomics (*Times of India*, February 29, 2004).

pension subscribers would remain fuzzy under the new plan. It is therefore imperative for the Government to provide a minimum benchmark benefit to those being covered under the modified pension plan. Certain Latin American countries like Argentina and Columbia provide insurance for financial risks by subcontracting private insurance companies either on a collective basis for financial risks or on an individual basis for the provision of lifetime pension benefit (Botka, 1998).

Clearly, the reforms initiated by The Government in its existing pension plan are an attempt to absolve itself by shifting all the trivial responsibilities to the employees—assuming that: (i) the private fund managers behave according to the market rules, keep the transaction cost at a level that allows account holders to earn decent returns over a multi-decade time horizon, follow sound investment decisions, and will not fudge their account books or make cartels, (ii) the IR account holders are homogeneously capable in handling finances or cope with all attendant risks in consultation with their investment counsellors, (iii) state has no need whatsoever to share some of these risks, and (iv) the monitoring and regulatory system in India can ensure the long term safety of IR contributions and their accruals. The past history of fund regulations in India is however somewhat contrasting.[26] Also, how far all this can be justifiable in the absence of the first two pillars of the social security is yet another issue that needs to be seriously debated.

7.4. Ageing and the Declining Interest Rate Regime: Is it Justifiable?

So far we were concerned in this discussion with inadequate social security provisioning in the country, and the recent attempts by the Government to reform the employees pension scheme. But these are not all, and the ageing process in India has to cope with the problems arising because of the declining rate of interest on small savings. A host of arguments have been offered to justify these declines. Notable among them are: (i) to bring down the capital cost of production, achieve international competitiveness and contribute towards a higher

---

26.   The point in argument is a number of financial scandals in the past—especially the problems that arose with the US-64, a flagship policy of the public owned Unit Trust of India with a large number of subscriptions meant for old age.

GDP growth, (ii) to reduce the debt burden on Government borrowings, and (iii) to ensure conformity between the low levels of national (and international) inflation and the nominal rate of interest (NRI) in the economy. The last, namely, the conformity between inflation and the NRI is considered helpful in keeping the real rate of interest (RRI) in line. We will, *inter alia*, concentrate on the RRI argument in most of the discussion to follow.

Three points need to be considered here. First, does the WPI, mostly used to judge the level of inflation in the economy, truly represent the market realities faced by the average consumers including the aged—especially from the lower stratums? Second, does the basket of commodities included in the WPI truly characterise the necessities of average persons, especially the older adults? And third, have the inflationary conditions, represented by the different price indices, remained stable over the preceding years? We argue that the instability in prices and inflationary conditions adversely affect the savings' reliant elderly persons. We will also attempt to crosscheck the official claim that the RRIs (i.e. inflation adjusted NRI) remained generally higher during the previous decade.

Methodologically, the questions raised above pose several difficult issues. Often, for instance, the price faced by individuals for an identical commodity varies according to their socio-economic status, buying practices, quantity purchased and place of purchase. A study of some or all these issues may indeed take us far beyond the scope of this work. Intuitively, however, it may well be surmised that many individuals from the lower stratums and with irregular work opportunities would generally buy in smaller quantities, and from the local shopkeepers with credit arrangements. Obviously, they might face a different price stream—perhaps higher than the usual ones. The shop owner might charge extra as a risk premium on possible credit losses. It may therefore be argued that inflation judged on the basis of the WPI may not hold for the bulk of the ordinary consumers—especially the poor.[27]

---

27.   For a discussion on this, see Chapter 3 of the Expert Group Report on the 'Estimation of Proportion and Number of Poor,' (Planning Commission, July 1993).

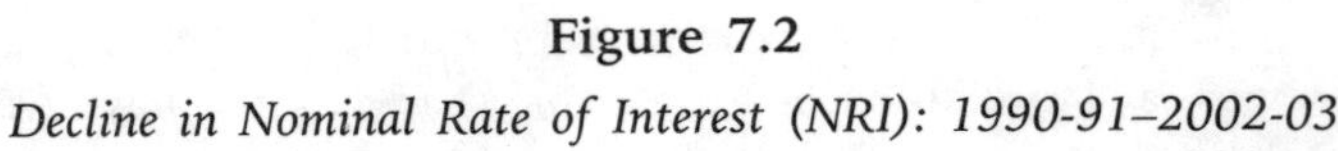

Figure 7.2

Decline in Nominal Rate of Interest (NRI): 1990-91–2002-03

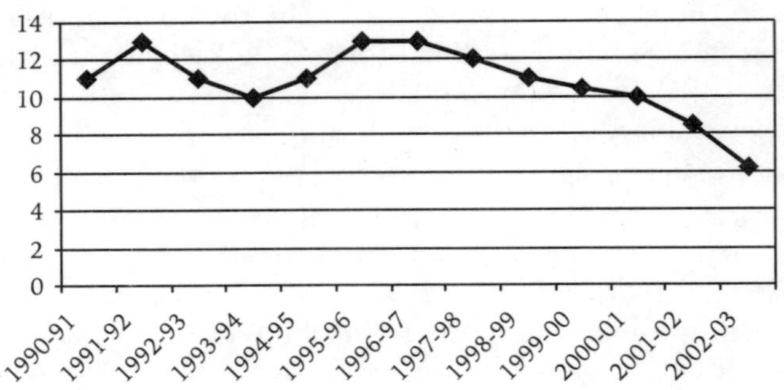

Source: Reserve Bank of India (2002-03) (Appendix Table A-7.1b).

Compared to the WPI, the CPI (consumer price index)[28] is a better indicator of the level of inflation faced by ordinary persons. This is particularly true because the CPI basket includes a combination of both goods and the services. In contrast, the WPI basket is entirely comprised of industrial commodities and simply represents the producers' cost.[29] Yet another indicator to observe the level of inflation in the economy is the GDP deflator. We provide a time series of all the three indices to supplement our earlier arguments implying erratic price behaviour in the country, affecting the real rate of interest earned by depositors (Appendix Tables A-7.1a, A-7.1b and A-7.2).

Variations in Inflation and Real Rates of Interest: Comparisons Based on WPI, CPIIW and GDP Deflator

Using all the three major price indices—i.e., the WPI, the CPI and the GDP deflator—and a common base, Figure 7.3 compares the over-

---

28. Because of its wider application, we have relied here on the time series of consumer price indices for industrial workers (i.e., CPIIW). An important use of CPIIW, for example, is to make periodic adjustments in the dearness allowance of government employees owing to inflationary changes.

29. Baskets of the WPI (revised in April 2000 with 138 new additions) and the CPI are given in Appendix Tables 7.3a and 7.4, respectively. Appendix Table A-7.3b provides over-time changes in inflation rates drawn by using the modified WPI basket, and 1993-94 as the base. This table also compares changes in inflationary condition owing to shifts in: (i) WPI basket, and (ii) the base year from 1980-81 to 1993-94.

time changes in annual inflation rates for a period from 1991-92 to 2001-02. Two observations emanating from this figure are significant. One is the higher level of inflation in the economy if judged on the basis of the CPI for industrial workers (CPIIW). At times, for example, the inflation measured by the CPIIW is higher than that of the WPI. The time series of GDP deflators reconfirm this (Appendix Tables A-7.1a and A-7.1b). Besides, this figure also suggests instability in levels of inflation overtime. These variations make the savings-reliant elderly more vulnerable.

Figure 7.3

Inflation Rates Based on WPI, CPIIW and
GDP Deflator: 1991-92 to 2001-02 (Base: 1993-94 = 100)

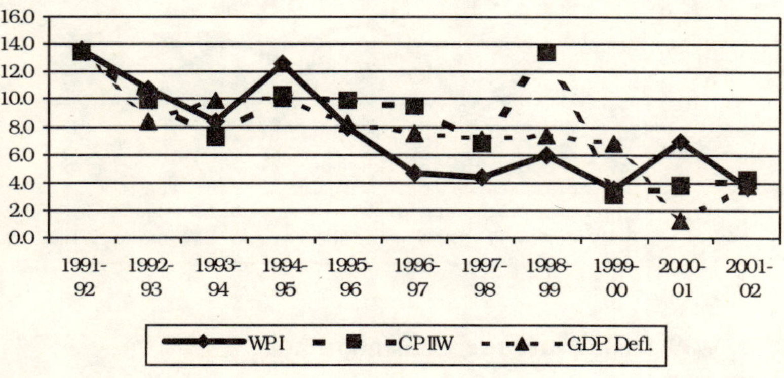

Source: Appendix Table A-7.1b.

How did these inflationary variations affect the RRIs over-time? Or, in other words, how big were the differences between the NRIs and the RRIs over the years under consideration? In order to make an assessment about these issues, we tried to compute the real rates of interest (RRIs) by using two price indices—namely, the WPI and the CPIIW. Figure 7.4 exhibits these rates and their differences (also see Appendix Table A-7.2). Clearly, this figure helps to shed an oft-repeated fallacy, namely that the reduced levels of inflation in the economy keep the RRIs high. Contrasting this, Figure 7.4 (and Appendix Table A-7.2 too) reveals negative RRIs in several years. Also, this figure suggests near convergence between the nominal and the real rates of interest in recent years.

As a whole, these details are a pointer to the hardship faced by the aged in India—they lose in both ways. On the one hand, for example, they lose on account of declining interest earnings, and on the other hand they are made to put up with fluctuating inflationary conditions —mostly owing to enhancements in administered prices of water, power, transportation, and so on. Seemingly, the Government needs to take this factor into consideration.

Figure 7.4

Gaps between Nominal and Real Rates of Interest Using WPI and CPIIW 1991-92–2002-03 (Base: 1993-94 = 100)

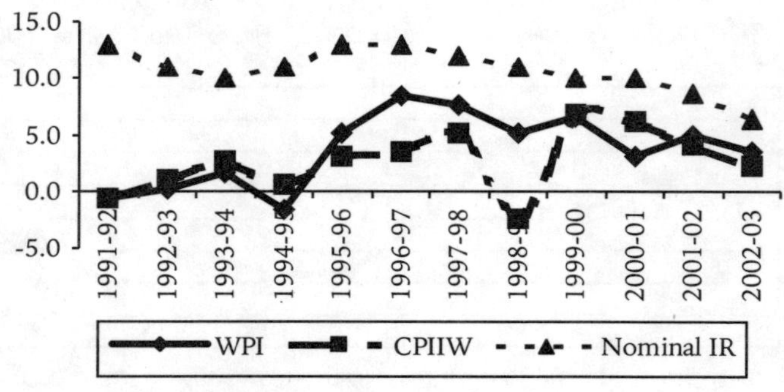

Source: Appendix Table A-7.2.

7.5. WPI Basket and the Consumption Requirements of the Aged

The question whether or not the needs basket of older persons tallies with the WPI—used by monetary institutions to fix the deposit rate—becomes irrelevant if judged on the basis of the WPI basket given in Appendix Tables A-7.3a and A-7.3b.

A question may then be asked here. Why is the WPI mostly used to reflect inflation, and why not some other appropriate measure of inflation?[30] This question may partly be explained by the

---

30. Initially, adjustments in poverty line because of changes in price level were obtained by using the wholesale price indices. This practice was however discontinued since 1984 on the recommendation of the Study Group on The Concept and Estimation of the Poverty Line, constituted by the Planning Commission (PPD, November 1984). The Study Group recommended the use of a price index appropriately weighted by the consumption basket of the poor. The private consumption deflator, derived from the National Accounts Statistics (NAS), was considered more appropriate.

computational ease of the WPI and its faster data availability. In addition, this measure suits industry as well as the Government—the former to minimise the capital cost of production, and the latter to reduce its debt burden. But does it or doesn't the WPI represent the ordinary consumer, especially the elderly? It needs to be further debated with greater understanding about its underlying issues. From some of the results presented in this study, especially the expenditure preferences revealed by the elderly, WPI might not be an appropriate indicator of inflation for them.

7.6. Concluding Observations

Our preceding analysis was largely related to the financial security of the aged, a statutory public responsibility, reiterated on various occasions by the Government—both nationally and at various international fora. While there have been some recent policy initiatives in this direction, the details emanating from this analysis expose several chinks and limitations—risking people to face serious financial difficulties at later ages. To illustrate, the destitute elderly— despite being covered under the National Social Assistance Scheme— run the risk of being left out owing to under coverage and arbitrary ceiling formula capping the size of the beneficiaries. Also, destitution is defined as per the norms drawn by the Central Government.

Likewise, a very large majority of the aged from the unorganised economic sectors remained outside the purview of any credible income security cover provided by Government. The Project OASIS did of course suggest a contributory pension fund for these workers. The OASIS Committee also suggested bringing the fund under private management, regulated by a centrally appointed authority. Unfortunately, however, it does not cover the existing old. Also, given the questionable past of the regulatory system in the country, the privately managed fund system is fraught with performance risks and, therefore, needs public guarantee.

A reformed and individually contributed pension plan for civil servants is now already in the offing, but it severely dilutes the role of Government. Also it renders many of the subscribers—especially from lower job categories—to face the risks of asymmetric information and system failure. That the high transaction cost of fund managers may eat away a good proportion of yields cannot be completely ruled out. While competition among the fund managers is used as a guarantee to ensure higher returns, the onus of responsibility for selection of good fund managers and investment portfolios lies with the individuals.

Alongside, there is no trace of a multi-pillared social security system in the country as suggested almost a decade ago in one of its studies by the World Bank (World Bank, 1994).

Finally, the soft interest rate regime—justified as a mechanism required for configuring between the real and the nominal rates of interest—seems less ingeniously designed, especially in the case of small savings and retirement plans. The time series of the real rate of interest, generated on the basis of the WPI and the CPIIW with a common base, confirm this. Further, there are instances when the real rate of interest has become negative owing to the nominal rate of interest falling short of inflation. Also, the price stability argument bears limited justification. Admittedly, while there has been no run away inflationary condition in the country for the past several years, our results indicate considerable variations in prices if measured separately by the WPI and the CPIIW.

Given this perspective, there is perhaps a need to debate some of these issues further at the policy level. Also, attempts may be made to design special and long-term deposit schemes for retirement purposes with provisions of higher and tax-free interest earnings. An example may be the LIC's Varishtha Pension Bima Yojna yielding nine per cent rate of interest annually.[31]

We also infer from some of our results that a decline in the nominal rate of interest below nine per cent may not work well given the current inflationary conditions—especially in major services including water, power, transport, medical care, etc.

---

31. Without making changes in interest yield, the Varishtha Pension Bima Yojna has now been replaced by a close-ended Senior Citizens' Saving Plan (2004).

Appendix Table A-7.1a

WPI, CPI and GDP Deflators: 1990-91–2001-02

Year	WPI*	CPI*	GDP Deflator*
1990-91	73.3	74.8	74
1991-92	83.3	84.9	84
1992-93	92.3	93.2	91
1993-94	100.0	100.0	100
1994-95	112.6	110.3	110
1995-96	121.6	121.3	119
1996-97	127.2	132.7	128
1997-98	132.8	141.8	137
1998-99	140.7	160.8	147
1999-00	145.6	165.9	157
2000-01	155.7	172.2	159
2001-02	161.3	179.7	165
2002-03	165.8	-	-

Source: Reserve Bank of India (2002-03).

Note: * The WPI, CPI, and GDP deflator are converted to the base 1993-94 = 100.

Appendix Table A-7.1b

Yearly Change in Inflation Rates: (WPI, CPIIW, CPIAL & GDP Deflator) and Nominal Interest Rate: 1990-91–2002-03

Year	Inflation Rates Based on			Nominal Interest Rate
	WPI	CPIIW	GDP Deflator	
1990-91	-	-	-	11
1991-92	13.64	13.48	13.51	13
1992-93	10.76	9.86	8.33	11
1993-94	8.33	7.27	9.89	10
1994-95	12.60	10.28	10.00	11
1995-96	7.98	9.97	8.18	13
1996-97	4.62	9.43	7.56	13
1997-98	4.39	6.83	7.03	12
1998-99	5.95	13.39	7.30	11
1999-00	3.53	3.18	6.80	10.5
2000-01	6.90	3.82	1.27	10
2001-02	3.62	4.31	3.77	8.5
2002-03	2.76	4.06	-	6.25

Source: Computed on the basis of Appendix Table A-7.1a.

Appendix Table A-7.2

Variations in Real and Nominal Rates of Interest

Year	Real Rate of Interest Based On:			Nominal Rate
	WPI	*CPIIW*	*GDP Def.*	*of Interest*
1990-91	-	-	-	11
1991-92	-0.64	-0.48	-0.51	13
1992-93	0.24	1.14	2.67	11
1993-94	1.67	2.73	0.11	10
1994-95	-1.60	0.72	1.00	11
1995-96	5.02	3.03	4.82	13
1996-97	8.38	3.57	5.44	13
1997-98	7.61	5.17	4.97	12
1998-99	5.05	-2.39	3.70	11
1999-00	6.47	6.82	3.20	10.5
2000-01	3.10	6.18	8.73	10
2001-02	4.88	4.19	4.73	8.5
2002-03	3.49	2.19	NA	6.25

Source: Computed on the basis of Appendix Table A-7.1b.

Appendix Table A-7.3a

*WPI Basket of Commodities (Based on the
Revised Series with Effect from 1st April, 2000)*

1. (A) Food Article

    (B) Non-food Article: Fibers, oil seeds and other non-food articles

    (C) Minerals: Metallic mineral, other minerals

2. Fuel, Power Light and Lubricants.

    (A) Coal Mining

    (B) Mineral oils

    (C) Electricity

3. Manufactured Products

    (A) Food products: Dairy products, Canning, preserving and processing of fish, Grain mill products, Sugar, khandsari and gur, Manufacture of common salt, Cocoa chocolate, Sugar, Bakery products, Edible oil, Oil cakes, Tea and coffee products,

Other food products, Beverages tobacco and tobacco products, textile, Wood and wood products, Paper and paper products, Leather and leather products, Rubber and plastic products, Chemicals and chemical products, Non-metallic mineral products, Basic metal alloys and metal products, Machinery and machinery tool, transport equipment and parts.

(B) Electricity for Railway Traction

(C) Purified Terephathalic Acid (PTA)

(D) Oxygen Gas in Cylinders

(E) Jelly Filled Telephone Cables

(F) Colour TV Sets

(G) Computer and Computer-based Systems

Appendix Table A-7.3b

Inflation Rates Drawn on the Basis of the New and the Old WPI Series

Year	Old Series: 1981-82 = 100		Revised Series: Base 1992-93 = 100	
	All Commodities Index	*Rate of Inflation*	*All Commodities Index*	*Rate of Inflation*
1993-94	100.0	-	100.0	-
1994-95	110.9	10.9	112.8	12.8
1995-96	119.4	7.7	121.6	7.8
1996-97	127.0	6.4	127.3	4.7
1997-98	133.1	4.8	132.8	4.3
1998-99	142.2	6.8	140.8	6.0
1999-00	146.4	3.0	144.9	2.9

Change in Commodity Weights: New and Old Baskets

Commodities	Old Series (1981-82)	Revised (1993-94)
(i) Primary Articles	32.30	22.02
(ii) Fuel, Power, Light, Lubricants	10.66	14.23
(iii) Manufactured Products	57.04	63.75
All Commodities	100.00	100.00

Source: Government of India, Press Information Bureau: Introduction of Revised Series of Index Number, Wholesale Price In India (Base: 1993-94), *http://industry. nic.in/ pib.htm*

Appendix Table A-7.4

Basket of CPI (Industrial Workers)

1. Food including non-alcoholic beverage
   - (A) Cereals and products
   - (B) Pulses and products
   - (C) Oils and fats
   - (D) Meat, fish and egg
   - (E) Milk and milk products
   - (F) Condiments and spices
   - (G) Vegetables and spices
   - (H) Other food (sugar, beverage, prepared meals and refreshment etc).
2. Tobacco, pan, supari, liquor and intoxicants
3. Fuel and lights
4. Clothing: bedding, footwear and headwear but excludes services like washing, cleaning and tailoring.
5. Housing: rent, water charges, house repair and upkeep.
6. Miscellaneous
   - (a) Medical care
   - (b) Education, recreation and amusement
   - (c) Transport and communication
   - (d) Personal care and personal effects
   - (e) Others (household furniture, appliances, furnishing, utilities and services, tailoring, cleaning etc.)

8

Highlights of the Study
and Areas of Policy Interventions

8.1. Highlights

Unlike the developed world, large scale ageing of population is a recent phenomenon for most of the developing countries—many of them however suffer from an inadequate policy regime; arguably, owing to insufficient empirical literature. With its perpetual demographic transition and growing life span, India is already among the countries with ageing as one of its core public issues. And yet, this issue remains in oblivion or, at best, in its infancy. This study basically draws its justification from this lack of concern, and attempts to explore demographic ageing in India—especially against the backdrop of old age poverty, serious health issues, changing social environment, erosion in traditional values, muted public response to old age income security, and growing prominence of pro-market institutions. Besides, this study also attempts to examine another interesting phenomenon of emerging demographic realities in the country—namely, the growing bulge in the size of working age adults, a situation used deftly by many Southeast Asian countries to their economic advantage. Such a deft utilisation of human resources is however less visible in India, especially owing to the decelerating opportunities in high productivity employment, and persistent demand-supply constraints affecting the labour market and its clearance mechanism. Given some of these realities, this study contemplated a difficult situation for both the bulging segments of population—aged for lack of worthwhile economic and health security, and younger adults owing to lack of quality employment. In such a constraining situation, can the familial transfer—a major plank of the ageing scenario in the country—work? This study delved into this issue to a considerable extent. Another issue of major concern relates to the dichotomy between the alarming health conditions of the aged and the increasing slogans of healthy and active ageing. As observed in the study, any such endeavour needs serious efforts at the policy level with attempts to control or bring down early life diseases.

8.2. Underpinnings and Structure

The underpinnings behind this analysis emanate from the situations evolving owing to:

(i) Demographically mediated age structure changes in the country with a growing bulge in young and old age population segments. The younger, *inter alia*, needing better income opportunities, while the aged would be looking for social security arrangements.

(ii) A pro-market paradigm shift in the economic regime together with an almost non-existent health and income security provisioning for the aged—over three-fourths of them reside in rural areas and suffer from considerable disparities in health and socio-economic standards.

(iii) Decelerating employment in higher productivity sectors along with large-scale casualisation of the work force. This makes the general premise that families may necessarily be able to support their aged a difficult proposition—at least for low-income households.

(iv) Growing erosion in multigenerational family arrangements.

(v) Downsizing of the family. It was argued that cutting the family size might lose some of its logical moorings in the absence of publicly provided protective safety provisions.

Obviously, an in-depth analysis of each of these issues was difficult for variety of reasons—both conceptual and for lack of relevant information. Yet, we tried to examine a few of the more significant ones, and structured the underlying study around the following questions:

1. Are we risking the bulk of our ageing population to face the threat of exclusion—especially given their weak financial status, high prevalence of multiple diseases and pulverised functional status?

2. Would this risk be over with the phasing out of the current cohorts of the aged?

3. Is the aged in India a homogeneous cross-section of the population? If not, what are the health and other outcomes of their heterogeneities? Further, do these heterogeneities also suggest the need for different support mechanisms for different groups of the aged?

4. Is the inter-generational transfer—or holding the families solely responsible for elderly care—a viable proposition given the changing socio-moral environment, persistent lifetime poverty and poor work opportunities?

5. Does old age poverty imply the same as general poverty? Or, in other words, would the basic requirements of the older persons conform to the general concept of basic needs and its underlying bundle of goods and services or weighting mechanism?

6. Is India facing a situation of economic-demographic mismatch? Demographically, for instance, the country is fast heading for significant age structure changes. Economically, however, these changes are not fully accounted for—younger adults are faced with decelerating employment opportunities, while the aged are devoid of a worthwhile social safety net, and

7. Is care providing to the aged altruistic?

It was postulated that an empirical investigation of these issues would help in drawing a more realistic policy regime for the older population in India and its neighbouring South Asian economies. Given this perspective, the entire study was broadly organised into eight major chapters, each running into several sections and sub-sections. Chapter 1, for example, relates to a number of conceptual issues. It was argued that the process of societal ageing and its economic or health management involve understanding about many issues including conceptual, social, economic, geriatric and those dealing with the community responses to ageing. Conceptually, for instance, it is perhaps important to go into the question of old age poverty. It was argued that the general concept of poverty could not be totally paraphrased to the old age poverty. It needs to give some weightage to the special needs of the older persons while conceptualising their poverty norms. Similarly, large-scale ageing in a society has important macro- and micro-economic implications. Health issues of ageing also need special treatment because they involve severe co-morbid and degenerating conditions, affecting the functional capabilities of the sick. These incapacitations may have major implications for care providers— especially working women. We tried to examine these issues with an implicit argument that a worthwhile old age security regime hinges on some of these details and their proper understanding.

An attempt has also been made to provide a macro situational assessment of older persons relying mostly on household level data obtained from the NSS 52nd Round for 1995-96. This analysis was to vindicate the argument that aged suffer from the severe disparities— spatial, socio-economic and gender wise—with major health and livelihood implications.

Following these instances of intra-aged disparities and their health and non-health outcomes, an obvious question relates to the recent socio-economic changes in the country and its interface with the process of ageing and the aged. For example, with declining fertility and family size, how does the non-aged perceive their own ageing and its related issues—particularly the need for retirement savings? Similarly, is filial support to the aged altruistic? Alongside the non-aged, the aged are also facing a number of upcoming issues. Frailty, poor health and non-senescent changes causing functional dependence are one. Expenditure preferences by the aged—used as a surrogate to make assessments about some of their basic requirements—come next. A third issue of considerable merit relates to the financial status or earning sources of the older persons. Yet another question of some consequences is about their living arrangements. Do they, or don't they, prefer to live with children? Also, there are issues linked with the declining interest earnings. All these questions assume significance with the ongoing neoliberal changes in the economy. As many of these issues have not been covered by the NSS or other secondary data sources, we decided to carry out a survey of 1000 households in Delhi with elderly co-residents. The results based on this survey comprise the set of empirical data from which conclusions have been drawn.

Data Sources

As may be clear from the preceding description, the study relied on both secondary and primary data sources. Secondary data sources —in particular the digital data diskette containing the household level information from 52nd Round of the NSS—were used to obtain a macro situational assessment and the prevailing levels of intra-aged disparities by major states. The micro level field based data, on the other hand, was generated to elicit views from four different socio-economic categories of the old (60+) and the young (14-59), and relate to a number of old age issues and their inter-face with emerging socio-economic changes in the country. A survey of one thousand households was conducted from all the nine districts of Delhi, with sample design, stratifications and other relevant details decided in close consultation with the Delhi Directorate of Census, and the Office of the Registrar General and Census Commissioner.

Besides the small sample size, an important limitation of this analysis is the non-coverage of the rural population. Hence, any generalisation of the results needs precaution.

8.3. Major Findings

This study has brought out many interesting results and may therefore help to drive several inferences about the problems of ageing over the coming years. Besides, the study was also designed with an intention to obtain views on ageing from a mix of respondents cross-classified into four socio-economic categories: high-income group, slum dwellers, aged co-residing with civil servants, and others comprising middle and lower-middle income people.

The beginning of the analysis was basically devoted to highlight the major conceptual and empirical issues of ageing such as old age poverty, age-dependency burden, macro-economic implications of ageing, health standards of the aged, certain incongruities between changes in major demographic parameters and pro-market shifts in the economy, inadequate communal support for the aged and so on. A re-look of the basic concept of old age poverty has been taken by discussing basket of goods and services required by the older persons. It was postulated that the weights assigned to the health care in the basic needs of an elderly person would be far different from the non-elderly. Hence, an increase in health care tariff or non-availability of public health care services would make the aged poorer. This may or may not happen with other age groups.

Owing to the fast growing share of the younger adults, India is relatively in a much comfortable position than other graying societies. Similarly, for quite some time, India is far from facing the labour market implications of ageing.

There is a very high prevalence of diseases among the aged, more than half of the aged, both in the rural and urban areas, suffer from chronic conditions—compounded by multiple ailments. Major issues are lack of even basic health care facilities in rural areas, and second, acute poverty among the rural masses including the aged. Yet another issue may be the high rural to urban migration by the non-aged—leaving the aged to cope with all the anomalies.

Community support to the aged is currently far from adequate in the country. Adequate data are lacking to comment on the quality of these supports and their beneficiaries. Hence the need to carry out a more detailed study on quality of support provisions, especially by demarcating the profit and non-profit organisations. In addition, while many big charities like the HelpAge India and such other non-government organisations are now expanding their activities and are engaged in helping the aged, most of them are usually concerned with the poor and destitute elderly. Private and profit making NGOs, who can work to look after the middle and higher income lonely aged, need to be promoted on a much bigger scale.

Two important aspects examined are: (i) the intra-aged disparities in terms of selected socio-economic characteristics, and, (ii) its health and livelihood outcomes. An assessment of the intra-aged disparities was made by profiling the aged in terms of their age, sex, spatial distribution, health standard and literacy levels in 15 major states in the country. Our results indicate that barring Delhi, Punjab and Kerala, the share of young old in most other states is very high. Majority of them are however suffer from co-morbid conditions. Hence, the general premise that the aged could help to provide cheap and experienced labour may not be entirely true. Our results also indicate that a big majority of the aged—or about three-fourth of the total—live in rural areas, and over half of them (i.e., 52 per cent) are in poor health conditions. It's true for the urban aged as well. This makes the old age health as the biggest challenge for the health planners in coming years. Also, in a situation like this, hoping to make ageing healthy and active is a moot point. Elderly females outnumbering the males are a common phenomenon in most countries, and true for India too.

While analysing poverty and economic standards—judged on the basis of the per capita monthly consumption expenditure (PCMCE) of the households with elderly members—we noticed that the aged in most states suffer from diverse economic conditions and very poor consumption levels.

How do these variations affect them socially and health-wise? A series of econometric exercises based on household data from the NSS 52nd Round were conducted separately for rural and urban areas. Illiteracy, age, poverty and sex are some of the important causal factors making the aged suffer from severe health conditions and multiple diseases. Being female and poor are also associated with certain social disadvantages. The analysis also indicated lack of altruism in elderly care. This was particularly true for women. Also, the share of women loners (i.e., women living alone) is far higher than for males. Some of these results were however later contrasted by our survey data.

Information was obtained from a survey of 1000 households in Delhi with elderly co-residents. These households were subsequently classified into four socio-economic categories, and two groups of the respondents comprising young (15-59 age groups) and the old in 60+ ages.

Younger respondents were asked to comment on two major issues. One of them was related to their own perceptions about ageing, especially planned ageing with emphasis on old age saving. This was followed by their views on care providing for the aged. Was caring for the aged a burden—especially in a new economic dispensation with fast pro-market changes, greater role of capital and deceleration in good quality employment? If not, what really induces them to take care of the aged? More surprising results were drawn on the latter. A very big majority of them—more than four-fifths—responded in favour of the aged. Also, they felt that caring the aged was their socio-moral and religious responsibilities. These responses were later substantiated by our detailed econometric exercises. Socio-moral and religious dummies used in these exercises turned out to be highly significant at 1 per cent level. Women were found to be better inclined to help the aged. To a certain extent, this blurs the son preference ideologies of a large number of people in the country.

In regard to planned ageing, there were two diverse opinions. While a fair majority of the respondents agreed with the idea of planned ageing and savings for their old age, those from the lower economic segments including slum dwellers had different views. They generally favoured public funded measures of social security to pay for retirement. Yet another group of these respondents favoured families as care providers. They were however much less in number.

The economically better off respondents were the ones who showed awareness of old savings instruments. Also, the products sold by the Life Insurance Corporation was far better known when compared to the Unit Trust of India. High-income respondents knew about private annuities too.

A total of 1,385 elderly persons were approached to elicit views on a large number of issues they used to confront on a day-to-day basis. Five of them, considered more relevant for further debate and policy initiatives, are described below. These include: (i) the income sources and financial status of the aged, (ii) their expenditure preferences, (iii) choice in living arrangements (iv) frailties, functional dependence and availability of filial support in their activities of daily living (ADL), and (v) implications of soft interest rate regime for a good fraction of savings reliant older persons.

A majority of respondents, over two-thirds in size, were highly vulnerable, completely dependent on their respective families, and didn't have any own source of income to fall back upon. We also tried to develop a financial security index (FSI) for the elderly males and females. As can be expected, females were highly vulnerable and short of own source income. It was clear from the index that women would remain more critically dependent on familial altruism. Persons with one independent source of income constituted 31 per cent of the total sample. Of the rest, 65.6 per cent had nothing to report on this count. The number of persons drawing destitute pension in Delhi appears to be relatively large. Though, there are instances of using unfair means by the pensioners. This suggests the need to scrutinise the pension system and its beneficiaries—not only in Delhi but in other states as well.

Expenditure preferences of the older persons were asked with a view to impute inferences about some of their basic consumption requirements. In all, eight different items were included. These were: food, doctors' fees, medicines, medical investigations, housing, clothing, entertainment, and items of socio-religious obligations/ expenses. The respondents were asked to rank these items according to their choice. Our results broadly indicate the food as the highest preferred expenditure item followed by the medical care, shelter and clothing. Entertainment and the socio-religious expenses drew the lowest ranks. Seemingly, the basic needs basket, used to compute the general level of poverty in the country, does not fully correspond with these ranks and choices, and may therefore suggest the need to debate the concept of old age poverty afresh.

Interestingly, low-income respondents and slum dwellers have preferred medicine to food. Unfortunately, the wholesale price index (WPI), used to indicate the inflationary conditions in the economy, does not consider services in its basket. This poses a few questions: one, does the WPI makes sense for the older populations in the country. If not, does it suggest the need to think about some alternative mechanism to account for the old age poverty?

On living arrangements, the aged are apparently losing interest in co-residing with children. A majority of them preferred to live independently, though close to their siblings. Those with no such choice, wished to rotate their residence. Some respondents, especially slum dwellers, however negated these views. The reasons are obvious.

Most respondents did not agree that a large family with too many children help to ensure old age security. These results clearly indicate the change in perceptions among the aged—at least those living in a metropolitan city like Delhi. Any further generalisation of these results—especially for the rural areas—may however not be possible due to data limitations.

An important extension of this analysis was to examine the prevalence of poor health, frailty and functional dependence in ADL among the aged. We conducted this analysis broadly on the lines suggested by the WHO with an assumption that the frailties or poor health are followed by disabilities, which is followed by death. The bottom line of this exercise was to suggest the poor quality of survival in later life years. We also tried to go into their causalities.

In short, our results indicate that a very large majority of the aged suffers from curtailed functional abilities in physical (eating, bathing, dressing, walking, climbing stairs, getting-up from a sitting position, etc.) as well as in sensory (hearing and vision) health domains. This forces them to rely on formal or informal help in their day-to-day activities. These problems of incapacitations are found to be particularly acute among the lower income groups. Women are especially the worst sufferers, with lesser amounts of filial support. Some of the causal factors with greater risks of functional impairments and dependencies are the income status (as proxied by an index suggesting the living standards of the respondents), sex, initial health stock and sedentary habits of living. To prevent or forestall these conditions, and preserve the health stock of individuals, we suggested some important public health interventions.

On issues such as the soft interest rate regime and its fallouts for the elderly depositors, opinions remained divided, especially according to the respondents' socio-economic background and their personal needs. Those guided by business interests or seeking personal loans were in favour of interest cuts, and *vice versa*.

This part of the analysis was entirely devoted on two crucial issues: one, public provisions for old income security—both relating to the destitute and the non-destitute. We found that the country is lagging far behind on this important issue of ageing. While the social assistance programme for the destitute elderly is in place, and run by the state governments with financial support received from the Centre, they generally suffer from serious anomalies. The biggest issue is the coverage of this programme. Every attempt has apparently been made to minimise the size of beneficiaries. The ceiling formula, used to determine the programme beneficiaries, is flawed. Given the size of old age poverty in the country, and examples of neglect by families for the aged—especially women—the ceiling formula appears to rely on over-simplified assumptions.

The pillars of income security for the non-destitute elderly are completely missing in the country, except for civil servants and public sector employees. Even this provision will soon be reformed on Peruvian model by making the old age pension an entirely private affair: funded by individuals at a rate decided by the finance department, managed by a group of specialised public and private investment agencies, and monitored for smooth functioning by a pension regulatory watchdog (PFRDA). Further, in these reforms, government has tried to dilute its responsibilities and decided to provide no guarantees against investment risks. Nor there is an assured minimum pension benefit. As pension funds are a multi-decadal venture, the lack of public guarantees on capital losses is a serious issue, especially for lower level public sector employees.

A similar programme for workers employed in unorganised segments of the economy is also under consideration. However, none of these measures can serve to provide an answer to the question: where is public pillar of income support to the aged?

The idea of giving way to funded private old age retirement provision will not only help the government to tide over its growing financial commitments arising due to pay-as-you-go system, it may as well help in raising the aggregate savings rate in the economy, boosting long-term capital accumulation, contribute to a more rapid development of efficient financial markets, and facilitate the process of privatisation. It may however leave the pension fund contributors in a state of uncertainty if they are not insulated against the risks of capital diminution, cost overrun or other forms of fund management risks. Given the poor record of regulatory system in the country, these risks may not simply be treated as imaginary and, therefore, deserve serious attention.

On declining interest rate regime, we have come across with two specific issues. One is related to the measure of inflation. We have argued that despite all its advantages and ease in computation, the wholesale price index (WPI) might not be a good indicator of the price conditions faced by an ordinary consumer—especially the aged. The second point was the instability in prices and sharp variations in inflation over the past decade. At times, it dropped considerably the real rate of interest in the economy. This makes the savings reliant elderly vulnerable. We therefore favoured special long-term savings instrument for the aged with higher returns.

8.4. Areas of Policy Interventions

Clearly, a range of policy intervention follows from this analysis. A few of them are summarised below for possible consideration as also for further debate.

- Accelerating growth in size, and very poor socio-economic conditions of the aged need serious consideration by planners and policy makers—especially given the neoliberal pro-market economic regime. Failing this the non-market traditional institutions may be taken over by the market leaving the aged at the margin.

- The aged being a highly diverse group, need different policy responses.

- Elderly women are faced with severe difficulties. Among those left to live alone, the share of women is considerably large. Gender discrimination is evident from many of our empirical analyses. Women also face serious functional incapacitations with a good proportion lacking filial support in activities of their daily living.

- The rural aged needs much greater consideration not only because of their size, but also for their serious poverty issues with very high socio-economic disparities. In most policy debate, however, the rural aged seem to draw limited attention or none at all.

- The health aspect of ageing is the most critical issue to be tackled—particularly in the rural areas. With very high prevalence of chronic diseases, positively associated with the risks of functional impairments, the idea of active and healthy ageing is becoming a moot point. The public health apparatus should be geared very aggressively to promote the significance of health stock, which is extremely important to ensure old age health. Special programmes need to be devised for the rural aged.

- A sense of familial support for the aged is shown as strongly rooted into the socio-moral and religious values of individuals. These values may be promoted further through moral teaching in early years of schooling. Religious institutions may also be roped in to give discourses on care providing to the aged. NGOs may especially work towards this.

- From the evidence, it appears that the government is trying to dilute its role in income security for the aged. The ceiling formula used by government to reduce the number of destitute pensioners is a point in argument. Similarly, the reforms introduced in the civil servants pension plan need further debate. Without disagreeing with the basic rationale, this study makes out a case in favour of: (i) public guarantees against capital risks, and (ii) a minimum return on pension fund contributions. The need to evolve a public pillared old age income security is essential. Pure privatisation may not work.

- Financing of old age income security needs to be examined. Especially, a range of health hazardous consumer items may be identified (paan masala may be one of many such other items) and taxed at higher rates to generate necessary finances for meeting the income and health security requirements of the aged.

- The political economy of ageing is likely to follow soon in the country and ensure the welfare of the elderly population, which is likely to accelerate in the coming decades.

- Old age savings instruments with differential rates of return are suggested.

- The proposed legislation (The Older Persons Maintenance, Care and Protection Bill, 2005) making food, shelter, clothing, medical requirements and other basic items of elderly maintenance mandatory for younger siblings may not work effectively in case of many low-income families, especially if they have to bear the younger dependencies as well. Between the two, i.e., the younger and the older dependencies, the former often gets precedence. Further, the medical cost of old age diseases may also be problematic for average families unless subsidised or brought under some form of universal insurance cover.

- Health system in India severely lacks geriatric health care infrastructure—both physical and in terms of human skills. The country therefore needs to evolve a framework at both the level. Especially, with shrinking families, growing migration and participation of women in income generating activities, the need for long-term care (LTC) may start growing sooner than later. While public opinion regards LTC as part of health care, LTC services in fact are quite distinct from health care services. Most health care involves highly trained medical professionals. In contrast, most long term care services require lesser trained people to helping ADL disabled aged in their routine activities like eating, dressing, bathing, toileting and so on. This difference between LTC and health care services has important implications for the role of the government in provision and financing of LTC services. There is thus a need to evolve a clear-cut strategy on this important issue of ageing and health in the country.

References

Agarwal, Bina (1990). "Social Security and the Family: Coping with Seasonality and Calamity in Rural India," *The Journal of Peasant Studies*, Vol. 17(3), pp. 314-412.

Aiyar, Swaminathan S.A. (2004). "Disinvestments as Soap Opera," *Times of India*, Sunday, February 29, Delhi Edition.

Alam, Moneer (1997). "Health Sector Financing by States: An Exploration," *Demography India*, Vol. 26(2), pp. 177-206.

————. (2000). "Ageing in Indian Society: A Country Profile, BOLD," *Quarterly Journal of the International Institute of Ageing*, Vol. 10(3), May 2000, pp. 5-22, United Nations (Malta).

————. (2001a). "Looking Beyond the Current Demographic Scenario: Changing Age Composition, Ageing and Health Security Issues in India and South Asia," paper presented at the Institute For Human Development and the UNDP organised *Consultation Meeting on Health Security in India*, July 26-27, *mimeo*, New Delhi.

————. (2001b). "Population, Ageing and Social Security: Analysing Changes in Population Structure for its Economic and Social Security Implications," in Srinivasan K. and Michael Vlassoff (eds.), *Population-Development Nexus in India: Challenges for the New Millennium*, pp. 142-174, Tata McGraw Hill, New Delhi.

Alam, Moneer and M. Mukherjee (2005). "Ageing, Activities of Daily Living Disabilities and Need for Public Health Initiatives," *Asia-Pacific Population Journal*, Vol. 20(2), pp.47-76.

Alam, Moneer and Piush Antony (2001c). "Social Security for the Aged," in Dev, S. M., Piush Antony, *et al.* (eds.), *Social and Economic Security In India*, pp. 340-66, Institute for Human Development, New Delhi.

Alam, Moneer and R.N. Agarwal (1999). "Ageing, Macro-Economic Implications and Health Insurance Requirements in India: An Exploratory Analysis." *The Indian Journal of Labour Economics*, Vol. 42 (3), pp. 471-99.

Alam, Moneer and S.N. Mishra (1998). "Structural Reforms and Employment Issues in India: A Case of Industrial Labor," *The Indian Journal of Labor Economics*, Vo. 41(2), pp. 271-92.

Albert, S.M. (2004). *Public Health and Aging: An Introduction to Maximizing Function and Well-Being*, Springer Publishing Company, New York.

Albert, S.M., Im A., Raveis, V. (2002). "Public Health and the Second Fifty Years," *American Journal of Public Health*, Vol. 92(8), pp.1214-1216.

Anant, T., K. Sundaram and S. Tendulkar (1999). *Employment and Labour in South Asia*, SAAT, International Labor Organisation (ILO), New Delhi.

Auerbach, Alan J.L.J. Kotlikoff, *et al.* (1989). "The Economic Dynamics of an Ageing Population: The Case of Four OECD Countries," *OECD Economic Studies*, No. 12 (Spring), pp. 28-29.

Barrientos, A. (2002). "Old Age, Poverty and Social Investment," *Journal of International Development*, Vol. 14, pp. 1133-1141.

Becker, G.S. (1974). "A Theory of Social Interactions," *Journal of Political Economy*, Vol. 82, pp. 1063-1093.

————. (1991). *A Treatise on the Family*, Harvard University, Cambridge, MA.

Bengston, V.L., and Schrader, S.S. (1982). "Parent-Child Relations," in Mangen, D.J. and W.A. Peterson (eds.), *Handbook of Research Instruments in Social Gerontology*, Vol. 2, pp. 115-185, University of Minnesota Press, Minneapolis.

Bhattacharya, B.B. and S. Sakthivel (2004). *Economic Reforms and Structural Changes in Employment: A Comparative Analysis of Gender Specific Employment Behaviour in Organised and Informal Sectors in India*, Institute of Economic Growth, March 2004, *mimeo*.

Bhavani, T.A. (2001). "Small-Scale Units In the Era of Globalisation: Problems and Prospects," *Discussion Paper Series* No. 41/2001, Institute of Economic Growth, Delhi.

Binstock, R.H. and E. Shanas (1976). *Handbook of Aging and the Social Sciences*, Van Nostrand Reinhold Company, New York.

Biswas, B.K. (1985). "Dependency and Family Care of the Aged: A Case Study," *Journal of the Indian Anthropological Society*, Vol. 20, pp. 238-257.

Bongaarts, J. and Z. Zimmer (2001). "Living Arrangements of Older Adults in the Developing World: An Analysis of DHS Household Surveys," *Working Paper*, Population Council.

Bose, Ashish and M. Kapoor Shankardass (2004). *Growing Old in India: Voices Reveal, Statistics Speak*, B.R. Publishing Corporation, Delhi.

Botka, A. Uthoff (1998). "Pension System Reforms in Latin America: How much Privatisation?" in Marmor Theodore R. and De Jong, Philip R. (eds.) *Ageing, Social Security and Affordability* (FISS, Volume 3), pp. 203–222, Ashgate, England.

Bream, J. (2003). *The Labouring Poor in India: Patterns of Exploitation, Subordination, and Exclusion*, Oxford University Press, New Delhi.

Breman J. and Arvind N. Das (2000). *Down and Out: Labouring under Global Capitalism*, Oxford University Press, New Delhi.

Burch, T.K. (1979). "Household and Family Demography: A Bibliographic Essay," *Population Index* 45: 173-195

Burholt, Vanessa, G. Clare Wenger, *et al.* (2003). *Families and Migration: Older People in South Asia*, Department for International Development Project (DFID), ESA315, January.

Cameron, A.C. and P.K. Trivedi (1986). "Econometric Models Based on Count Data: Comparisons and Applications of Some Estimators and Tests," *Journal of Applied Econometrics*, Vol.1, pp.29-53

Cain, M. (1985a). "The Fate of the Elderly in South Asia: Implications for Fertility," Population Council, Centre for Policy Studies, *Working Paper* No. 116, November.

———. (1985b). "Consequences of Reproductive Failures: Dependence Mobility and Mortality among the Elderly in Rural South Asia," Population Council, Centre for Policy Studies, *Working Paper* No. 119, November.

———. (1981). "Risk and Insurance: Perspectives on Fertility and Agrarian Change in India and Bangladesh," *Population and Development Review*, Vol. 7(3), pp. 435-474.

Census of India (2001). "Provisional Population Totals, Paper 2 of 2001," *Rural-Urban Distribution of Population*, Series-8 (Delhi), Directorate of Census Operations, Delhi.

———. (2001). *Final Population Tables* (Series I, India), Registrar General of India, May 2004, pp. 6-7.

Clark, A.E., and A.J. Oswald (1994). "Subjective Well-being and Unemployment," *Economic Journal*, Vol. 104, pp. 648-59

Cox, D. (1987). "Motives for Private Income Transfers," *Journal of Political Economy*, Vol. 95, pp.508-546.

Cox, D., and M.R. Rank (1992). "Inter-vivo Transfers and Intergenerational Exchange," *Review of Economics and Statistics*, Vol. 74, pp. 305-314.

Dandekar, K. (1996). *The Elderly in India*, Sage Publications, New Delhi.

DFID (2003). *Inequalities in Health in India: The Methodological Construction of Indices and Measures*, DFID (India), New Delhi, *mimeo*.

Dreze, Jean (2003). "Praying for Food Security," *The Hindu*, Editorial Page, Monday, October 27.

Dreze, Jean and Amartya Sen (1991). "Public Action for Social Security: Foundations and Strategy," in E. Ahmad, Jean Dreze, John Hills and Amartya Sen (eds.) *Social Security in Developing Countries*, Clarendon Press, London.

Duggal, R. (1995a). "Health Expenditure Patterns in Selected Major States," *Radical Journal of Health*, Vol. 1 (New Series), January, pp. 37-47.

———. (1995b). "Public Health Budgets: Recent Trends," *Radical Journal of Health*, Vol. 1 (New Series), July 1995, pp. 177-182.

Dunlop, D.D., S.L. Hughes, and L.M. Manheim (1997). "Disability in Activities of Daily Living: Patterns of Change and a Hierarchy of Disability," *American Journal of Public Health*, Vol. 87(3), pp. 378-383.

Eggebeen, David J., and Davey Adam (1998). "Do Safety Nets Work? The Role of Anticipated Help in Times of Need," *Journal of Marriage and Family*, Vol. 60(4), pp. 939-950.

Ellis, Randall, P. Moneer Alam and I. Gupta (2000). "Health Insurance in India, Problems and Prognosis," *Economic and Political Weekly*, Vol. 35(4), January 22, 2000, pp. 207-17.

Evandrou, M. (2000). "Social Inequalities in Later Life: The Socio-economic Position of Older People from Ethnic Minority Groups in Britain," *Population Trends*, Vol. 101, pp. 11-18.

Friedlander, D. and K.R. Malul (1980). "Ageing of Population, Dependency and Economic Burden in Developed Countries," *Canadian Studies in Population*, Vol. 7(1), pp. 49-55.

Fries, J.F. and L.M. Crapo (1981). *Vitality and Ageing: Implications of the Rectangular Curve*, W.H Freeman, San Francisco, CA.

Gaiha, R. (1991). "Structural Adjustment and Household Welfare in Rural Areas: A Microeconomic Perspective," *FAO Economic and Social Development Paper* No. 100, Rome.

Ghosh, A.K. (1994). "Employment in Organised Manufacturing in India," *The Indian Journal of Labour Economics*, Vol. 37((2), pp.141-162.

Gilbert, C.L. (1979). "Econometric Models for Discrete Economic Processes," *Discussion Paper*, University of Oxford

Goldar, B. (2000). "Employment Growth in Organized Manufacturing in India," *Economic and Political Weekly*, April 1, 2000, pp. 1191-95.

Gordon, D., Adelman, A., *et al.* (2000). *Poverty and Social Exclusion in Britain*, Joseph Rowntree Foundation, York.

Government of India (2002). *High Level Expert Group on New Pension System*, (Bhattacharya Committee Report), February.

————. (2002-03). Economic Survey, *Department of Economic Affairs, Ministry of Finance*.

————. (2001-02). Economic Survey, *Department of Economic Affairs, Ministry of Finance*.

Green, W.H. (2002). *Econometric Analysis*, Pearson Education Press, Delhi.

Grootendrost, Paul V. (2002). "A Comparison of Alternative Models of Prescription Drug Utilization," in Jones Andrew M. and Owen O'Donnell, (eds), *Econometric Analysis of Health Data*, John Wiley & Sons, pp. 74-86.

Gumber, A. and Peter Berman (1995). "Measurement and Pattern of Morbidity and Utilization of Health Services–A Review of Recent Health Surveys in India," *Gujarat Institute of Development Research Working Paper Series*, No. 65, March 1995.

Gupta, I. and D. Sankar (2002). Health of the Elderly in India: A Multivariate Analysis, *IEG Discussion Paper* No. 45/2002

Gwatkin, Davidson R. (2000). "Health Inequalities and the Health of the Poor: What Do We Know? What Can We Do?" *Bulletin of the World Health Organisation*, Vol. 78 (1), pp. 3-17.

Hashimoto, A. (1991). "Living Arrangements of the Aged in Seven Developing Countries: A Preliminary Analysis," *Journal of Cross-Cultural Gerontology*, Vol. 6(4), pp.359-382.

Hausman, J. Hall, B.H. and Griliches, Z. (1984). "Econometric Models for Count Data with an Application to the Patents-R&D Relationship," *Econometrica*, 52, pp.909-938

HelpAge India (1998). *Directory of Old Age Homes*, Research and Development Division, HelpAge India, New Delhi.

————. (2000). *Senior Citizen's Guide*, Research and Development Division, HelpAge India, New Delhi.

————. (2003). "Non-contributory Pension In India: A Case Study of Uttar Pradesh," Research and Development Division, June, *mimeo*, HelpAge India, New Delhi.

Hogan, D.P., D.J. Eggebeen, and C.C. Clogg (1993). "The Structure of Intergenerational Exchanges," *American Journal of Sociology*, Vol. 98, pp. 1428-1458.

Holzer Jerzy Z. and Ewa Fratczak (1994). "The Ageing of the Population in Poland: 1959-2020," in George J. Stolnitz (ed.) *Social Aspects and Country Reviews of Population Ageing: Europe and North America*, United Nations Economic Commission for Europe and United Nations Population Fund, Economic Studies No. 6, United Nations, New York and Geneva, pp. 245-68.

Horioka, Charles, Yuji (1991). "The Determinants of Japan's Saving Rate: The Impact of the Age Structure of the Population and other Factors," *Economic Studies Quarterly*, Vol. 42(3), pp. 237-53.

Horioka, Charles, Yuji (1992). "Future Trends in Japan's Saving Rate and the Implications thereof for Japan's External Imbalance," *Japan and the World Economy*, Vol. 3 (4), pp. 307-30.

Hurd, M. (1997). "The Effects of Demographic Trends on Consumption, Saving, and Government Expenditure in the United States," in Hurd D. Michael and Naohiro Yashiro (eds.), *The Economic Effects of Ageing in the United States and Japan*, (A National Bureau of Economic Research Conference Report), University of Chicago Press, pp. 39-57.

Insurance Regulatory and Development Authority (2001). Pension Reforms in the Unorganised Sector, *IRDA Report*, New Delhi.

International Labour Organisation (2005). *World Employment Report 2004-05: Employment, Productivity and Poverty Reduction*, February, ILO, Geneva.

Jackson, William A. (1998). *The Political Economy of Population Ageing*, Edward Elgar Publishing Limited.

Katz S. Ford, A.B. and Moskowitz, R.W. Jackson, B.A. Jaffe, M.W. (1963). "Studies of Illness among the Aged," *JAMA*, Vol. (185), pp. 914-919.

King, M. and S.H. Preston (1990), Who Lives with Whom? Individual versus Household Measures, *Journal of Family History*, Vol. 15, pp. 117-132

Kotlikoff, L.J., and J. Morris (1990). "Why Don't the Elderly Live with their Children? A New Look," in D.A. Wise (ed.), *Issues in the Economics of Aging*, Chicago, University of Chicago Press.

Kulkarni, P.M. (2001). "Prospective Changes in the Size and Structure of India's Population: Implications of PFI's Projections up to 2051," in K. Srinivasan and Michael Vlassoff (eds.), *Population-Development Nexus in India*, Tata McGraw Hill, New Delhi.

Kumar, P.V. (1999). "Elderly Women in Rural India: Need for Policy Intervention," *Research and Development Journal*, HelpAge India, 5(3), pp.27-30.

Kumar, V.S. (1998). "Responses to the Issues of Ageing: The Indian Scenario," *BOLD*, Vol. 8(3), pp. 7-26.

Lamb, Sarah (2000). *White Saris and Sweet Mangoes: Ageing, Gender, and Body in North India*, Berkeley, University of California Press.

Logan, John R., Peter D. Hoff and Michael Newton (1999). "Estimation for the Marriage Model," Center for Demography and Ecology, Working Paper 99-31, University of Wisconsin, Madison.

Manton Kenneth G. and Eric Stallard (1994). "Medical Demography: Interaction of Disability Dynamics and Mortality," in Linda G. Martin and Samuel H. Preston (eds.), *Demography of Ageing*, National Academic Press, Washington, D.C.

Martin, L. (1990). "The Status of South Asia's Growing Elderly Population," *Journal of Cross-Cultural Gerontology*, Vol. 5(2), pp.93-117.

Masson Paul R. and Ralph W. Tyron (1990). "Macro-Economic Effects of Projected Population Aging in Industrial Countries," *IMF Staff Papers*, Vol. 37 (3), pp. 453-85.

Mathiyazhagan, M.K. (2001). *Household Characteristics and Health Expenditure among the Rural People in India*, Economics Unit, ISEC

Mehrotra, P.K. and Alok R. Chaurasia (2001). "Population and Social Development: Higher and Technical Education," in K. Srinivasan and Michael Vlassoff (Eds.) *Population-Development Nexus: Challenges for New Millennium* Tata McGraw Hill, New Delhi.

Ministry of Rural Development (2000). *Annual Report of the Ministry of Rural Development 1999-2000*, Government of India, New Delhi.

Montgomery, Mark R., Michele Gragnolati, Kathleen Burke and Edmundo Paredes (1999). "Measuring Living Standards with Proxy Variables," Policy Research Division, Population Council, *Working Paper* No. 129.

Mor, V., V. Wilcox, R. William, J. Hiris (1994). "Functional Transitions among the Elderly: Patterns, Predictors, and Related Hospital Use," *American Journal of Public Health*, Vol. 84, pp. 1274-1280.

National Sample Survey Organization (1996). *The Aged In India-A Socio-Economic Profile*, NSS 52nd Round, 1995-96, Report No. 446, Ministry of Statistics and Programme Implementation, Government of India.

National Sample Survey Organization (2001). *Employment and Unemployment Situation in India, 2000-01*, NSS 56th Round, Report No. 476, Ministry of Statistics and Programme Implementation, Government of India.

Natrajan, K.S. and V. Jayachandran (2001). "Population Growth in 21st Century India," in Srinivasan K. and Michael Vlassoff (eds.), *Population-Development Nexus in India: Challenges for the New Millennium*, Tata McGraw Hill, New Delhi, pp. 35-57.

NFHS (1998-99). *National Family Health Survey: Delhi*, International Institute for Population Sciences, Bombay (India), March 2002.

Noguchi, Yukio (1990). "The Age Structure of the Population and the Saving/Investment: An Analysis Based on Cross-Country Comparisons," *Financial Review*, Institute of Fiscal and Monetary Policy, Ministry of Finance, Government of Japan, August.

Nolan, B. and C.T. Whelan (1996). *Resources, Deprivation and Poverty*, Clarendon Press, Oxford.

OASIS Project Report (2000). "First Report of the Expert Committee for Devising a Pension System for India," *The Project OASIS Report*, Ministry of Social Justice and Empowerment, Government of India, January 2000, New Delhi.

Oswald, A.J. (1997). "Subjective Well-being and Economic Performance," *The Economic Journal*, Vol. 107, pp. 1815-31.

Padgaonkar, Dileep (2002). "Hard Times Ahead," *Sunday Times of India* (Delhi Edition), December 1.

Palloni, Alberto (2001). "Living Arrangements of Older Persons," *Population Bulletin of the United Nations*, Special Issue Nos. ST/ESA/SER.N/42-43. pp. 54-110.

Parikh, K.S. (2002). "Social Infrastructure as Important as Physical Infrastructure," in K.S. Parikh and R. Radhakrishna (eds.), *India Development Report 2002*, Oxford University Press, New Delhi.

Piliavin, Jane Allyn and Charng, Hong-Wen (1990). "Altruism: A Review of Recent Theory and Research," *Annual Review of Sociology*, Vol. 16, pp. 27-65.

Planning Commission (2002). *Report of the Special Group on Targeting Ten Million Employment Opportunities Per Year Over the Tenth Plan Period*, Government of India, Planning Commission, New Delhi, May.

————. (1993). *Report of the Expert Group on Estimation of Proportion and Number of Poor*, Perspective Planning Division, Planning Commission, Government of India, July.

————. (1984). *Study Group on The Concept and Estimation of the Poverty Line*, Perspective Planning Division, Planning Commission, Government of India, November.

Prabhu, Seeta K. (2001). *Socio-economic Security in the Context of Pervasive Poverty: A Case Study of India*, The Indian Journal of Labour Economics, Conference Number, Vol. 44(4), pp.519-558, October-December.

Pradhan, M. and M. Ravallion (2000). "Measuring Poverty Using Qualitative Perceptions of Consumption Adequacy," *Review of Economic and Statistics*, Vol. 82, pp. 462-71.

PROBE (1999). *Public Report on Basic Education in India*, Oxford University Press, New Delhi.

Rajan, I. S., U.S. Misra and P.S. Sharma (1999). *India's Elderly: Burden or Challenge*, Sage Publications: Delhi.

Rajan, I.S. (2002). "Social Security for the Unorganised Sector in South Asia," *International Social Security Review*, Vol. 55 (4), pp. 143-56.

Raju, Siva S. (2002). *Health Status of the Urban Elderly: A Medico-Social Study*, B.R. Publishing Corporation, Delhi.

Reddy, K.N. (1996). "Social Security for the Elderly in India: Need for Reform," *Research and Development Journal*, Help Age India, 3(1), pp. 8-26.

Reserve Bank of India (2002). "State Finances: A Study of Budgets of 2000-2001," December, Bombay.

————. (2002-03). *Handbook of Statistics on Indian Economy*, 2002-03, Bombay.

Retherford, Robert D. and Minja Kim Choe (1993). *Statistical Models for Causal Analysis*, John Wiley & Sons, USA.

Saad, Paula M. (2005). "Informal Support Networking among Older Adults in Latin America: Comparative Studies of SABE Surveys," paper presented in the *25th IUSSP International Conference*, Tours (France), 18-23 July.

Sample Registration System (SRS) (1980, 1991 and 1998). "Statistical Report," Registrar General, India, Ministry of Home Affairs, Government of India, New Delhi.

————. (1999). "SRS Based Abridged Life Tables," Registrar General and Census Commissioner Office, Ministry of Home Affairs, Government of India, New Delhi.

Sankar, Deepa (2001). "Access and Utilisation of Health Care Services: Patterns and Determinants in Kerala". Unpublished Ph.D dissertation submitted to the Jawaharlal Nehru University through the Centre for Development Studies, Thiruvananthapuram.

Sen, A.K. (1984). *Research Policies and Development*, Oxford University Press, London.

Severson, M.A., Smith G.E. Tangalos, E.G. *et al.* (1994). "Patterns and Predictors of Institutionalization in Community-based Dementia Patients," *Journal of American Geriatric Society*, Vol.42, pp. 181-185.

Shah, A. (2003). "Investment Risk in Indian Pension Sector and Role for Pension Guarantees," *Economic and Political Weekly*, Vol. 38(8), pp. 719-729.

Singh, P. (1997). *Social Security System in Developing Countries: Asia, Africa and South America*, Friedrich Ebert Stiftung, New Delhi.

Sokolovsky J. (2001). "Living Arrangements of Older Persons and Family Support in Less Developed Countries," *Population Bulletin of the United Nations*, Special Issue Nos. 42/43, pp. 162-192.

Spitze, G. and J.R. Logan (1989). "Gender Differences in Family Support: Is There a Payoff?," *The Gerontologist*, Vol. 29, pp. 108-113.

Sarvekshna (1991). *Journal of the National Sample Survey Organisation* (NSSO), Ministry of Statistics and Programme Implementation, Government of India, Issue No. 49, p.116.

Srinivas, P.S., and Susan Thomas (2003). "Institutional Mechanisms in Pension Fund Management: Lessons from Three Indian Case Studies," Special Article, *Economic and Political Weekly*, Vol. 38(8), pp. 706-17.

Srinivasan, K. (2001). "The Population Issues in the New Millennium: The Legacies and the Challenges," in Srinivasan K. and Michael Vlassoff (eds.), *Population-Development Nexus in India: Challenges for the New Millennium*, pp. 12-34, Tata McGraw Hill, New Delhi.

Stern, E. (1991). "Evolution and Lessons of Adjustment Lending," in V. Thomas and A. Chibber (eds.), *Restructuring Economies in Distress—Policy Reforms and the World Bank*, Oxford University Press.

OASIS Project Report, The (2000). Submitted to the Ministry of Social Justice and Empowerment, Government of India, New Delhi.

Townsend, P. (1979). *Poverty in the United Kingdom*, Allen Lane and Penguin Books, Harmondsworth, Middlesex and Berkeley, University of California Press.

United Nations (1999). *World Population Prospects–The 1998 Revision*, Volume II: Sex and Age, ST/ESA/SER.A/180, United Nations Publications, New York.

————. (2003). *World Population Prospects–The 2002 Revision*, Volume II: Sex and Age, ST/ESA/SER.A/223, United Nations Publications, New York.

Van Praag, B.M.S., P. Frijters and A. Ferrer - i - Carbonel (2002). "The Anatomy of Subjective Well-being," *The Tinbergen Institute Discussion Paper*, TI 2002-022/3.

Van, Gelder S., D. Johnson (1989). *Long Term Care Insurance: Marketing Trends*, Washington, DC: US Health Association of America.

Visaria, P. (1998). "Unemployment among Youth in India: Level, Nature and Policy Implications," *Employment and Training Paper*: 36, Action Programme on Youth Unemployment, International Labour Office, Geneva.

————. (1980). "Poverty and Living Standards in Asia," *Population and Development Review*, Vol. 6(2), pp. 189-223.

World Bank (2001). "India: The Challenge of Old Age Income Security," Finance and Private Sector Development, South Asia Region, Report No. 22034-IN., April 5, 2001.

————. (1998). *Reducing Poverty in India: Options for More Effective Public Services*, A World Bank Country Study, The World Bank, Washington, D.C.

————. (1994). *Averting the Old Age Crisis: Policies to Protect the Old and Promote Growth*, Published for the World Bank by the Oxford University Press.

————. (1993). *World Development Report-Investing in Health*, published for the World Bank by the Oxford University Press, Delhi.

World Health Organisation (2001). *International Classification of Functioning, Disability and Health*, Geneva, WHO.

Q

quality of survival in later ages/
years 77, 175

R

Rajan, I.S. 64, 223, 232, 233
Raju, Siva S. 171
Rank, M.R. 214
rational choice 213
Ravallion, M. 38
Raveis, V. 190
rectangularised survival curve
46, 47
record keeping system, centralised
236
reforms and income security
issues 136
regression analysis, multivariate
89
regulatory mechanism 56
replacement level 32
reproductive ages, persons in 32
report of the technical group on
population project 231
reproductive health 30
reproductive life 32
Reserve Bank of India 226, 245
Retherford, Robert D. 113
retirement benefits 37, 223
retirement income security plans
222
retirement linked benefits 40
revenue generation, low levels of
226
risk bearing funds 235
risk factors associated with
functional impairment 185
risks of physical disabilities
among the aged 185

rotating residence 157
run away inflationary condition
246
rural elderly 49
rural-urban differentials in the
value system 97

S

Saad, Paula M. 213
safety net 93
Sakthivel, S. 63
sample design 107
multi-stage 116, 123
sample households, variability
across the 115
sampling manual 116
Sanjay Gandhi Niradhar Anudan
Yojna 229
Sankar, Deepa 53, 89
Sarvekshna 48
savings, aggregate private 44
saving, declining returns to 59,
161
to small savings 37
savings, private 45
domestic 43, 44
saving instruments 43, 143,
162, 165
saving potentials 40
scams in the financial market 237
scheduled caste/scheduled tribe
101
Schrader, S.S. 213
Second World Assembly on
Ageing 66, 73, 221
sedentary life style 188
self employed women's association (SEWA) 209
self-ageing 71

INSTITUTE OF ECONOMIC GROWTH
Studies in Economic Development and Planning
List of Publications

1. Dhar, P.N. and H.F. Lydall (1961). *Role of Small Enterprises in Indian Economic Development.* Asia Publishing House, Bombay.

2. Sahota, G.S. (1961). *Indian Tax Structure and Economic Development.* Asia Publishing House, Bombay.

3. Rao, V.K.R.V. (ed.) (1962). *Agricultural Labour in India.* Asia Publishing House, Bombay.

4. Rao, V.K.R.V. and Dharam Narain (1963). *Foreign Aid and India's Economic Development.* Asia Publishing House, Bombay.

5. Chopra, V.P. (1965). *India's Industrialisation and Mineral Exports 1951-52 to 1960-61 and Projections to 1970-71.* Asia Publishing House, Bombay.

6. Dharma Kumar, S.P. Nag and L.S. Venkataramanan (1965). *Resource Allocation in the Cotton Textile Industry.* Asia Publishing House, Bombay.

7. Rao, C.H. Hanumantha (1965). *Agricultural Production Functions, Costs and Returns in India.* Asia Publishing House, Bombay.

8. Goyal, S.K. (1966). *Some Aspects of Cooperative Farming in India with Special Reference to the Punjab.* Asia Publishing House, Bombay.

9. Rao, C.H. Hanumantha (1966). *Taxation of Agricultural Land in Andhra Pradesh.* Asia Publishing House, London.

10. Dhar, P.N. and D.U. Sastry (1967). *Demand for Energy in North-West India.* Asia Publishing House, Bombay.

11. John, P.V. (1968). *Some Aspects of the Structure of Indian Agricultural Economy 1947-48 to 1961-62.* Asia Publishing House, Bombay.

12. Krishnamurty, K. and D.U. Sastry (1970). *Inventories in Indian Manufacturing.* Academic Books, Bombay.

13. Sinha, J.N. and P.K. Sawhney (1970). *Wages and Productivity in Selected Indian Industries.* Vikas Publications, New Delhi.

14. Rao, V.K.R.V. (ed.) (1972). *Bangladesh Economy: Problems and Prospects.* Vikas Publishing House, New Delhi.

15. Khusro, A.M. (1973). *Buffer Stocks and Storage of Major Food Grains in India.* Tata-McGraw Hill, Bombay.

16. Khusro, A.M. (1973). *The Economics of Land Reform and Farm Size in India.* Macmillan Co, Madras.

17. Joshi, P.C. (1975). *Land Reforms in India: Trends and Perspectives.* Allied Publishers, Bombay.

18. Krishnamurty, K. and D.U. Sastry (1975). *Investment and Financing in the Corporate Sector in India.* Tata- McGraw Hill, New Delhi.

19. Rao, C.H. Hanumantha (1975). *Technological Change and Distribution of Gains in Indian Agriculture.* Macmillan Co, Madras.

20. Mishra, S.N. and John Beyer (1976). *Cost-benefit analysis: A Case Study of the Ratnagiri Fisheries Project.* Hindustan Publishing Corporation, New Delhi.

21. Mishra, S.N. (1978). *Livestock Planning in India.* Vikas Publishing House, New Delhi.

22. Subbarao, K. (1978). *Rice Marketing System and Compulsory Levies in Andhra Pradesh: A Study of Public Intervention in Foodgrain Marketing.* Allied Publishers, Bombay.

23. Saini, G.R. (1979). *Farm Size, Resource-use Efficiency and Income Distribution: A Study in Indian Agriculture with Special Reference to Uttar Pradesh and Punjab.* Allied Publishers, Bombay.

24. Dasgupta, Sipra (1980). *Class Relations and Technical Change in Indian Agriculture.* Macmillan Co, New Delhi.

25. Siddharthan, N.S. (1981). *Conglomerates and Multinationals in India: A Study of Investment and Profit.* Allied Publishers, New Delhi.

26. Dhawan, B.D. (1982). *Development of Tube Well Irrigation in India.* Agricole Publishing Academy, New Delhi.

27. Kadekodi, Gopal K. (1982). *Economic Planning for Iron Ore in India.* Hindustan Publishing Corporation, New Delhi.

28. Kapila, Uma (1982). *Oilseeds economy of India: A Case Study of Groundnut.* Agricole Publishing Academy, New Delhi.

29. Rangaswamy, P. (1982). *Dry Farming Technology in India: A Study of its Profitability in Selected Areas.* Agricole Publishing Academy, New Delhi.

30. Sinha, Basawan and Ramesh Bhatia (1982). *Economic Appraisal of Irrigation Projects in India.* Agricole Publishing Academy, New Delhi.

31. Bhatia, Ramesh (1983). *Planning for the Petroleum and Fertilizer Industries: A Programming Model for India.* Oxford University Press, New Delhi.

32. Bose, Ashish and P.B. Desai (1983). *Studies in Social Dynamics of Primary Health Care.* Hindustan Publishing Corporation, New Delhi.

33. Bandyopadhyay, Arun Kumar (1984). *Economics of Agricultural Credit (with Special Reference to Small Farmers in W. Bengal).* Agricole Publishing Academy, New Delhi.

34. Bhattacharya, B.B. (1984). *Public Expenditure, Inflation and Growth: A Macro-econometric Analysis for India.* Oxford University Press, New Delhi.

35. Mishra, S.N. (1984). *Rural Development Planning: Design and Method.* Satvahan Publications, New Delhi.

36. Sastry, D.U. (1984). *The Cotton Mill Industry in India.* Oxford University Press, New Delhi.

37. Brody, Andrew (1985). *Slowdown Global Economic Maladiess.* Sage Publications, Beverly Hills.

38. Ray, S.K. (1985). *Intensification of Agriculture: A Study in the Plains of Uttar Pradesh.* Hindustan Publishing Corporation, New Delhi.

39. Agarwal, Bina (1986). *Cold Hearths and Barren Slopes: The Woodfuel Crisis in the Third World.* New Delhi: Allied Publishers; London: Zed Books; Riverdale Publishers. Reprinted 1988, Maryland.

40. Banerjee, Biswajit (1986). *Rural to Urban Migration and the Urban Labour Market: A case study of Delhi.* Himalaya Publishing House, Bombay.

41. De Janvry, Alain and K. Subbarao (1986). *Agricultural Price Policy and Income Distribution in India.* Oxford University Press, New Delhi.

42. Dhawan, B.D. (1986). *Economics of Groundwater Irrigation in Hard Rock Regions: With Special Reference to Maharashtra State.* Agricole Publishing Academy, New Delhi.

43. Goldar, B.N. (1986). *Productivity Growth in Indian Industry.* Allied Publishers, New Delhi.

44. Tilak, J.B.G. (1987). *The Economics of Inequality in Education.* Sage Publications, New Delhi.

45. Dasgupta, Rajaram (1988). *Nutritional Planning in India.* Navrang Publishers, New Delhi.

46. Dhawan, B.D. (1988). *Irrigation in India's Agricultural Development: Productivity, Stability, Equity.* Sage Publications. 2nd edition in 1994, New Delhi. Commonwealth Publishers, New Delhi.

47. Goyal, R.P. (1988). *Marriage Age in India.* B.R. Publishing Corporation, Delhi.

48. Gulati, S.C. (1988). *Fertility in India: An Econometric Analysis of a Metropolis.* Sage Publications, New Delhi.

49. Kadekodi, Gopal K. (1988). *Planning for Coal Sector: Issues in Exhaustibility, Technology and Benefication.* B.R. Publishing Corporation, Delhi.

50. Rao, C.H. Hanumantha, Sushanta K. Ray and K. Subbarao (1988). *Unstable Agriculture and Droughts: Implications for Policy.* Vikas Publishing House, New Delhi.

51. Dhawan, B.D. (1989). *Studies in Irrigation and Water Management in India.* Commonwealth Publishers, New Delhi.

52. Murty, M.N. (1989). *Redistributive Taxation and Public Sector Pricing.* Commonwealth Publishers, New Delhi.

53. Chopra, Kanchan (1990). *Agricultural Development in Punjab: Issues in Resource Use and Sustainability.* Vikas Publishing House, New Delhi.

54. Chopra, Kanchan, Gopal K. Kadekodi and M.N. Murty (1990). *Participatory Development: People and Common Property Resources*. Sage Publications, New Delhi.

55. Dhawan, B.D. (1990). *Studies in Minor Irrigation: With Special Reference to Groundwater*. Commonwealth Publishers, New Delhi.

56. Mishra, S.N. and R.K. Sharma (1990). *Livestock Development in India: An Appraisal*. Vikas Publishing House, New Delhi.

57. Sarap, Kailas (1991). *Interlinked Agrarian Markets in Rural India*. Sage Publications, New Delhi.

58. Dhawan, B.D. (1993). *Trends and New Tendencies in Indian Irrigated Agriculture*. Commonwealth Publishers, New Delhi.

59. Rao, C.H. Hanumantha (1994). *Agricultural Growth, Rural Poverty and Environmental Degradation in India*. Oxford University Press, New Delhi.

60. Dhawan, B.D. (1995). *Groundwater Depletion, Land Degradation and Irrigated Agriculture in India*. Commonwealth Publishers, New Delhi.

61. Agarwal, R.N. (1996). *Financial Liberalisation in India: A Study of Banking System and Stock Markets*. B.R. Publishing Corporation, Delhi.

62. Bora, R.S. (1996). *Himalayan Migration: A Study of the Hill Region of Uttar Pradesh*. Sage Publications, New Delhi.

63. Maria Saleth, R. (1996). *Water Institutions in India: Economics, Law and Policy*. Commonwealth Publishers, New Delhi.

64. Dhawan, B.D. (1997). *Studies in Minor Irrigation with Special Reference to Ground Water*. 2nd enlarged edition. Commonwealth Publishers, New Delhi.

65. Gulati, S.C., R.P. Tyagi and Suresh Sharma (2003). *Reproductive Health in Delhi Slums*; B.R. Publishing Corporation, Delhi.